Praise for *Exploring Topics in Non/Human Coexistence*

"This collection interrogates the human-animal studies field's seeming compulsion to focus on human interactions with nonhuman animals and its implicit centering of the human in doing so. By reframing human interactions with nonhumans as intrusions, this collection disrupts normative logics that ignore nonhuman realities at the expense of feel-good coexistence narratives and moves towards a liberatory framework on which the field can build."—**Zane McNeill**, editor of *Vegan Entanglements: Dismantling Racial and Carceral Capitalism*

"Nonhuman animals globally need all the help they can get in the Anthropocene, often called 'the age of humanity' but practically cashed out as 'the rage of inhumanity.' Meaningful work on behalf of other animals to help them deal with widespread human intrusions into their lives and diverse ways of being require academics and on-the-ground activists to work hand-in-hand to use what we know about these fascinating individuals to help them to thrive in an increasingly human-dominated world. *Exploring Topics in Non/Human Coexistence* clearly shows that coexistence between non/humans requires ongoing multispecies negotiations with humans showing far more respect for what other animals need to have the freedoms to express who they are and to live high-quality lives typical of their species."—**Marc Bekoff**, Ph.D., author of *The Animals' Agenda: Freedom, Compassion, and Coexistence in the Human Age, Dogs Demystified: An A-to-Z Guide to All Things Canine,* and *The Emotional Lives of Animals*

"To liberate. To leave alone. These seem like contradictory principles, one active and one passive. *Exploring Topics in Non/Human Coexistence* challenges us to see their complementarity, inviting readers to investigate non-interference as an active ethical principle and helping us recognize that non/human coexistence unfolds not only through 'encounter' but also, importantly, through deliberate non-encounter. This provocative collection of essays, with its diverse range of perspectives and wide thematic scope, is sure to make you think differently. The editors and authors should be applauded for their valuable contribution to non/human liberation."—**Jessica Pierce**, PhD, affiliate faculty, Center for Bioethics and Humanities, University of Colorado Anschutz Medical School, author of *Who's A Good Dog? And How to Be A Better Human*.

"Animal studies is a dynamic and vibrant area of contemporary scholarship. It thrives on crossing boundaries, not only intellectual boundaries but also boundaries between theory and practice. This volume celebrates that diversity, juxtaposing innovative ideas within and across chapters. Read it and you will have a sense of the excitement, the breadth and depth of thinking, that is emerging in work on non/human coexistence."—**Thomas Dietz**, author of *Decisions for Sustainability*

"*Exploring Topics in Non/Human Coexistence* makes an impressive contribution to the literature, not least through drawing meaningful attention toward an eclectic range of otherwise marginalized and little-understood intersectional areas of enquiry. This, together with the fact that the contributions include some of the most important international scholars and activists working at this time, will make it essential reading for many. In particular, its accessibility and breadth should have strong appeal across many critical academics, activists, and broader public communities alike: I really hope it is read widely!"—**Dr. Richard J. White**, associate professor in Human Geography, Sheffield Hallam University, co-editor of *Vegan Geographies: Spaces Beyond Violence, Ethics Beyond Speciesism*

"This edited volume critiques some of the most important issues preventing the success of animal liberation, including the failure of capitalism, consumerism, and lab-grown meat. In contrast, it argues for animal liberation as a social justice movement in solidarity with other social justice movements. It is a wonderful text, and I highly recommend it."—**Vasile Stănescu**, associate professor, Department of Communication Studies & Theatre, Mercer University

"This collection is provocative and accessible; it draws on ways humans and nonhuman animals coexist together from a vegan perspective. Each essay's unique perspective makes the whole book interesting and engaging. There is also zero compromise regarding human and nonhuman animal liberation. This is a book that might make anyone look at our relationship with other animals in an entirely different manner. I couldn't recommend it more to anyone interested in veganism, total liberation, or simply making sense of the way we share and view the world."—**John Tallent**, author of *How to Unite the Left on Animals: A Handbook on Total Liberationist Veganism and a Shared Reality*

"*Exploring Topics in Non/Human Coexistence* is an essential contribution to the growing field of scholarship daring to challenge deeply ingrained paradigms about shared non/human existence. With breathtaking scope and ambition, the editors have curated a body of scholarship spanning disciplines and worldviews that boldly break the mold, offering an expansive, thought-provoking collection interrogating and dismantling boundaries which have long limited the discourse on liberation for all life. The range of perspectives gathered here illuminates the often invisible yet profound 'entanglements of oppression' binding non/humans, revealing how these entanglements can potentially become the groundwork for genuine liberation. This volume transcends the usual frameworks to spark new ways of thinking about coexistence and resistance. It invites readers not just to imagine new futures, but to take seriously the urgent need to build them—futures where liberation is collective, holistic, and encompasses literally everyone."—**Emilia A. Leese**, author, podcaster, rewilder, and author of *Think Like a Vegan*

Exploring Topics in Non/Human Coexistence

Passion, Praxis, and Presence

Edited by Sarah Tomasello, Erin Jones,
Mark Suchyta, and Nathan Poirier

Lantern Publishing & Media • Woodstock and Brooklyn, NY

2025
Lantern Publishing & Media
PO Box 1350
Woodstock, NY 12498
www.lanternpm.org

Printed in the United States of America

Library of Congress Cataloging-in-Publication information is available upon request.

To "the snake" and "the deer," two nonhumans for whom unnecessary human interaction was deadly.
—Nate

To my friends, the pigeons, one of the most misunderstood and unfairly treated avian species. May we learn to coexist.
—Sarah

To all the dogs. Your worth is the sum of your existence.
—Erin

To my flock—Ren, Opa, Whimsey, Aspen, and Rainford—for continuing to inspire and support me in my advocacy.
—Mark

Collectively, we would like to specifically dedicate this book to Dr. Paul Waldau for his support and guidance throughout our academic and personal journeys, and for reminding us to continue questioning everything we think we know about the world around us.

Nathan would like to particularly extend this dedication to Paul because of Paul's direct influence on his life trajectory, which he continually reflects upon. Few people make such a difference that it is worth singling Paul out here. Without exaggeration, Nathan's almost entire life would have been different if not for Paul's overwhelmingly sincere, direct, and helpful encouragement, without which he certainly would have been intellectually and even emotionally bereft. Paul has always shown such earnest support of everyone's uniqueness and strengths—a rare characteristic that goes an immeasurably long way toward making individuals feel valued for who they are, something to learn from and to try to emulate. Nathan speaks for all of the editors in saying that he himself can only hope to have even a partial amount of that influence on others going forward. Publishing-wise, it was also Paul who first connected Nathan and Sarah in 2015, an intellectual pairing from which, ultimately, this book came about. Paul, this book is dedicated to you and exists in large part because of you.

Acknowledgements

It's good to be skeptical of something that everyone does, says, or thinks. In the case of acknowledgements for a book, though, seemingly every author/editor notes the inevitability of an incomplete list. So, rather than trying to list individuals and coming up short, we are keeping our acknowledgements quite general. Some individuals did play a rather key role in the development of this book, however. We would like to thank our friends and family (chosen and blood), human and nonhuman. We must acknowledge the contributors, without whom this book would not exist. They have made it what it is. Any praise should be directed toward them. We also thank those who have written editorial reviews ("blurbs") for the book: Thank you for your time and support. If we can help repay the favor in some way, we would be happy to. We must thank Brett Colley for lending us his image and designing the cover. A particular thank-you goes to Brian Normoyle from Lantern Publishing & Media for taking a chance on this book and encouraging us to recruit more contributors as it evolved. It was a suggestion that clearly came from experience, and we believe it helped to increase the impact of this book. A special acknowledgement for our friend Nicole Sokolov, who was always available to answer questions we had regarding the editing and publishing process. Last but not least, Mark would like to credit Tom Dietz for encouraging him to continue and boldly publish meaningful work.

Contents

Foreword

Joshua Russell, PhD

This book was edited by four emerging scholars, three of whom I have known and worked with in the anthrozoology program at Canisius University. One of the contributing authors was also a student of mine at York University in a course on animal studies. So it is with a great deal of gratitude and a sense of pride that I write the foreword to this diverse and critical contribution to the scholarship on human–animal interactions. It is perhaps cliché for me, as an educator, to hope and believe that my students will go on to make a positive impact in their communities and the world around them. For almost fifteen years, I have been teaching courses on human–animal relationships, many drawing on interdisciplinary and critical perspectives that inevitably raise ethical and political questions. While, in the realm of animal studies scholarship, the area of critical animal studies is most often associated with translating theory into action or activism, I argue it is difficult to teach any course emphasizing human–animal interactions without raising questions about the kinds of relationships we ought to have with other animals. I am excited to see that these four scholars—who have seriously tackled these considerations in their coursework and courses of study—are now moving forward in new directions.

The editors of this book are well situated to introduce readers to the topic of non/human coexistence. The book incorporates carefully chosen terms that consider how liberation takes many forms while also acknowledging that these forms are entangled, centering the reality that humans (in all their diversity) and other animals (in all the diversity that constitutes the word "animal" itself) are inextricably connected. These connections are a matter not just of ecology but also of shared interests in individual well-being, community peace or security, and a broader sense of flourishing. The editors demonstrate how these ideas from their previous and ongoing work have coalesced in this volume. Sarah Tomasello's contributions in my classes and in her capstone project consistently drew upon her extremely interdisciplinary background in the humanities and social sciences—namely religion, philosophy, and anthropology. When I worked with Nathan Poirier on an article considering the liberatory potential of in vitro meat, he had already established a refined sense of how movements for human and animal justice need alignment, collaboration, and shared visions despite the uniqueness of each. Erin Jones's important work around cooperative care in human–dog relationships builds on a sense of shared and relational contributions to multispecies well-being, which is critical for and central to this book's concept of coexistence. Lastly, while I have not worked with Mark Suchyta prior to this, both his previous work and his contribution to this volume demonstrate a commitment to utilizing sound social science to bolster the strategies of animal activists, ultimately benefiting animals and humans alike. Readers are therefore in good hands.

This volume is, as the editors point out, eclectic in its content. It is interdisciplinary, global, and—to borrow a term from Aph Ko's *Racism as Zoological Witchcraft: A Guide to Getting Out* (2019)—multidimensional in its point of view. There are chapters that integrate diverse and critical theoretical perspectives, including from Black, queer, trans, and disability studies. There are chapters that reflect on informal and formal education's crucial role in non/human coexistence. Various authors explore the nuances of veganism, vegetarianism, and alternative animal-based practices as enactments of liberatory ethics and politics. One chapter even encourages us to consider similarities between animal liberation work and sightings of UFOs—a timely addition, given the U.S. government's recent increased disclosure of investigations into unidentified aerial phenomena to the public (for whatever purposes).

In sum, I think readers of this volume will find it provocative and expansive. It makes important contributions that will be of benefit to animal studies scholars working in many different areas, and it provides several points of reflection around activism and the potentialities of activist scholarship at a crucial point in human history and global politics. I congratulate the editors and authors for their thoughtful work, and I am excited to see this book taken up by a wide readership.

Preface

Lea Lani Kinikini, University of Hawai'i West O'ahu

A week after the fires that ravaged the town of Lāhainā on the island of Maui on August 8, 2023, I'm contemplating the absencing of bare life—sacred life—from state and military–industrial discourses: the thousand human animals vanished, the three thousand nonhuman animals presumed vanished or dead. To states and militaries, these lives are mere biology—trivial, hardly worth mentioning, even ignorable. The island ecosystem environment that is Maui has been decimated to a toxic char as bare life—sacred life—becomes nothing more than life evincing a trace of the past. As I write, activists are identifying how bare life was reduced to such absence. For some, Lāhainā burned because of governmental incompetence; for others, the blaze is theorized to be a directed energy-weapons attack by the U.S. military–industrial complex that wanted the town of Lāhainā razed so as to convert it to a "smart city." For yet many others who have been protesting military–industrial occupation, the fires resulted not only from intensifying weather patterns related to climate change but moreover from the legacy of water theft by plantations and landholding corporations that have been diverting rivers for the past 150 years. No matter what you believe, please believe that we are all bare life: just hanging on. If government is structure, if territory is the limit, then bare life within the *terra* (or the *mare*, the ether, for that matter) is mere "zones of indiscernibility" as Gilles Delueze writes in *Francis Bacon: Logic of Sensation* (1981). Hyper-discernibility seems an essential part of the civilizing war mission—to civilize or become civilized means a carnivorous ritual, a spectacle of war and boundary making between enemy and friend, between those who will conquer *in hoc signo* and those who will submit. Even the *Inter Caetera* is run through with Admiral Christopher Columbus's circular journey of finding the factors who needed civilizing:

> [Christopher Columbus] with help from above and utmost perseverance while sailing the ocean, these [men] found certain very remote islands and even mainlands heretofore undiscovered by others and inhabited by an abundance of peoples who live peacefully and who go naked, as we are assured, and don't eat flesh [. . .]. (Pope Alexander VI 1493, n.p.)

The primary factors—being peaceful, naked, and non–flesh eating— were seen by the Roman Catholic world as requiring immediate change. Dress them up, make them eat our preferred food (flesh), and take their peace. I raise the specter of the smoldering ash of human animals and nonhuman animals and the absence of water in Maui in this preface because it's very important to read the chapters that follow with the lens of how carceral governance and global oligarchy on land and at sea look, feel, and operate. Lāhainā means "merciless sun." The attack—if that is what it was—obliterated an entire whaling town-turned-tourist mecca, with more than four thousand lives missing in action. Because of the oligarchical legacies of the insular possession, unsurprisingly, grassroots activists also have been suggesting that the Maui fires had been inten- tionally set by the military in order to "sandbox" the town and create a "smart city" ruled with artificial intelligence, to test technology on a small and remote population. Whether these suggestions rely on an evidence base or are primarily speculations remains a topic for future research. In the midst of this political "fire and furor," in a factually occupied Hawaiian Kingdom whose sovereignty has never been extinguished, I find myself re-editing this preface, wondering what this volume can say about bare life in the framework of the destructive politics of the state, the family of nations that refuses to acknowledge, let alone honor, the sacred inherent in the non/human. While this volume spans a cross-section of topics, what is on my mind today is disaster capitalism, whereby there is a hierarchy of death—with animals, air, and minerals being quite down the line on the great chain of being and human animals barely registering, particularly Black, Brown, and Indigenous bodies who have been displaced from their homelands prior to imperialization by Western law jurisdictions and states of perpetual war.

For one to theorize action, one ought to name the quality of coexistence. One might describe a coexistence whereby disagreements are disarmed and not harmful. Mutual care and reciprocity, love, liberation, and sovereignty are all part of coexistence and part of a radical politics of perpetual balance for peace versus perpetual war. Humans have been in the Heliocene and are heading into the Pyrocene—the age of fire. With this eventuality, humans are in dire need of a politics that unwrites the fallacy of laws *and* establishes a praxis of degrowth. Is it blasphemous if I say that all lives are sacred, that in the beginning and the end, all we are is bare life? Is it too metaphysical to say that we can live beyond the material and step into the unseen, invisible world beyond this world? Is it impossible to believe, as my ancestors do, that we humans descended first from the *limu* (seaweed), then from the taro plant, the coconut tree, and the kava plant, and only then from our first ancestor in animal form, the worm (*momo* in Tongan)? The word "sacred," from the Latin *sacer*, means "set off, restricted," and the English word "taboo" was adopted from the Hawaiian/Polynesian word *kapu* or *tapu*. English had to steal our Polynesian word for "sacred" to actually register. When we say "sacred," we mean, "HANDS OFF! Don't touch!" In order to understand and explain a whole new world, we are reminded that *tapu* is "restricted, respected, bounded by mystery," a cloak that says, "I am nothing but a worm," "who am I to 'know'?" "who am I to 'dominate'?" "I am a worm." A humble stance. We are worms. Worms we will become.

As you soak in these chapters, I want you to recall that in the context of Western law and Western subjectivity, based on the jurisdictions of Justinian Roman civil law, a civilization and empire crucified human animals designated as slaves or cult devotees (like Christians) and also pitted human animals against nonhuman animals in battles in large, circus-like arenas that kept the masses in a violent slumber. The same imperializing projection of power fashioned jurisdictions and orders— like dominions and states predicated by war and violent bloodletting, murderous life-taking rituals—to regulate humans as "things" and "entities." As I reflect on the collection in this book, I think of the ways in which the "Anthropocene" has made yet another terroristic threat to the earth, water, air, and the living beings therein. Some say *Terra* is entering a final phase of capitalism, one that echoes the end time revelations of the Pyrocene: that the Earth will be baptized with fire.

They say the mark of a good read is how much of you is left behind as you read it. When you read this volume, ask yourself: How much of *you* is dredged through the non/human paradigm? How attached are YOU to your human existence, and how much of your bare life would you sacrifice in the fire of change? And, more important, what part of *YOU* will your praxis be(come) as you contemplate the coexistence of non/human life, including the divine entities of the land, sea, water, and sky—the numen of all life, upon which we as bare life depend?

Introduction: A Clarion Call for Coexistence

Nathan Poirier, Sarah Tomasello, Mark Suchyta, and Erin Jones

In the last scene of the BBC natural-history documentary *Rise of Animals*, David Attenborough holds a newborn baby boy and delivers a piercing insight into just how animal humans are:

> His backbone and jaw came from the early fish, his limbs and lungs from amphibians; the reptiles gave him his water-tight skin; tiny nocturnal mammals donated a bigger brain, sharper senses, and the manner in which he was born; his hands and color vision came from the fruit-eating primates, and his larger brain and greater intelligence from the first humans (Lee 2013).

This scene well demonstrates how humans are anatomically, physiologically, and psychologically connected to nonhumans. All of us humans are pieced together from the nonhuman ancestors who paved the way. The connections run skin, bone, and cell deep. As Peter Kropotkin (1902) shows in *Mutual Aid: A Factor of Evolution*, non/human coexistence is also built into our common evolutionary history and shared across species.

Humans exist because of nonhumans. But *coexistence* of humans with other species is dependent on humans alone. However, while human behavior threatens the possibility of non/human *existence* (let alone true non/human coexistence), blaming all of humanity for planetary and climate destruction is racist, sexist, and ableist. This is because it is generally wealthy Western white men who have contributed the most to humanity's erroneous, dangerous, and socially constructed break from other species and the Earth. They are the ones who have benefited from the dramatic consequences of this thinking, at the expense of both other humans and nonhumans. Therefore, it is sensible to keep much of the rest of humanity (e.g., the global South, historically marginalized groups) out of our finger pointing and instead challenge this elite group and the culture and institutions associated with it. It is precisely this elite that is siphoning itself off from the rest of humanity by building shelters, gating off living communities (its own often literally and others' often figuratively, such as through "red-lining"), and fleeing to more agreeable climates, or even to less agreeable ones such as space. The ocean, too, has been a potential colony for capitalists, but as Oceangate and the orca attacks in mid-2023 showed, this may not be a welcoming home for the wealthy (Isfahani-Hammond 2023; Blanco 2023).

CONTRIBUTOR RELATIONSHIPS

This book came together via existing relationships between the editors and some of the contributors. Sarah, Erin, and Nate all obtained master's degrees in anthrozoology from Canisius College (now University). Because of this, we are exceedingly grateful to have Joshua Russell write the foreword, as the three of us who graduated from Canisius all worked with him in that program. Both Mark and Nate have a graduate specialization in animal studies from Michigan State University and thus shared a department for a few years. This book contains works from contributors who have also graduated from Canisius and Michigan State. The connections therefore extend significantly (but not only) in these two directions.

The cover art for this book—both the image and overall design— was created by artist Brett Colley. Brett earned his MFA in printmaking from the University of Iowa in 1994 and is currently an associate professor at Grand Valley State University in West Michigan. Brett teaches a variety of courses, including drawing, printmaking, and senior seminar. His recent writing and studio work have assumed a wide critical perspective on industrialized animal agriculture, examining how the tragedies of racism, sexism, ableism, and ecocide intersect with our exploitation of other species. Projects that he, as both an artist and a curator, worked on have been exhibited in over thirty states and six countries. Brett's work can be viewed at brettcolley.com. At a previous event that Nate organized (called Rewild! Protecting All Life), Brett presented on topics very similar to those of this book; their acquaintance began here. And to promote that event, Brett allowed Nate to use an image of his for free for publicity. It is this image that now graces the cover of *Exploring Topics in Non/Human Coexistence*. This is yet another meaningful connection that we as editors are grateful to have and to continue.

NON-INTERFERENCE AS A GUIDING PRINCIPLE

We would like to take this opportunity to think with and through a concept that is rarely discussed in animal-protection circles: that of non-interference. We like the idea of exploring direct non-interference particularly because the notion receives so much pushback. It seems the default reaction to any mention of "non-interference" is to assume it means leaving all nonhumans alone. This comes without asking the speaker what they mean by "non-interference" or considering that the term could be used in other ways. Our contention is that non-interference can be presented as a contextual yet widely applicable guiding principle for non/human interactions that can promote coexistence. Concerning non/human coexistence, we have lingering questions about the role(s) humans should play in the more-than-human world. More specifically, these would be "questions about the obvious fact that many nonhuman animals seem to want to choose for themselves something other than human domination" (Waldau 2013, 31). We particularly like the use of the word "obvious" here. This "fact" is indeed obvious, but only if we allow ourselves to see it in the first place. How involved with nonhumans should humans be?

Helena Pedersen and Vasile Stănescu (2011) echo Waldau when they write in their introduction to *Women, Destruction, and the Avant Garde* that "it is indeed a mild irony that so much of animal studies is invested in human/animal intersubjectivities and 'encounters,' when most nonhuman animals [. . .] are likely to flee as far away from us as possible if they had a chance" (x). They develop this idea through the concept of "negative space," which, in art, is the part of a work that is intentionally left untouched while still retaining a function to the whole. The authors then demonstrate how to generalize this notion of negative space to anthrozoology

> [by] questioning the taken-for-granted validity of the *encounter* between humans and animals as *the* central unit of analysis, and [exploring] what impact an absence of encounters with humans may have on animals' lives. Such a negative space may not only be more beneficial to a great number of animals, but may also bring us closer to the animals' perspective. (x)

This is a perplexing result, so it warrants closer examination. We proceed under the interpretation of "reality" as what it is like to be a nonhuman animal. Thus, the animal's perspective, along with their experiences and perceptions, makes up their reality. If a large portion of nonhuman-animal behavior consists of avoiding humans, then by trying to avoid nonhuman animals, we as humans are taking a significant step toward understanding their reality. We would be attempting to mimic their general behavior and, in that respect, empathizing. By being "absent" to them, we can get a sense of what it might be like to try to carry on with our lives while avoiding certain "others," which is precisely what many nonhuman animals decide on. This allows them to express their natural behavior in their natural environment. Plus, since this course of action is one less taken for us, it is ripe with possibility. It would seem correct, then, that a properly evolved form of non/human liberation should be able to recognize that a potential key action toward pursuing nonhuman realities is perhaps inaction—"quite simply, to leave them alone" (Pedersen and Stănescu 2011, xi).

A healthy relationship supports all parties involved. If we humans are to study our relationship with nonhumans, then we should also consider how that relationship is perceived from other sides—that is, take nonhuman realities into account. We have raised Pedersen and Stănescu's "negative space" metaphor as a positive guideline. Leaving "animals" alone would automatically mean, among other implications, experimenting on them less and not destroying their habitats—their homes (and ours). This proposition frames non/human coexistence in a

4

way that not only puts nonhumans at the center but also assumes their realities are vulnerable to intrusion. It not only grants nonhumans the freedom to be themselves but also allows us to become more fully human. A mature form of non/human coexistence and liberation would have us take a step back and observe what has worked so well for the other 99 percent of the animal kingdom.

We humans should be insightful enough to put aside our inclinations to be quite so involved with nonhumans. In *Dominion* (2003), Matthew Scully elaborates:

> Man [*sic*], guided by the very light of reason and ethics that was his claim to dominion in the first place, should in the generations to come have the good grace to repay his debts, step back wherever possible and leave the creatures be, off to live out the lives designed for them. (43)

Humility and honesty would indeed be superior values for non/human coexistence. When thought about, this is actually wise advice. Given our incessant tinkering with the more-than-human world, from ecosystems down to the very genes of our non/human relations, we are doing the exact opposite of leaving others alone. The onset of COVID-19 showed just how capable more-than-human nature is of restoring itself when left to its own devices. One might say it is always just awaiting the chance.

In *Pensées*, Blaise Pascal reckons that "the sole cause of man's [*sic*] unhappiness is that he does not know how to stay quietly in his room" (1995, 37). In using the phrase "stay quietly," Pascal was not referring to apathy; he was implying a mature use of restraint based on critical, reflexive thought. Simply "letting go" would not absolve us humans of the responsibility we have incurred by contributing to global warming in the first place. It would not be acceptable for us to continue to put pressure on other species with our destructive ways. What dropping our obsession with controlling life could lead to, though, is an awakening that we could apply widely in order to lessen our control over nonhumans, with the hoped-for goal of reducing the outsized negative global influence of (a select portion of) humanity. Nature's resiliency is showcased yet again in the case of polar bears in the western Hudson Bay of Canada. These polar bears are developing behavioral adaptations to attempt to cope with climate change. They are finding other food sources to supplement their mainstay of ice-caught seals (Gormezano and Rockwell 2013). What we find most intriguing and inspirational is that these behavioral modifications, though ultimately not sufficient to save the bears from unprecedented and rapid climate change, could be used as a model for what might be possible if we humans were to loosen "our" grip over Earth and its life forms and allow nature to take care of itself as it has always done. If allowed to, nature finds a way.

We must begin to think critically about what non-interference can bring to non/human liberation. Academically, most of the focus is on non/human interactions, many of which are precisely the problem. Instead of modifying harmful non/human interactions, we should instead abandon many of them. We could completely cease, say, industrial exploits or war. Not interfering in numerous ways would cut down on the vast majority of the harms inflicted on nonhumans. If we want nonhumans to recover and flourish, the easiest solution is also the most effective: to simply *let them*—that is, leave them alone to a reasonable extent. Even a reasonable extent would cover quite a bit of ground. Nonhuman populations would recover if left to their own devices, on their own and in their habitats, minimally disturbed. Nonhuman nature existed for millions of years before humans, which means it can take care of itself without our intervention.

The less critical reader will surely reply to this with something along the lines of: "We can't stop all interactions with non/humans. Some of our interventions are beneficial, such as in preventing suffering." Yes, of course. They absolutely are. We are not promoting the idea of never interacting with nonhumans in the absolute, or even as far as possible. Complete avoidance would be ridiculous and impossible (and racist, ableist, classist, etc.). Non-interference does not mean zero interference but less negative interference. The non-interference we are discussing is necessarily contextual. It is not our wish to outline a complete set of activities humans should refrain from doing or should do. That would be a futile and even dangerous pursuit for multiple reasons. No one is in a position to know such information. Besides, the world situation is constantly changing; relations between beings are constantly changing. While there may be some things we could completely cease doing, many things—such as resource extraction—we could simply do much less of. It may not be possible for all of us to stop buying commodities altogether (although we should not rule out what is possible a priori), but a good number of us can certainly buy a lot fewer. A reasonable start may be to stop purchasing from Amazon, Walmart, and the like, instead buying more locally, from independent, Black- or queer-owned establishments. This would constitute non-interference inasmuch as by doing and consuming less, we would proportionally lessen our individual and collective impact on the more-than-human world.

We are also not saying that anyone getting by on very little should give up what little they may have. The burden is always on those with more to lessen their impact. Non-interference says: cease the bad interactions. Non-interference does not prohibit positive interactions. If a nonhuman animal moves away from us during an attempted interaction, then that is an interaction we do not get to have—and both parties may be that much more liberated because of it. This is an interspecies consent culture. If you are in doubt as to whether a potential interaction may have negative consequences, or if you are not fully sure about or confident in your ability to successfully engage in a particular action, it may be best to err on the side of caution and not attempt it. However, neglect is a harmful form of non-interaction and is not precluded by non-interference. Neglect must be remedied whenever and wherever possible, by whatever means necessary.

On the flip side, positive interactions can be increased. Negative interactions can be scaled back or ceased altogether, creating room and time for positive ones: captive nonhuman animals can be released; those not able to be released can be homed in sanctuaries; instead of breeding nonhumans, we can pay acute attention to their lifeworlds, to their diverse experiences and means of communication, and we can work on adapting our behavior(s) to theirs; we can prevent—instead of causing or contributing to—harm. Non-interference does not lead to a less fulfilling life for any non/human involved. It is the quintessential case of less being more. Non-interference could be referred to as simultaneously harm reduction and joy creation. It also does not mean not intervening when abuse is witnessed or known to exist. In fact, it necessitates intervention in such a case.

On Publishing Meaningful Contributions

As the full manuscript was nearing completion, during a Zoom meeting, we, the four editors, started discussing our favorite chapters. We went in a round-robin fashion, each editor naming a chapter they particularly liked and explaining why. While it may seem (or be) taboo for editors to discuss "favorites," our reason for including this story is this: We had intended for each of us to name only one favorite chapter, but after going around once—with everyone having picked a different chapter— we spontaneously started going around again. This second go-round produced yet again different chapters that hadn't already been chosen. We quickly realized how each chapter has unique qualities and contributions to the book as a whole—picking a favorite became pointless as none of us were able to actually do it. We hope you (the reader) have a similar experience.

The variety of contributions that its chapters offer indicates that this book is not too tightly bound to a single theme. We prefer broad and varied topics because edited collections that center around too strong a central theme often become rather mundane as one reads through the chapters. Typically, the central theme is important and the introductions to such volumes are interesting, but subsequent chapters tend to, more or less, simply apply the theme to their particular subtopics. This engenders the effect of chapters feeling rather repetitive, not least of all due to multiple authors providing a review or overview of the main theme, frequently citing very similar literature (see the chapters in Dhont and Hodson 2020 for an example of this extreme repetitiveness). Whole chapters are written for what likely would require only a few paragraphs or less to explain, thus producing much superfluous material and providing little fodder for intellectual stimulation.

For instance, a book on the various types of harm caused by the animal–industrial complex would seem to be an unnecessary "contribution" to the study of non/humans. Numerous books (not to mention articles, websites, social media posts, etc.) already recount these atrocities. Another book that provides a sweeping overview of them provides nothing new. One that situates the same harms within a different theoretical framework also accomplishes little, certainly much less than a full book (edited or authored) would suggest. We understand there is an academic pressure to publish, but this is not a valid excuse nor a good reason. And while we understand the situation, it is not unreasonable to ask academics to pursue topics that are more meaningful and not what is more easily publishable, especially if it has already been well covered. Likewise, contemporary "updates" of a topic are not necessarily warranted either if they are rather minimal (like new editions of undergraduate textbooks). We—book editors, authors, and contributors—must all be careful not to saturate a given discourse.

Thus, while *Exploring Topics in Non/Human Coexistence* does have a central theme of non/human coexistence, this theme is loosely woven throughout the chapters, as well as mixed with additional motifs, such as, but not limited to, praxis, passion, and presence. We believe this makes for a more entertaining read and more meaningful contribution. It helps this book to stand apart from others. One edited book that does this well is *Vegan Geographies: Spaces beyond Violence, Ethics beyond Speciesism* (Hodge et al. 2022), whose chapters cover quite a bit of ground around the theme of veganism. Veganism is an exceedingly wide term and the chapters in *Vegan Geographies* reflect this. Veganism as a central theme works because there are so many ways to approach it while keeping the chapters quite distinct from each other—indeed, veganism is another sub-theme of *Exploring Topics in Non/Human Coexistence*. At the same time, we must be careful not to saturate the discourse around veganism and instead to produce meaningful works that push veganism forward and outward. Human geography, too, covers much territory (pun intended) as it deals with space and place—and who doesn't exist in some place? Thus, books on non/humans from a geographical perspective tend to be wide-ranging and therefore especially interesting (Urbanik 2012; Gillespie and Collard 2015).

Exploring Topics in Non/Human Coexistence does not focus solely on veganism as do vegan studies texts—such as *The Vegan Studies Project* (Wright 2015), *Critical Perspectives on Veganism* (Castricano and Simonsen 2016), and *Thinking Veganism in Literature and Culture: Toward a Vegan Theory* (Quinn and Westwood 2018). Vegan studies can have the effect of sequestering veganism into an academic space that is not necessarily infused with the mainstream. Our book tries to overcome this by stretching the dimensions and applications of veganism and connecting with literature in many fields beyond vegan studies.

Similar to the problem of repetitiveness in scholarship or academic literature, another trend we've noticed is that a slew of books seem to simply place an adjective in front of "capitalism" and then assert that this represents a particularly novel form of or insight into a world problem. Some examples are *Carceral Capitalism* (Wang 2018), *The Age of Surveillance Capitalism* (Zuboff 2020), *Colonial Racial Capitalism* (Koshy, Cacho, Byrd, and Jefferson 2023), *Technocapitalism* (Suarez-Villa 2009), and *Gore Capitalism* (Valencia 2018). There are many more similar titles. Essentially, what each of these books does is focus on a different aspect of capitalism. However, such works are not necessarily particularly novel contributions. The abundance of "(blank) capitalism" literature may be explained by what's known as "prism publishing." A prism fragments light into its different frequencies, which are perceived as different colors; while the colors may appear distinct, they actually represent a continuum of frequencies highly related to each other. "Prism publishing" is akin to "salami slicing"—slicing up a topic to generate abundant publications.

Attaching different adjectives to the word "capitalism" is a fairly repetitive move. Anyone with experience in activism knows that capitalism and its offshoots pervade all aspects of social life, which is why even social movements, including the animal liberation movement, quite unfortunately and counterproductively, can and do suffer from things like internal (and outward) sexism and racism. Similar to edited collections heavily focused on a central theme, books that are titled *(blank) Capitalism* and that follow the mold of "capitalism applies to this area of life too" could probably be summed up in the space of a single chapter. But please do not get us wrong: the books mentioned above are all enlightening and all provide a thoughtful critique of a deeply problematic phenomenon. They are not bad or invalid texts, just somewhat repetitive. Simply pointing out an overlooked component of a larger discussion is an "expected rhetorical move that implicitly garners one a kind of validity" (Bey 2020, 12). Carceral capitalism *is* racial colonial capitalism *is* gore capitalism *is* surveillance capitalism, etc. These are all dimensions (different "frequencies" or "colors") of capitalism that show its malleability and evolutionary potential. Capitalism, in its ruthless quest for expansion, will inevitably reach into hitherto untapped domains to acquire the resources needed for ever-increasing domination in existing domains.

With *Exploring Topics in Non/Human Coexistence*, we avoid this "(blank) capitalism" dilemma by not explicitly centering the book around capitalism, although plenty of chapters are (rightly) critical of capitalism. We do not wish to misconstrue capitalism as *the* root of all non/human oppression; we believe there is no single root of all of anything. Instead, by centering the book around the notion of coexistence—a theme that we believe is broad enough also not to constrict the chapters—we highlight an aspect of non/human relations that has been largely overlooked, at least explicitly. Coexistence, after all, is the goal of our efforts to end non/human oppression.

DECONSTRUCTING THE MEANING(FULNESS) OF THIS BOOK

In this book's title and throughout its contents, we emphasize the term "non/human" instead of other, similar ones. We first encountered the use of "non/human(s)" in the book *Screening the Nonhuman: Representations of Animal Others in the Media*, edited by Amber E. George and J. L. Schatz (2016, xiii). Although the term is not explained, the intention is clearly to call attention to the interconnections between humans, nonhuman animals, and the environment. Word choice is definitely a key issue concerning liberation, as well as the topic of much ongoing conversation among those involved in non/human justice causes. The rhetorical separation of "human" and "nonhuman" indicates the asymmetry created and enjoyed by humans (some more than others), which ultimately precludes non/human coexistence. Meanwhile, use of the phrase "human and nonhuman" privileges one species out of millions. Therefore, "non/human" is the best combination of "nonhuman" and "human" that we know of so far in the English language. Of course, the situation would differ for other languages; incidentally, some languages do not even have this problem as they were developed without such a separation to begin with (see Nguyen 2019).

Sometimes, "non/human(s)" may read as slightly confusing as to just who is being referred to. But this is largely the point. Non/human liberation struggles are all entangled with each other, and there is no real—meaning moral—difference between one and the next. If the reader prefers language that makes the intended subject(s) of a sentence clearer, perhaps they should ask themself why. What does it really matter? What are the material consequences of linguistically (that is, symbolically) separating humans from nonhumans? What are the (material) consequences of combining them and always thinking of them together? Indeed, non/human justice struggles should be conflated to the point of consistent anti-oppression (Feliz and McNeill 2020), as liberation would require.

The title of this book emphasizes coexistence, which we take to refer to non/humans living peacefully together. Yet coexistence does not imply perfect harmony. There will always be disagreements, which is not necessarily a bad thing. Jeremy Bendik-Keymer (2020) takes disagreement as the starting point for ethical relations in what is termed "anthroponomy." Disagreement, when properly attended to, opens possibilities for mutual aid, relationship formation and strengthening, and exposure to new ideas and modes of life. Coexistence is something to always be striving toward. We do not take coexistence to encompass any sort of "separate but equal" (as if that were ever truly possible to begin with) paradigms that suggest diverse groups can thrive in mutually exclusive social and physical environments. Such paradigms do nothing to foster out-group empathy, which is a requirement for coexistence. Our conceptualization of coexistence is best captured by this saying from the French anarchist geographer Elisée Reclus: "Live your own life, but allow others the complete freedom to live theirs" (cited in Clark and Martin 2013).

The subtitle of this book consists of the words "passion," "praxis," and "presence." "Passion," in the English language, is often used to refer to—yet its meaning extends far beyond—feelings of intense emotion and commitment. As Donald Senior (1990, 8) explains, "passion" comes from the Latin word *patior*, which means "to suffer," "to endure," or "to bear"—to care about something so deeply that one is willing to accept and endure the hardships that come along with it. These various layers of meaning contained within the word really illuminate the experiences of those involved in non/human liberation work. Committing oneself to helping end the oppression and marginalization of non/human others means being hyperaware of their exploitation and, oftentimes, being directly exposed to their suffering. As some of the authors within this book describe, this knowledge, while extremely important, can be a distressing and even traumatic burden to bear. Many activists feel particularly distressed and overwhelmed thinking about the suffering they will not be able to prevent (Granovetter 2021). Additionally, when one chooses to partake in non/human activism, one is also choosing to put oneself at odds with well-established societal norms. As a result, one not only finds it more challenging to reach others, convincing them to care and take action, but often receives direct backlash and ridicule, which can be isolating. This theme of deep commitment to activism despite the suffering one may endure is present all throughout the chapters of this book, which is why we chose to highlight it in our subtitle.

"Praxis" refers to the use of theory to inform action and of action to inform theory. It encapsulates the idea that theory and action are inseparable from each other and, thus, that one without the other is incomplete and bereft of something meaningful. We would even assert that action in the absence of theory (if, indeed, this were even possible in the absolute), or theory in the absence of action, can be dangerous. We think it is rather obvious that an action that is not guided by some overarching ideal is likely to be arbitrary, almost random, and could have negative implications not only for the actor but also for those toward whom the action is directed. Thus, the actor may needlessly put themself or others in harm's way. Further, an action that is without intention or purpose can be meaningless, which is a waste of resources that could have been used toward achieving non/human coexistence.

Finally, we chose the word "presence" because it denotes being fully conscious, mindful, and aware—a skill that is critical to non/human liberation. A present individual is actively engaged in the work at hand, in both the immediate and the ultimate sense, and is reflexive. It is essential that, when engaged in activism, one take a step back to see things holistically so that one can make the most informed choice. Thus, one may be able to reflect on outreach strategies and educational models to better understand which are the most successful, become aware of and challenge one's own biases and assumptions, and know where and when not to interfere.

DESCRIPTION OF CHAPTERS

This book's contents could be described as eclectic. Some chapters cover traditional animal studies topics, such as vivisection; others push into territories that are still unfolding, such as that of in vitro—more commonly, cultured—meat. Some chapters are written in an academic fashion, but most are more free-flowing. Some deal primarily with ideas, and some focus on actions (not to imply that these are necessarily distinct). Indeed, some chapters are written by academics and some are written by activists (again, not to imply that these should be considered separate positions). Some chapters are shorter and some are longer. And the final chapter deals with a topic that is almost never discussed, even by those invested in animal protection, let alone by anyone else.

Despite their diversity, all the chapters are connected through the themes of passion, praxis, and presence, as well as various subthemes. Each chapter serves to make this book unique and meaningful. Because of this, we chose not to break the book into sections; each categorization we attempted betrayed segmentation, often in more ways than one. The chapters are intentionally ordered, though, to invoke a loose ebb and flow of themes. For instance, Chapters Two, Three, and Four all engage with ecofeminism and assert the place of veganism in fostering non/human coexistence, and Chapters Ten to Thirteen all revolve around education and outreach to some degree. Many chapters are solution-oriented, as critique alone is insufficient to achieve liberation.

With the support of Lantern Publishing & Media, we continually reached out to people and asked them to contribute to this book. We wanted more voices in the mix. This is why this book contains a foreword, preface, and afterword—all three being the most esteemed parts of any book in our view. To open and close a book—framing its contents—with the words and perspectives of someone who is not an editor is especially valuable. These preliminary and closing thoughts can do wonders in terms of providing clarity, summing up the book's message(s), and provoking further reflection.

Chapter One, "Black Trans Feminism and the Nonhuman," by Marquis Bey, explores the ways in which Black trans feminism contributes to the liberation of the more-than-human world. Marquis explains that Black trans feminism is not confined to a specific demographic. Rather, it is linked to no subject at all, viewing liberation as the very base from which we should relate to the world. Marquis describes the exclusion of certain subjects from liberatory frameworks as "carceral thinking" and argues that this is linked to various forms of non/human oppression. Marquis's chapter sets the tone for the rest of the book by positing from the outset that no one is left outside of non/human liberation.

Chapter Two, "The Reproduction of Violence in Resistance to Brahminical Vegetarianism," by Varun Joshi, explores the complex interconnections between non/human rights, as well as the many considerations that need to be made in order to achieve total liberation. In his chapter, Varun illustrates how cow protectionism in India has resulted in violence toward and marginalization of certain non/human communities and perpetuates harmful hierarchical ideologies. Additionally, Varun critiques the inherent hypocrisy of cow protectionism, which vilifies the slaughter and consumption of cow flesh but continues to frame cows as resources and sources of valuable milk and manure.

Chapter Three, "The Place of Veganism in Multispecies Justice," by Darren Chang, discusses the limitations of ecofeminism as a framework for total liberation since many ecofeminist thinkers perceive there to be an unavoidable need to use and kill nonhuman animals in various contexts, or they even actively support these violent practices. Alternatively, Darren argues that Multispecies Justice is a more appropriate tool for dismantling the roots of oppression, especially because it is well suited to accommodate the multiple forms of veganism(s) that have developed to meet local needs. Similar to Marquis Bey's description of Black trans feminism, Multispecies Justice calls for justice/liberation at a very base level, which therefore encompasses all, both human and nonhuman.

Chapter Four, "Veganism as a(n) (Overlooked) Component of Anarchafeminism?" by Nathan Poirier, builds upon the work of Chiara Bottici to illustrate how veganism can be included within anarchafeminism. Using eco-Black-feminist theory, Nathan shows how veganism can be seen as a rejection of current hierarchical and authoritarian systems and, therefore, is a logical and necessary addition to anarchafeminism, which seeks to oppose all forms of domination. Nathan also considers how veganism may already be implicitly present in Chiara's anarchafeminism.

Chapter Five, "Interbeing: A Spiritual Insight of the Suffering of Nonhuman Animals," by Lucrezia Barucca, draws upon personal experiences as well as Buddhist philosophy and the work of Leo Tolstoy to explore the concept of interbeing. In doing so, Lucrezia argues that while witnessing the suffering of nonhuman others is important, it is essential that we not internalize it too much. Instead, we should also focus on relieving the suffering of those in close proximity to us (i.e., those to whom we have access) as well as finding ways to encourage others to actively work to reduce suffering.

Chapter Six, "Animal Liberation under Capitalist Realism," by Richard Giles, explores the relevance of Mark Fisher's theory of capitalist realism to animal liberation theory. Capitalist realism is the belief that capitalism is the only viable system of economic organization and that it is impossible to even imagine an alternative. Richard examines both how the exploitation of nonhuman animals is encouraged by capitalism and how it could still exist in alternative, non-capitalist regimes, as speciesism could pervade any economic system. Similar to Marquis Bey's argument against "carceral thinking," Richard promotes an ethic of "care without community," encouraging us to care for others regardless of whether they belong within the confines of our "community" (e.g., our species, class, racial group).

Chapter Seven, "Black Anarchy through Urban Agriculture as a Potential Alternative and Resistance to State-Regulated Cell-Based Meat," by Nathan Poirier, provides a critical analysis of a letter written to then-U.S. president Donald Trump calling for federal regulation of cell-based meat products. Through his analysis, Nathan argues that cell-based meat is being used to further support U.S. nationalism and imperialism, its main goal being to keep the United States a world leader in protein production. Using Black anarchist theory, Nathan argues that localized, grassroots efforts, such as urban agriculture, should be used as an alternative to federally regulated cell-based meat.

In Chapter Eight, "The Kurdish Diet and Vegetarianism: A Journey of Rediscovering Wild Food Plants," Jihan Mohammed reflects upon her experience as a vegetarian Muslim Kurd and how some of her peers have struggled to understand her beliefs and dietary choice, emphasizing traditions of meat and dairy consumption in both Kurdish culture and Islam. Jihan's chapter encourages readers to consider the ways in which religion, social class, and ethnicity shape and intersect with our relationships with nonhuman animals as well as calls for open conversations on these important ethical issues. She also celebrates the food of her culture, which she notes is actually very vegan- and vegetarian-friendly.

Chapter Nine, "On Total Liberty: Species Privilege and More-than-Human Autonomy," by Amanda R. Williams and Paislee House, brings to light the extreme limitations faced by nonhuman animals that prevent them from moving and acting as they please. Amanda and Paislee show how these limitations are influenced by human exceptionalism as well as other oppressive systems, such as ableism, racism, classism, and sexism.

Chapter Ten, "What Animal Liberation Activists Need to Know about Values: Debunking Three Common Myths," by Mark Suchyta, highlights the importance of understanding values in order to make non/human activism as strategic and effective as possible. Mark explains that values are the guiding principles that influence a person's beliefs and behaviors; therefore, having an understanding of how values function can help activists create messaging that is received well by its audience.

In Chapter Eleven, "Humane Education: A Pathway to Compassionate Coexistence," Emily Tronetti and Macy Sutton highlight the important role that humane education can have in cultivating compassion and reverence for the more-than-human world. Humane education encourages people to reexamine their values, model compassionate choices, and educate their communities and, as such, as Emily and Macy argue, is essential for fostering non/human coexistence. While humane education has traditionally been geared toward youth, Emily and Macy suggest that by integrating it into adult education, we can achieve greater and more accelerated social change.

Chapter Twelve, "Building an Effective Animal Liberation Movement: Beyond Educational Outreach," by Kiana Avlon, examines the effectiveness of animal activists' strategies. Kiana specifically calls attention to the hegemonic ideas of leadership found within the movement, such as those promoted by vegan celebrities, and the overreliance on educational outreach. Kiana argues that animal liberation activists should instead focus on building coalitions and forging connections based on values shared with allies and the general public. She also highlights the importance of developing useful criteria to evaluate successes and failures within the movement so that we can learn and adjust strategies accordingly.

Chapter Thirteen, "Teaching and Learning Critical Animal Studies: Treading and Shredding the Line," by Sarah May Lindsay, is a critical auto-ethnography that reflects on Sarah May's experience introducing critical animal studies to students in a graduate-level animal studies program. Sarah May walks us through her emotional, intellectual, and cognitive experience, including her anxieties and struggles with imposter syndrome. She also discusses the reactions that her students had to course material, which included both criticism and positive ontological shifts. This very personal account of her fears and her highs and lows while teaching highlights her passion for animal activism, as well as the pain and grief that can often accompany it.

Chapter Fourteen, "Nonhuman Animals: Laboratory or Liberation? A Critical Analysis of the Defense of Vivisection," by Lynda Korimboccus, challenges the modern arguments for vivisection held by philosopher Carl Cohen. Lynda argues that the dilemma of needing to rely on nonhuman animals in order to cure human diseases is a false one. Highlighting the work of philosophers Nathan Nobis and Alix Fano, Lynda shows that vivisection is actually a scientifically flawed practice—that in fact, relying on animal experimentation over alternative technologies is holding us back from discovering successful treatments to various human ailments.

Chapter Fifteen, "UFOs and Animal Exploitation: The Rhetoric of Ridicule," by Seven Mattes, explores the parallel experiences of ridicule faced by two groups challenging societal norms: animal liberationists and those who have experienced UFO phenomena. While experiencing such ridicule can be isolating and burdening, Seven suggests that by coming together to share knowledge and find strength in community, these groups can rise above the ridicule and work to challenge the dominant narrative of human exceptionalism. This is an excellent concluding chapter because of its novelty in the connection being made. We hope it will inspire readers to think about how to push the boundaries of academics, advocacy, and collective liberation and to act—by whatever means necessary—on that inspiration.

CHAPTER ONE

Black Trans Feminism and the Nonhuman

Marquis Bey

Time and again, there is a logic of parochialism—or more, a logic of categorical cordoning—that pervades the discourses of radicalism we find ourselves advocating, inventing, and participating in. That is, so often, it is observed that *this* movement or mode of thought concerns *these* things specifically, sometimes solely; hence, other things—things rendered outside of this mode of thought—are, at worst, improper to this space or, at best, valid but "not what we do over *here*." On the one hand, this appears quite fine, even sensible and courteous: yes, save for those moments of rudeness or imprecision, to assert that "here we do this and if over there y'all do that, that's cool" is perfectly within the scope of justice movement thought and praxis. To be sure, it is not quite the aim of this perhaps too-brief meditation to lambaste such a logic; on the whole, it has and has had immense utility. On the other hand, it strikes me that this logic nevertheless forecloses what might be, to put it in crass teleological language, an additional, further, (we might even say) radical step toward another (il)logic—that of refusing the categorical cordoning altogether.

At base, one thinks, of course, that this is a difficult—even impossible—gesture. Reams of neuroscientific articles, not to mention laysubjects' pop-sci pontificating, hammer home how our brains are "just hardwired" that way, predisposed to categorizing as a means of semiotic survival and understanding. There is nothing wrong with categorizing and thus making discrete this thing over or relative to that thing; indeed, it is well within our species' evolution. But this chapter, "Black Trans Feminism and the Nonhuman," seeks another framework, or perhaps that which precisely vitiates the delimitations of the "frame" of such work. If black trans feminism, as I've theorized in my eponymous monograph (2022), asseverates—via radicality, abolition, and liberation—an unfixing of blackness, transness, and feminism from the normative constituents of "Man" (Wynter 2003) and posits these terms as modalities and postures (rather than attributes of a certain kind of subject), and if it also seeks a thoroughgoing reimagining of what is possible for us and the world to be, then it does not "include" but rather definitionally *refuses to exclude* the nonhuman. Thus, this brief chapter seeks to meditate on the ways a black trans feminist project contributes to the liberation of the nonhuman—the liberation and lively proliferation of nonhuman animals, of land, of other modes of life and being. What relevance, this chapter asks, does black trans feminism—ostensibly "human" nominatives—have for the nonhuman? A tentative answer might be: an insistence on other modes of life as possible, as already existing, and as necessary for the overturning of the world as we know it.

At base, perhaps this might be said to be a matter of starting point. Whereas many, one would assume, erect a philosophical or ideological framework and then, when met with critiques, seek to include those critiques into it, here the attempt is to begin from a place of not having excluded in the first place. With the former method, one maintains a sense of gatekeeping, of deeming oneself the arbiter of what can validly enter or exit. And of course, as noted, this is sensible: there are certain criteria for what "counts," and it is not a bad thing to determine what does or does not count based on those criteria. But again, the purpose here is to interrogate such a logic. It is precisely the gesture of *taxonomizing*—and we can hear how this veers deeply into the territory of *species*, much closer to the topic at hand, at least for those expecting certain topics in this volume—that proves problematic. To taxonomize means that one, by virtue of defining the very thing one is creating, is excluding things from the jump, before they even emerge onto the scene to be evaluated or considered. They are a priori excluded, as folks in my philosophical circle would say. But what if we did not even utilize this logic, that of excluding from the jump? What if, instead, we maintained an openness to anyone and non-one, anything and non-thing? What if we presupposed liberation instead of determining a criterion from which liberation came?

That is where black trans feminism enters, though it has already been here, as has everything. Black trans feminism is not a parochial project, concerned only with the *people* implied by its titular nominatives. Black trans feminism is not only and simply *for* a certain demographic: "Black trans feminism is not *about* black trans women. The radical politics that black trans feminism names are not beholden to 'being' a presumed type of subject" (Bey 2022, 32). As such, it is delinked not even simply from an anthropomorphic subject but *from a specific subject altogether.* It posits liberation in the first instance; it posits liberation as the ground on which we begin to emerge into relationality. The various categorical apparatuses we have available to us—being human and all the identificatory requirements that inhere in that hegemonic modality; being animal and the assumptions that lie therein; being of this demographic or that demographic, this culture or this region—confine and cordon us such that "us" is the product not of choice and experimentation and agency, but of the legible entrapment imposed onto us before we had a say. Black trans feminism, in its abolitionist penchant, cannot abide such confinement—which is to say, it cannot abide carcerality.

And maybe that's the thing. We, at least some of us, rightly oppose the confining of nonhuman animals in captivity (from animal trafficking to factory farms to zoos). But we do not often link this to a general landscape of carceral logics that are not simply cages with bars and barbed wires but also include (or don't exclude) the very ways in which such species delimitations incarcerate the possibilities we have for relating and being and imagining. That is to say, what is also carceral is that we taxonomize and thus hierarchize a certain conception of this or that category—whether of animal or plant or what have you—and that taxonomization cages that which it categorizes by definitionally, ontologically disallowing exit from or "improper" entry into its categories. That taxonomization has myriad disciplinary rules for being a valid inhabitant and consequences (exile or punishment or policing) when those rules are flouted—as seen by how the platypus was once deemed wrong (not the Linnaean taxonomy that made no room for the platypus) or how a given species is deemed fit for only slaughter or consumption or entertainment. All of this is carceral. There is the specter of hyperbole here, for sure, and let me not join the ranks of animal liberationists past who, say, made analogies and comparisons that, even if intellectually apt, struck most as lacking in awareness and compassion for other forms of life (like that "dreaded comparison" Marjorie Spiegel wrote about in 1988). The aim is not a collapsing but an expanding, not to say that "killing animals should be on par with killing humans; both are murder!" (not that this assertion is without merit) but rather, more robustly, to ask ourselves: what if we think about just how the underlying logics of authorizing ourselves to end the lives of others find expression in numerous forms and pervade how we relate to one another under cisheteropatriarchal, white-supremacist capitalism?

All this to say: yes, the language of carcerality and incarceration to speak to jailing human people, and jailing nonhuman animals and ontologically, categorically jailing subjects in order for said subjects to be legible as subjects at all is in *all* instances a manifestation of a logic of jailing as natural and good. And if black trans feminism is an abolitionist project, a project that does not understand the titular terms as tethered to "humans," a project that seeks radical liberation, then it is deeply fitting to assert not an inclusion but an a priori non-exclusion of the nonhuman.

The project at hand is, then, a bit more than what Tiffany Lethabo King calls a "mutual coexistence and relationality with nonhuman, animal, and plant life that radically respatializes the body and notions of the self" (2019, 130). I deeply agree with the sentiment as one that attempts to dissolve the hierarchies embedded in the taxonomizing of species and, in turn, to dissolve the anthropocentric normativities that constitute "being human." The vitiation of taxonomization *is* in service of liberation of the nonhuman—not merely the nonhuman animal. Taxonomizing is not innocent, is not a mere transparent description of extant, distinct entities. The distinctions are not natural (as if something's purported "naturalness" is to be conflated with positive moral valuation); thus, taxonomy is always an endeavor imposed and laden with political weight. For those of us adhering to this iteration of black trans feminism, we must "giv[e] up the ghosts of an easy taxonomic identity, be it racial, gendered, or whatever"; we are to commit to "an interspecies [or better, *trans*species] communion that attempts to go beyond taxonomic structures, beyond taxonomizing gestures, and find the kinship between those entities said in no way to be kin," a "nontaxonomic betrayal of the regime of Man"—a regime that is not merely descriptive of a gendered (human) subject but has authorized itself to adjudicate taxonomic impositions in the first place (Bey 2002, 95). A regime, that is, that incarcerates.

What, then, does all this do? Or a better question: why make this fuss? It seems that, very often, philosophical, perhaps even ontological, epistemological, and metaphysical questions are cast as too lofty and removed from "reality." That to concern oneself with these kinds of questions distracts one from "on-the-ground" work, which is, of course, hierarchized as much more important. At times, maybe detractors have a point—insert armchair-philosopher and navel-gazing insults here. So often, I, as a theorist and philosopher given to radical politics, have personally been charged with not attending (enough) to lived experience and movement work and organizing. "What are you even doing, then? How can you say you are a radical [*that* I've never said, but rather that I adhere to and move through radical politics—an important distinction] when all you do is make shit up?" This is almost literally what has been said, not *to* but *around* me. And with that I take great issue. It is because the very sinew of the organizing and movement work many do is predicated on having thought, having theorized and intellectualized, having imagined something radically otherwise. All the material and experiential, it seems to me, has emerged from desiring and feeling. Do not dare denigrate thought and philosophy—it has cultivated and cared for exactly the ground on which you all work.

I say all this, and conclude with this, because this talk about categorical cordoning and the ontological might appear at first blush as too up in the clouds. There are nonhuman subjects, objects, and beings suffering right now, in this world, and we must tend to that. And you are right.

I want to assert here that the suffering is not after the fact, however; I want to assert that the suffering—which is not the only effect to which we must genuflect in our radicality—stems from how we distinguish and categorize and think about things, and that how we choose to act stems from what we've theorized and how we've theorized liberation. I am not interested in a hierarchy here. This is not to say that what I've done is more or less important than what others do. We all are in this, and that is what black trans feminism, as I understand it, has been saying all along. It is not that this one discourse or position wins and all else either needs to follow or loses. No, we are all in this, because black trans feminism "allows for other projects of radicality to serve not as competitors but goons and accomplices in the struggle together" (Bey 2022, 63).

CHAPTER TWO

The Reproduction of Violence in Resistance to Brahminical Vegetarianism

Varun Joshi

Nonhuman-animal (herein referred to as animal) rights efforts in India face multiple systems of violence, especially caste-based oppression. Hindus who practice vegetarianism link their dietary choice to active justice aligned with contemporary interpretations of Hinduism. However, current state-level Hindu nationalism spearheaded by the governing Bharatiya Janataya Party (BJP) provides a very narrow form of animal rights that excludes non-Hindus, non-Brahmin Hindus, animals aside from cows, and the environment. Meanwhile, resistance to Brahminical vegetarianism in India manifests as the production of an absent referent pertaining to animals, using the commodification of cows and the consumption of cow flesh to protest state-administered violence in the name of animal rights. This chapter juxtaposes how animal rights are appropriated by Hindu nationalism within India and how resistance to Hindutva reproduces violence against animals.

By viewing cow protection through an ecocentric lens, this chapter builds on Yamini Narayanan's (2018a; 2018b; 2019) focus on considering the vulnerabilities of animals. Ecocentrism, a theoretical framework from green criminology, is applied to examine how cows, as social agents, are used by various social actors in contemporary India. Thus, I identify strategies used to reject state violence, along with the consequences of viewing cows as social actors in discussions surrounding violence and cows in India. This chapter begins with an analysis of animal rights in Hinduism to situate how the predominant religion in India engages with animals. Then, I examine how current Hindu nationalism weaponizes cow protection, along with state-administered violence in response to perceived threats to cows. Next is an account of contemporary resistance by victims of Hindutva-aligned cow vigilantism, demonstrating the dissemination of violence by the state against minority groups in India. This is followed by a critique of resistance to cow vigilantism that identifies the production of violence against cows. Finally, I outline alternative strategies to counter both state violence under the guise of cow vigilantism and further perpetuation of violence against animals. This discussion brings forth the emancipatory power of both veganism and anti-caste animal rights.

INDIA AND COW SLAUGHTER

Whether Hinduism, the predominant religion in India and religion of the current Hindu nationalist government, prohibits or allows the consumption of cows is beyond the scope of this chapter. (Arguments can be made that the term "Hindu" is a colonial imposition with a complex history.) There is evidence for both the consumption of cows and the rejection of animal consumption in Vedic literature (Gundimeda and Ashwin 2018; Sunder 2019; Akram, Nasar, Safdar, and Sher 2021). Nonetheless, as noted, the *Sanātana Dharma*'s (herein referred to as Hinduism for convenience) stance on cow consumption is beside the crux of my argument. Instead, this section briefly outlines cow protection in the Indus region and identifies the current relationality toward cows in India.

Since the start of the nineteenth century, Hindu political groups have recognized the potential for cows to be mobilized as a symbol of unity to highlight commonalities among peoples in the Indus region, due to their utility in providing labor and milk products (Jaffrelot 2008; Adcock 2010; Chigateri 2010). *Gaurakshini Sabhas* (cow protection organizations) facilitated a unification that transcended nationalist identity, class, caste, and religion to protest British industrialization; cow protection was mobilized as resistance against the British Raj, which was opening abattoirs to address its military needs (Adcock 2010; Gundimeda and Ashwin 2018). Along with the *Swadeshi* (anti-foreign cloth) movement and civil disobedience against the British Raj, cow protection was a tool used by both Hindu reformists and nationalists to fight colonialism (Dharampal and Mukundan 2002; Adcock 2010; Gundimeda and Ashwin 2018; Narayanan 2018b). This has not historically been the domain of solely Hindu groups, however, as Muslims, castes that followed Islamic traditions, and lower-caste Hindus who predominantly ate beef also participated in cow protection to fight the British Raj and strive for upward caste mobility (Dharampal and Mukundan 2002).

Hindu reformists such as Swami Dayanand, Mohandas Gandhi, and Jayaprakash Narayan recognized Vedic history's violent relationality toward cows and that cow protection was an ongoing practice that was producing a new Hinduism based on *ahimsa*, or nonviolence (Adcock 2010; Narayanan 2018a; Akram et al. 2021). On the one hand, Hindu reformists asserted that legal sanctions were ineffective due to the potential for conflict between Hindu and non-Hindu communities; on the other hand, cow protection was seen as admirable in that it was fostering a new Indian identity. Again, Hindu nationalists have not been the sole proprietors of cow protection, as cow protection rituals have been accessed by leaders, non-Hindus, and non-Brahmin castes to allow participation in regional cultures. Until the late nineteenth century, cross-participation in cultural practices, including cow protection was common among Hindus and non-Hindus, especially Sikhs, a reality that is further explored later in this chapter (Dharampal and Mukundan 2002).

Although India has a large percentage of Hindu vegetarians, not all Hindus are vegetarian, and it is important to note that India is the world's second largest exporter of beef (Chigateri 2008; 2010; Sathyamala 2019; Akram et al. 2021). As households' incomes rise, so does the consumption of animal products and animals, including cows (Srinivasan and Rao 2015). Cow slaughter is banned in several Indian states, and there is an overpopulation of abandoned cows in every region, which results in both public health concerns and concerns about the cows' welfare (Adcock 2018; Narayanan 2018a; 2018b; Sharma et al. 2019). Various prohibitions on cow slaughter have resulted in cow slaughter and beef production transitioning underground, where it is difficult to regulate (Chigateri 2008; 2010; Qureshi 2012; Narayanan 2018b). The mechanization of agriculture, bans on cow slaughter and euthanasia, and lack of state support in housing abandoned cows in *gaushalas* (designated cow sanctuaries) contribute to the presence of cows throughout India (Narayanan 2019; Sharma et al. 2019). *Gaushalas* often are overpopulated and lack the resources to appropriately care for abandoned cows, and there are no federal-level standards of care for *gaushalas* to follow (Narayanan 2019). *Gaushalas,* in addition to soliciting donations, are encouraged to cover the costs of operations by selling milk and dung; when bulls are not available, shelter employees reenact the cruelties of the dairy industry (artificial insemination of cows, separation of calves and mothers, etc.) (Narayanan 2018b; 2019; Sharma et al. 2019). Moreover, *gaushalas* reproduce the caste status of cows in preferring to care for cows rather than buffaloes, considered lower-caste due to various features and their historical association with impurity (Gundimeda and Ashwin 2018; Narayanan 2018b; 2019). *Gaushalas* are not restricted to caring for cows; they can also farm milk products for sale and use, justifying the process by citing the purity associated with milk and the fact that foods prepared from cow milk are considered inherently *prasad*, or holy offerings (Narayanan 2018b; 2019; Sharma et al. 2019). Managers of *gaushalas* rarely recognize the connection between dairy production and cow slaughter. Milking cows for consumption in vegetarian communities is seen as nonviolent while anything related to cow slaughter is considered violent, even in documented instances of *gaushalas* selling cows to butchers (Narayanan 2018b; 2019). It is not uncommon for vegetarians to raise cows to knowingly sell them to butchers (Staples 2017; Narayanan 2018).

While constitutional protection of cows (under Article 51A) is rationalized by invoking both the political and commercial worth of the bovine species, buffaloes, despite their use value, do not receive the same caste privileges that cows do (Gundimeda and Ashwin 2018; Narayanan 2018; 2019). In addition to the marginalization of buffaloes due to their alleged impurity, the individualization of cow guardianship demonstrates the Hindu nationalist state's attempt to absolve itself of responsibility for cow welfare and relegate this responsibility to the public instead of providing the necessary infrastructure to ensure that cows are cared for. Lastly, Article 48 of the Indian Constitution stipulates that cows ought to be protected from slaughter due to their value in providing labor, organic manure, and milk products (Adcock 2018; Gundimeda and Ashwin 2018; Sunder 2019). Article 48 was designed to align with secular conceptions of animal relationality, but there is room for interpretation as to how to act in accordance with improving animal and human welfare, and those who slaughter cows are portrayed as shortsighted, not able to see the economic value of cows (Chigateri 2008; 2010; Adcock 2018; Sunder 2019). Thus, the value of cows as implied in the Indian Constitution ultimately stems from their commodification, which is antithetical to the goal of providing them with rights. Furthermore, the designation of utility and sacredness that helps place cows in a higher caste than other animals results in the denial of moral consideration to these other animals (Srinivasan and Rao 2015; Narayanan 2018b).

Currently, cow slaughter is banned in twenty out of India's twenty-eight states; for the remaining states, there are variations in how cows can be slaughtered (Sathyamala 2019). India is currently among world leaders in cow slaughter, with lower-caste Hindus and Muslims making up a significant portion of this industry (Gundimeda and Ashwin 2018; Narayanan 2018a; 2018b). Some BJP politicians, such as the head of Chhattisgarh, wish to see cow slaughter-ban offenders subject to the death penalty, with expressed support from popular BJP politicians like Uttar Pradesh chief minister Yogi Adityanath (*The Wire* 2017).

HINDUTVA APPROPRIATION OF ANIMAL JUSTICE

Hindutva refers to Hindu nationalism, which advocates an Indian state based on a Hindu nation and religion and which excludes Muslims and other non-Hindu Indians from society due to their categorization as foreign invaders (Jaffrelot 2008; Rao 2011; Adcock 2018; Gundimeda and Ashwin 2018). Hindutva frames cow protection in multiple ways, with multiple motivations, ranging from economic interest (due to the utility of cows as sources of labor and food) to reverence for their sacred status (Jaffrelot 2008; Chigateri 2010; Gundimeda and Ashwin 2018; Narayanan 2018b; 2019). The BJP government has been explicit in its promotion of violent means to protect cows from those deemed enemies of the Hindu state (Narayanan 2019; Akram et al. 2021).

Hindutva groups have a convenient blind spot: the violent relationality between the consumption of dairy products, something a large portion of upper-caste Hindus indulge in, and participation in sending cows to slaughterhouses (Qureshi 2012; Adcock 2018; Narayanan 2018b; 2019; Reddy 2022). Moreover, the sacrificial killing of goats or chickens in Hindu festivals practiced by upper-caste Hindus and the sale of cows to non-Hindu butchers are overlooked. Also, in times of food scarcity, Hindu communities do not have issues with consuming cows (Chigateri 2008; 2010; Adcock 2018; Narayanan 2018b; Reddy 2022). The Hindutva conception of animal welfare produces a social hierarchy that has been challenged in the Indian legal system. In this hierarchy, cows are at the top of the spiritual ladder due to their use value, but other animals can be subject to violence (Chigateri 2008; 2010; Adcock 2010; 2018; Gundimeda and Ashwin 2018; Narayanan 2018a; 2018b; 2019). Moreover, the placement of cows in dairy production undermines Hindutva philosophy given the harms inflicted by the industry and the abandonment of cows who are too old to produce milk (Jaffrelot 2008; Srinivasan and Rao 2015; Narayanan 2018a; 2018b). The lack of state policy in caring for abandoned cows further highlights the inconsistency in Hindutva animal welfare (Srinivasan and Rao 2015; Narayanan 2018a; Sharma et al. 2019). Guardianship of abandoned cows is transferred over to individuals, and *gaushalas* are rendered dependent on donations from the public. Indeed, cow protection bolstered by Hindu nationalist rhetoric is a veil to disguise state activity that further consolidates Hindu nationalist power over the Indus region (Rao 2011). The BJP has made efforts to ban literature geared toward various levels of education that outlines Vedic consumption of beef. It has also attempted to make offenders of cow slaughter bans punishable under the Prevention of Terrorism Act (Chigateri 2008; Rao 2011; Narayanan 2018a; Akram et al. 2021). Nevertheless, Hindutva cow protection policy becomes impossible to administer as it targets the slaughter of cows without considering the breeding of animals for dairy production (Narayanan 2018a; 2018b).

Cow Vigilantism

Cow vigilantism is central to this analysis as it demonstrates how state appendages reinforce themselves through mobs that forcibly enact Hindutva ideology pertaining to cow rights. Self-proclaimed *gau rakshaks* (which translates to "cow protectors") take action against any individual allegedly participating in violent relationality toward cows (Prabhu 2016; Gundimeda and Ashwin 2018; Sunder 2019). This vigilantism manifests as financial extortion of cow traders, lynching or beating of those suspected of consuming beef, physical and sexual violence against their families, and various societal othering methods (Chigateri 2010; Ashraf 2017; Sathyamala 2019; Akram et al. 2021). Victims of *gau rakshaks* are often Dalits, other lower-caste Hindus, and non-Hindus who work in professions wherein cows or their corpses are harmed, including but not limited to butchery, leather tanning, and livestock transport (Chigateri 2008; 2010; Ashraf 2017; Gundimeda and Ashwin 2018; Narayanan 2018b; Sunder 2019; Chandra 2022). *Gau rakshaks* exploit the fact that the Indian judicial system enforces cow slaughter bans due to the use value of cows, thereby upholding Hindu values, to enjoy immunity from the law (Chigateri 2008; 2010; Chandra 2022). There have been numerous instances of violence administered against those deemed by *gau rakshaks* as offenders of cow slaughter bans, including but not limited to the lynching of five Dalit men in Haryana in August of 2003, the stripping of two Muslim cow traders in South Canara in 2005, the killing of Mohammad Akhlaq in Dadri in 2015, and the flogging of four Dalit youths who were transporting cow corpses in Gujarat in July of 2016 (Chigateri 2008; 2010; Chandra 2022).

As Sunder (2019) describes, alleged transgressors of beef bans facing violence from *gau rakshaks* are a grotesque caricature of *homo sacer*, and how these victims of cow vigilantism experience violence is represented by the production of bare life, as conceptualized by Agamben (Nikolopoulou 2000). Bare life is the life of one who can be killed by anyone (but not sacrificed), outside the law and without legal consequences (Nikolopoulou 2000; Sunder 2019). Lower-caste Hindus are siloed into such hereditary professions as animal slaughter and leather tanning by Brahminical Hindus, only to be vilified and subjected to violence for performing the professions designated for their social status (Sathyamala 2019; Sunder 2019; Reddy 2022). Muslims, Christians, and other non-Hindus who are employed in positions that involve harming cows thus become subject to cow vigilantism, even if they do not follow Hindu beliefs (Sunder 2019). Anyone involved in cow slaughter is ensnared in Hindutva policy and the Hindutva framework, punished as a transgressor against Brahminical Hinduism and rendered an outsider, worthy of being socially and physically destroyed—all to uphold a Brahminical Hindu societal order (Sunder 2019). The transgressor is placed outside the law, only to be dragged into Hindutva structures again so that violence against them is justified. A state of exception emerges: to reinforce Hindutva ideology, alleged cow harmers are trapped in a flux that subjects them to extrajudicial forms of violence facilitated by the state.

A peculiar governmentality is witnessed whereby political and judicial forces create the conditions for *gau rakshaks* to uphold cow protection policy and to police non-Hindus who allegedly participate in cow slaughter (Rao 2011; Fletcher 2017). "Governmentality" refers to the art of governing and controlling populations through disciplinary power from afar, with subjects appearing to participate in the reproduction of discipline to uphold state logic (Fletcher 2017). In the case of cow protection violence, *gau rakshaks* act as informal state agents to reproduce Hindutva ideology by enforcing cow slaughter bans, with violence against anyone deemed guilty of transgressing against Hindu nationalism deployed as a disciplinary measure.

RESISTANCE TO COW SLAUGHTER BANS

Resistance to cow slaughter bans has involved the consumption of cows in various ways. During the Sukoon festival at Hyderabad Central University (HCU), the Dalit Students' Union (DSU) challenged the university's executive body by establishing a stall that distributed dishes with cow flesh (Gundimeda 2009). Cow flesh was identified as an important element of the food practices of the Dalit community and was therefore required in the festival to ensure that India's cultural diversity was represented (Gundimeda 2009). The HCU unsuccessfully attempted to shut down this stall. The DSU viewed this moment as an opportunity to invite upper-caste Hindus to try the food and to re-evaluate their perception of cow consumption (Gundimeda 2009). This move was inspired by the observation that Dalits' attempts to adopt strict vegetarian diets did not protect them from violence and that affirming their identity through food and providing a space for dialogue with communities that disagreed with them was a means for conflict resolution (Gundimeda 2009). Indeed, some Dalit women adopt vegetarianism to be recognized as clean, but changes in conduct cannot break Hindutva conceptions of caste (Chigateri 2008; Gundimeda 2009). Meanwhile, Dalits who become vegetarian may be considered inauthentic Dalits (Chigateri 2008). In Chigateri's (2008) research, members of the Dalit Mathu Mahila Chaluvali, or Dalit and Women's Movement (DMC), talked about the consumption of rat meat by the Vadda community alongside the consumption of beef to disrupt conceptions of disgust and what constitutes good and bad food.

In Kerala, where cows have been a part of the regional culinary culture, Indians protested cow slaughter bans by hosting parties and events where cow flesh was consumed (Ehsan 2015; Doshi 2017; Narayanan 2018b). In the words of locals in the city of Kozhikode, beef is not merely food but "a deep-seated emotion" (Doshi 2017). Lawyers in Chennai protested cow slaughter bans at the Madras High Court by bringing and sharing dishes with cow flesh with fellow protestors, arguing that the state did not have any business deciding what citizens could eat unless public health concerns were relevant (Subramani 2015). Protestors referenced Article 21 of the Indian Constitution, which states that one cannot be denied their personal liberty, under which eating falls (Subramani 2015). After the Delhi police raided a restaurant called Kerala House following reports from Hindu nationalists that the restaurant served cow on its menu, various Keralites participated in eating cow flesh as resistance (Mathew 2015; Nair 2015). Politicians like Ritabrata Banerjee and other citizens who would normally avoid red meat on the recommendation of their doctors visited Kerala House to join the protest (Mathew 2015). Anirudhan Sampath, a politician from the Communist Party of India, questioned: "How can someone dictate what should I eat or what should I cook in my kitchen[?] Today it is beef, tomorrow it could be fish. Where will this end?" (Nair 2015). The Member of Legislative Assembly (MLA) of Jammu and Kashmir, Engineer Rashid, hosted a "beef party" and expressed support for the Kerala House protest, stating that governments should respect the sentiment of local communities concerning food (Ehsan 2015).

"You keep the cow's tail, give us our land" was a phrase coined by Dalit political activist Jignesh Mevani while at the vanguard of the Dalit Asmita Yatra (literally "Dalit March for Self-Respect"), organized in response to an incident of cow vigilantism violence against Dalit youths in Gujarat (Jha 2016; Prabhu 2016). Mevani organized communities to collectively refuse to perform traditional Dalit professions like animal-corpse disposal, scavenging, and gutter cleaning until the state agreed on a policy of providing each Dalit family in Gujarat with five acres of land (Jha 2016; Prabhu 2016). At the Dalit Asmita Yatra, Mevani asked the crowd, "Do you still want to continue skinning dead animals?" to which the crowd responded, "No!" (Jha 2016).

In Rajasthan, the Banjara community faces physical violence and financial extortion perpetrated by *gau rakshaks* from the Bajrang Dal for transporting oxen and handling sales of oxen to farmers, a profession they have historically performed (Ashraf 2017). Banjara women were at the forefront of protests to raise awareness of cow vigilantism affecting Hindu trading communities (Ashraf 2017). Victims of financial extortion by *gau rakshaks* are accused of selling cows to slaughterhouses, even though they sell oxen and only to farmers needing animals for labor (Pande 2016; Ashraf 2017). In response to these accusations from *gau rakshaks*, members of the community have argued: "We Banjaras trade in oxen, not in cows. These oxen are used to plow the rocky terrain of South Rajasthan. Trading oxen is our identity, our right. And, mind you, we too are Hindus. But the vigilantes have turned the cow into an emotional issue for their dubious ends" (Ashraf 2017). Some dairy farmers in Rajasthan have resorted to breeding and trading goats instead of oxen to avoid persecution by *gau rakshaks*, but these farmers acknowledge that this is not a realistic option for everyone (Ashraf 2017).

Although Christians in South India eat largely vegetarian diets, they still hold certain cow dishes in high esteem as cow being served would mark special days—Sundays, holidays, or other festive occasions (Staples 2017). Christian Indians have adopted beef consumption as a symbol of resistance against Hindu hegemonic dissemination and because state attempts to legislate food products appeared undemocratic to them. Consumption of cows was also fueled by attempts to achieve certain health-related goals, with Ayurvedic texts being referenced as justification, as consuming cows was thought to have medicinal benefits (Staples 2017).

Lastly, a Delhi-based photographer, Sujatro Ghosh, photographed women wearing a mask of a cow head in an attempt to raise awareness of the insufficient state response to violence against women as well as to protest the political support for cow vigilantism (Pandey 2017). Given the lack of justice for victims of sexual violence, Ghosh's message is that even cows are considered more important than women. Ghosh's is a silent but visually distinct form of protest (Pandey 2017).

CURRENT CRIMINOLOGICAL ENGAGEMENT WITH COW PROTECTION

Contemporary frameworks toward restorative justice in criminology appear insufficient for addressing the harms produced by cow vigilantism in India. "Restorative justice" refers to the systematic consideration of the needs of offending and victimized parties in a conflict to ensure that the needs of all are met in a collaborative effort. In line with this approach, Akram et al. (2021) call for collaboration between Hindus and non-Hindus, overlooking Hindutva influences in the cultivation of violence in cow protection debates. It is problematic to frame Hindu nationalists as being economically exploited by Muslims involved in the beef industry, as Hindu nationalists concerned with cow protection are already prohibited from participating in cow slaughter for any reason, financial or spiritual. Ownership in institutions that slaughter cows conflicts with an ethic of care toward cows that is central to Hindu ideology and that Hindutva embraces. At first glance, the Hindu–Muslim cow protection committees suggested by Akram et al. seem to hold value, but their ethnocentric bias toward Hindu beliefs lies in the protection afforded to cows but not other animals. Moreover, violence inflicted on cows would still occur, just in a mutually decided-upon manner. The call for increased police response to incidents of cow vigilantism, including the monitoring of communication channels like WhatsApp, underestimates the insidious connection between law enforcement and surveillance techniques. Increased police activity has the potential to both further marginalize victims of cow vigilantism and justify violence against *gau rakshaks*. Meanwhile, the call for complementary legal intervention to support community collaboration overlooks the propensity of the Indian judicial system to uphold cow protection laws using the logic of use value in Article 48, while dismissing claimants who are non-Hindu (Chigateri 2008; 2010). Lastly, it is unclear what protection for cows looks like in practice. Criminology scholars engaging with the phenomenon of cow protection need to determine if cow protection is an extension of animal welfare only, allowing cows to still be eventually harmed, or if an animal rights position should be articulated to ensure cows are truly safeguarded. An inability to conceptualize animals as social actors in discussions of cow protection demonstrates the shortcomings of traditional criminological approaches in engaging with complex issues like cow protection violence.

Gundimeda and Ashwin (2018) offer five suggestions in response to the inconsistency of current cow protection laws. First, cows are to be treated as other domestic animals are, with the responsibility lying with their owners, who could do whatever they wanted with the cows. Second, the constitutional status of the Supreme Court of India's reinterpretation of Article 48 is upheld, so that cows and their progeny above seventeen years old are allowed to be slaughtered. Third, the slaughter, along with the consumption, of all cows and their progeny is otherwise prohibited. Fourth, the enforcement of cow slaughter bans is left to state-level governments. Lastly, cow slaughter is banned, but the slaughter of bulls and oxen at a certain age is permitted (Gundimeda and Ashwin 2018). These suggestions warrant this chapter's call for a more critical approach to cow protection in India. Each of the solutions suggested leads to more violence against both cows and Indians involved in their slaughter. The most radical of the solutions, which is to ban the slaughter and consumption of cows, reproduces casteist speciesism by elevating cows, through legal protection, above other animals who are consumed.

Moreover, the conditions that would cause a ban on cow slaughter and consumption to be perceived as unfavorable are not questioned, which limits the potential for achieving justice for those who are enmeshed in the cow protection debate against their will. At the same time, the economic, social, and cultural structures that allow for the infliction of violence upon animals in India are not challenged.

GREEN CRIMINOLOGY AND ECOCENTRISM

Coined in the 1990s, "green criminology" refers to an interdisciplinary field continuously informed by environmental sociology, psychology, labor studies, feminist criminology, public health studies, and many more (Lynch and Stretsky 2014). The critical theory underlying green criminology identifies the dominant frameworks in society that uphold processes of domination and moreover recognizes land and animals as social actors capable of experiencing victimization (Lynch and Stretsky 2014). By adopting an ecocentric framework, green criminology recognizes the interconnectedness of humans and other animals based on a common capacity to experience harm, to affect one another (Halsey and White 1998; White 2018). Ecocentrism incorporates elements of both anthropocentrism and biocentrism. Anthropocentrism privileges humans and their interests, such that nonhuman entities are seen as means to attain those interests and harm is measured by how those interests are affected (Halsey and White 1998; White 2018). Meanwhile, biocentrism sees the preservation of nonhuman entities as a moral imperative, regardless of consequences to humans (Halsey and White 1998). As such, ecocentrism recognizes that human institutions produce negative consequences for animals and other nonhuman entities and a holistic lens is required to identify the origins of harm. Nonhuman entities are viewed as social actors who can experience harm, with both biophysical limits and social constructs taken into consideration (Halsey and White 1998; White 2018). An ecocentric lens through which to view cow protection in India provides a consistent framework that treats land, animals, and humans as interconnected, yet also as distinct social actors with unique experiences.

ECOCENTRIC ENGAGEMENT WITH RESISTANCE TO COW PROTECTIONISM

Yamini Narayanan's (2018a; 2018b; 2019) vegan feminist critique of Hindutva and cow protection outlines the numerous ways in which the discourse surrounding cow vigilantism needs to address structural violence produced against humans in addition to failures in providing protection for cows. Both Hindus and non-Hindus suffer under cow protection laws (Pande 2016; Ashraf 2017; Narayanan 2018a; 2018b; 2019). Narayanan's focus on the vulnerability of social actors who are animals is vital given the highlighting of the different structural forces that exercise violence against various individuals. However, highlighting just the violence experienced by animals and humans due to cow vigilantism results in discourse centered on the animal–human divide without recognizing the land as a dynamic actor instead of a static element in the background of sociological debate.

LIMITATIONS IN CONTEMPORARY RESISTANCE

This section examines the rationale underlining current attempts to protest cow protection laws. Resistance to Hindutva cow vigilantism has manifested as the organization of festivals to distribute meat, as well as the continued consumption of cows to affirm one's heritage and to reify elements of one's regional or religious culture (Gundimeda 2009; Doshi 2017; Staples 2017). However, consuming meat as a means of mobilizing against Hindutva undermines vulnerable communities residing in social and physical spaces where animal flesh is a vital source of nutrition and livelihood (Sunderland 2019). In order that animals who have been hidden by industrialized animal slaughter are made visible, violent relationality toward them is nevertheless maintained (Sunderland 2019). The binary of human versus nonhuman animals is reinforced, along with violence associated with the consumption of cows, even within lower-caste Hindu, Muslim, and various other communities with traditions that incorporate cow consumption in the Indus subcontinent. When policy meant to protect cows is met with their increased consumption, the phenomenon of cow vigilantism emerges, reifying the violence imposed upon cows, buffaloes, and other bovine animals, as well as the land upon which they are farmed given the resources required to raise bovine animals as food sources (Brent, Neff, Santo, and Vigorito 2015; Winders and Abrell 2021). Moreover, violence experienced by individuals who must slaughter bovines is reproduced, which adds to the psychological harm already inflicted by the act of killing (Winders and Abrell 2021). By applying an ecocentric lens, we can identify three actors: humans, animals, and land. Humans suffer due to the processes inherent in the production of food products from bovines. Animals suffer from being exploited in life and eventually killed. Land suffers given the impact that rearing bovines for food has on the natural environment.

Continuing to use bovines as food as a means of rejecting current Hindu food hierarchies ends up reifying the very hierarchy that harms non–upper caste Hindus. As Dalit rights activist Kancha Ilaiah argued, buffaloes are more sacred than cows as more Indians drink buffalo milk than cow milk (Chigateri 2008). In this instance, appealing to the use value of buffaloes reproduces the same structural violence as that resulting from Article 48 of the Indian Constitution, which stipulates that bovine animals are protected from slaughter due to their use value related to agricultural practices. The hierarchical Hindutva caste order that places one animal above another is disrupted by one Dalit's (Ilaiah's) perspective that a low-caste animal like the buffalo is more productive than a high-caste animal like the cow. However, this merely creates a new caste order in which buffaloes are above cows, while both animals are still commodified for their utility and neither is afforded any consideration based on moral value. Meanwhile, when one argues that all bovine animals, not just cows, should be valued ("glory to the cow, the bull, and the buffalo that give us such rich food at a low cost"), the societal structures that inflict harm upon land due to the strains of dairy production are reified (Chigateri 2008). Once again, the application of an ecocentric lens illustrates not only how animals and land are harmed in distinct ways, but also how humans are subject to harm by maintaining practices that uphold violent structures.

Hindu victims of financial extortion from *gau rakshaks* as well as the Banjara community have engaged in two practices to resist cow vigilantism. Some farmers with access to enough resources transition from farming oxen to farming goats to avoid scrutiny from *gau rakshaks*. Nevertheless, two hierarchical orders remain standing. First, the Hindutva caste system that treats cows as sacred is reinforced: the sacred can exist only if there are other, non-sacred animals present to demarcate the limits of the caste order applied to animals. Second, a hierarchy based on human exceptionalism and speciesism is also strengthened when farmers swap oxen for goats. "Human exceptionalism" refers to the ontological and ethical distinction between human and nonhuman forms of life to assert the uniqueness of human life (Srinivasan and Kasturirangan 2016). "Speciesism," akin to racism or sexism, refers to a socioecological phenomenon in which humans assign greater value to certain species while devaluing others (Narayanan 2018b). Whether oxen or goats are involved, a system that commodifies animals and renders them vulnerable to the harms associated with animal agriculture is upheld. Alternatively, when other Banjara individuals argue that oxen trading is integral to their rights and identity, the commodification of animals is reproduced, entrenching the Banjara identity in a single idea. Banjaras have not engaged solely in animal trade, but rather have also traded spices, produce, flora, and various other goods. The reduction of the Banjara identity to only animal trade denies Banjara genealogy rooted in trading goods that did not exploit animals and that promoted nonviolent relationality (Sinha 2008).

Lastly, Ghosh's photography project aimed at advocating for survivors of sexual violence creates a predicament. The comparison with Hindutva scrutiny of actions concerning cows is apt in that *gau rakshaks* will defend a cow over a woman. However, making the claim that cows are treated better than women does a disservice to both survivors of sexual violence and cows. Cows and women experience failed legal protection in different ways. A cow is not dealing with human sexual harassment any more than a woman is facing the suffering associated with being a dairy cow and facing eventual slaughter. A false equivalence is constructed, which undermines the respective experiences of cows and women.

Conclusion

Future scholarship on cow vigilantism can benefit from adopting an ecocentric lens to ensure a more complete engagement with the topic. Discourse on the violence produced by Hindutva policies can benefit from calls for a more critical examination of Hindu mythology. Narayanan's (2018a) reinterpretation of the *Samudra Manthana*, or the tale of the Churning of the Ocean of Milk, constitutes a possibly unintended attempt at reclaiming Hindu mythologies. Such reinterpretations align with an ecocentric perspective, presenting the religion of Hinduism as a human construct and not essentializing it by arguing for a simplistic rejection of it. Rather, a discursive process occurs in which stories and the natural world are examined to include excluded animals, humans, and land. These attempts at reclamation are vital in the fight against Hindutva cow protection and the violence it produces. Narayanan's ecofeminist engagement with cow protection is a nuanced and critical one, identifying how cows, as social actors, are subject to a "disassembly line" of animal production whereby their biological bovine motherhood, their children, milk, flesh, skin, and bones, are taken from them to sustain a Hindu nation aligned with Hindutva (2019). Such ecofeminist analyses can benefit from taking into consideration an additional social actor: land. Narayanan situates both humans and animals, along with their complex social positions, but it is easy to overlook land in India given the breadth of the topic of cow protection. Guided by an ecocentric approach, scholars can continue to identify the harms experienced by land, specifically from resource extraction and methane emissions. Lastly, scholarship on cow vigilantism can benefit from consideration of the voices of marginalized communities affected by cow vigilantism, like Dalits, by further including the perspectives of vegan Dalits engaged in grassroots activism to resist and reject the structural violence produced by Hindutva cow protection (Mukherjee 2022). Indeed, veganism facilitates an ecocentric lens in engaging with complex topics like cow protection. The perspectives of those resisting Hindutva caste structures through veganism can offer robust contributions to the fight against cow vigilantism.

CHAPTER THREE

The Place of Veganism in Multispecies Justice

Darren Chang

Multispecies Justice (MSJ) is an emerging field of study that aims to theorize what the inclusion of more-than-humans in our justice considerations might require. One group of scholars who have mapped the research terrain for MSJ traces its intellectual and political origins to animal rights, environmental justice and political ecology, and posthumanism, as well as Indigenous philosophies and decolonizing justice theories (Celermajer et al. 2021). Although proponents of veganism and animal liberation exist in all of the aforementioned intellectual traditions, veganism has generally not been widely accepted as an integral part of securing justice for nonhuman animals (with the exception of animal rights); in fact, it has often been critiqued and resisted within these traditions. Moreover, the diverse theories that MSJ brings together often diverge on what the approaches and priorities are that ought to guide us in striving for a more just world. Understanding these tensions allows us to situate veganism in at least two spheres of contention within MSJ: (1) internal to each distinct intellectual tradition or theoretical position and (2) between one tradition and the next.

In this chapter, I consider how the contentious status of veganism within MSJ might help us clarify the relations between veganism and different epistemologies. I also examine the implications this has for organizing across divergent values and frameworks. I begin by engaging with Richard Twine's (2022) summary and analysis of the debates surrounding veganism within ecofeminism, particularly around the question of universalism. I argue that while the ecofeminist debates on contextual veganism and vegan universalism are generative in revealing key points of tension between positions that are difficult to reconcile, both the contextual-versus-universal framing and an intersectional ecofeminist perspective ultimately present a limited understanding of the actual relational dynamics between veganism and different worldviews and contexts. Furthermore, although ecofeminist analysis has produced painstaking approaches that attempt to critically and creatively move beyond the impasse of the veganism debate, its limitations emanate from the fact that the framework remains trapped within a single intellectual tradition (i.e., feminism) and that ecofeminism lacked diversity during the specific era when the debates took place.

Following from the lessons of the ecofeminist debates on veganism, I propose that adopting an MSJ approach as the starting point of analysis could effectively circumvent the challenges revealed by the ecofeminists. The key advantage of MSJ is that its framework allows for the recognition of a multiplicity of veganism(s) that either exist or have the potential to exist within any of the epistemologies that have something relevant to contribute to the goal and agenda of achieving justice across species. Here, I have parenthesized the plural "s" in "veganism(s)" to emphasize the existence of veganism in multiple forms, understood through a plurality of worldviews, and to signify the interplay between these different forms of veganism. By examining how different veganism(s) might influence one another within the field of MSJ through the concept of vernacularization (a process whereby local actors adopt and present globalized ideas in their local contexts, to be expanded on later), I argue that compared to the contextual-versus-universal and intersectional framings that came out of the ecofeminist debates, the Gramscian concept of hegemony (and counter-hegemony) might be more productive in getting at the power relations and radical, transformative potentials between different veganism(s), as well as their relations to the broader anthropocentric and speciesist norms they seek to contest.

Lessons from the Ecofeminist Debates

In *Ecofeminism: Feminist Intersections with Other Animals and the Earth*, edited by Carol J. Adams and Lori Gruen, Richard Twine (2022) revisits the ecofeminist debates over veganism. Twine's overview shows that "ecofeminists have historically been cautious towards universalism," given their critiques of masculinist and rationalist approaches to animal ethics, which tended to be articulated in universalistic terms, disavowing everyday lived realities and emotionality in ethical decision-making (2022, 235). Given that, historically, Western cultures have been globally dominant and dominated by Enlightenment rationalism, in practice, veganism and animal advocacy shaped by Western rationalist universalism risk reproducing imperialist and colonial patterns, along with all the oppressive power dynamics they entail. Twine highlights examples of these oppressive tendencies in animal advocacy by looking at various critiques, such as Greta Gaard and Claire Jean Kim's (separate) analyses of the conflicts between animal advocates and the Makah over the Makah Whale Hunt; Maneesha Deckha's examination of the connections between nationalism, masculinity, and animal exploitation; as well as Dinesh Wadiwel's account of how Australian animal advocates coded the animals they sought to protect as "Australian" in opposing the live export of cattle to Indonesian slaughterhouses, thereby representing Australians as civilized and Indonesians as racialized, barbaric others (2022, 233–35). In response to such issues, ecofeminists and those aligned with the tradition have opted for contextual approaches to promoting veganism or advocating for animals as a means to acknowledge the socioeconomic and cultural contexts that might make nonhuman-animal exploitation unavoidable and to navigate the nuances of power relations between privileged and marginalized groups in relation to changing nonhuman-animal use practices.

However, as Twine goes on to show, the concept of "contextual" is itself highly contested and deployed differently among ecofeminists (2022, 240–44). On one hand, there is the position taken by those such as Deane Curtin (1991) and Marti Kheel (2004), who recognize both the contextual restrictions to practicing veganism and "the compulsory nature of norms of animal consumption as universals in need to critique" and therefore uphold vegetarianism/veganism as an ideal that Twine argues is "not far from universalistic," meaning an "ecofeminist ethic of care [that] argues against the consumption of animals" under most circumstances (2022, 236, 243–44). On the other hand, Val Plumwood's (2000; 2003; 2004) contextual approach "[espouses] an anti-vegan stance" that limits itself to opposing industrial animal agriculture but not all animal consumption because, as Twine argues, Plumwood has "incorrectly framed veganism as precluding [the] possibility" of situating the "human" in ecological relations wherein humans and other animals are all deemed edible (2022, 241). Despite efforts such as Twine's to clarify and challenge misconceptions and misplaced critiques of veganism, these seemingly irreconcilable positions have become increasingly entrenched, reflecting the type of tensions that exist over veganism in various communities and movements, including ecofeminism and posthumanism—tensions that persist to this day. For example, in the same collection, *Ecofeminism*, Susan Fraiman's (2022) chapter tracking feminist interventions in animal studies shows that decades since these debates first emerged, influential posthumanist feminist thinkers like Donna Haraway (2008) continue to champion a position similar to Plumwood's, which accepts the perceived unavoidable need to use and kill nonhuman animals in various contexts or even actively supports these violent practices.

At the same time, the contemporary vegan landscape has drastically transformed since the earlier days of the ecofeminist debates. Thanks to the decades of social justice advocacy work done by marginalized peoples, the predominantly privileged vegan communities and movements in the Global North have embraced greater gender, economic, racial, and cultural diversity. This change is reflected in the literature by the growing number of anti-oppressive Black, Indigenous, and People of Color/People of Global Majority (BIPOC/BIPGM) vegan voices that have produced published works over the years. Notable examples include works that articulate Black veganism, such as *Aphro-ism* by Syl Ko and Aph Ko (2017), as well as the collections *Sistah Vegan* (2010) and *Brotha Vegan* (2021), edited by A. Breeze Harper and Omowale Adewale, respectively. Similarly, Indigenous vegans such as Mi'kmaq scholar Margaret Robinson (2013) and Māori scholar Kirsty Dunn (2019) have shared their perspectives on how veganism fits in with their decolonial worldviews and practices.

This changing reality also attests to just how much of the earlier debates regarding the place of veganism in social justice was dominated by whiteness, both in ecofeminist circles and beyond. In my view, this whiteness is embodied by the very terms of the ecofeminist debates; that the early ecofeminists were arguing within the conceptual confines of a universal–contextual continuum, or even creative attempts to move past the deadlock, such as Marti Kheel's "'invitational approach' to veganism" (Twine 2022, 243), speaks to their inability to theorize beyond their standpoints and their intellectual tradition.

To be fair, I do acknowledge that it is important to keep in mind the contexts of the ecofeminists' conversations, specifically with regard to their target audiences and the interlocutors they were speaking back to (predominantly white, privileged Global North scholars in various traditions and the equally white, privileged animal rights and environmental movements) in attempts to make advocacy efforts more sensitive to nuances. This is where MSJ, conceived in an era when the compositions of various intellectual traditions and cultures have become more inclusive of veganism and when veganism itself has become more inclusive and diverse, has an opportunity to learn from the limitations revealed in the ecofeminist debates and to altogether shift the conversation about veganism.

VEGANISM(S) AND MULTISPECIES JUSTICE

In the introduction to a symposium on the value of MSJ, published in the journal *Environmental Politics*, Māori political theorist Christine Winter (2022) writes that the contributors examine how MSJ can help us "rethink, reorder, and revitalize the field of justice studies in order to make it more relevant to the reality of climate change impacts, ecosystem collapse, land- and water-scape degradation, human–ecology dependencies, and social dislocations" (251). Winter suggests that among the strengths of MSJ is that it includes humans and thus "has utility for social justice too," that it "addresses, or has the potential to address, the 'racial-sexual-species-ableist-colonial' contract" in order to "enhance the foundations of justice" beyond addressing what Charles Mills describes as "epistemologies of ignorance" at the roots of certain just oppressions (2022, 252).

It appears, then, that in terms of analysis and the agenda of identifying and simultaneously challenging multiple interconnected forms of oppression, ecofeminism and MSJ are practically indistinguishable. For example, Greta Gaard (1993) has argued that "the insights of ecology, feminism, and socialism" inform "ecofeminism's basic premise that the ideology which authorizes oppressions such as those based on race, class, gender, sexuality, physical abilities, and species is the same ideology which sanctions the oppression of nature" (1). Carol J. Adams and Lori Gruen (2022) have likewise stated that ecofeminism "addresses the various ways that misogyny, heteronormativity, white supremacy, colonialism, and ableism are informed by and support pernicious anthropocentrism, and how analyzing the ways these forces interconnect can produce less violent, more just practices" (xxi). Indeed, elsewhere, Danielle Celermajer and I (forthcoming) have traced and acknowledged how ecofeminists have laid a vital foundation with profound impacts on the formation of MSJ.

Yet, ultimately, both the changes within vegan communities as mentioned earlier and the different starting positions of ecofeminism and MSJ matter significantly with respect to the differences in what the two theoretical frameworks could enable and accommodate. Global North feminism has always been entrapped within institutionalized privileges, such that all the marginalized peoples whom the ideals of feminism sought to represent have had to fight their ways to inclusion and/or visibility. This means that historically, in practice, (eco)feminism advanced in an additive fashion, such that it struggled to become increasingly inclusive of other standpoints and epistemologies.

Meanwhile, MSJ, having been conceived at a historical moment built on past struggles, in an intellectual environment already made mindful of radically different epistemologies and standpoints, has a fundamental commitment to diversity and multiplicity that offers spaces of cooperative contestation and facilitates the engagement of all perspectives relevant to the fight for justice from the outset. This early effort at inclusion has been reflected not only in the multiple intellectual traditions that MSJ relies on but also in works such as *The Promise of Multispecies Justice* (Chao, Bolender, and Kirksey 2022), an edited collection featuring a diverse lineup of contributors. To be clear, there is no guarantee that MSJ would succeed in maintaining its commitment to a collective reimagining of justice through diverse theoretical traditions. It may very well fall short due to institutional constraints. Nonetheless, MSJ is currently construed in such a way that it should theoretically be a field of study, as well as an intellectual and political project, wherein multiple veganism(s) stemming from different traditions and epistemologies stand a chance of finding their places and productively working within and across their respective bases of knowledge.

To conceptualize how different veganism(s) might interact with each other within MSJ, we must first understand the development of different veganism(s) as a process of vernacularization. In their interrogation of how global ideas about women's rights actually get adopted and used in local contexts, Peggy Levitt and Sally Merry (2009) offer this description of vernacularization:

> As women's human rights ideas connect with a locality, they take on some of the ideological and social attributes of the place, but also retain some of their original formulation. We see this as analogous to the ways in which organic molecules connect with each other. New pieces attach at points of similarity, producing a new overall structure. Even though the features of the original core do not necessarily change, the new composition of elements is different. How vernacularization actually works varies according to a number of factors. These include where its communicators are located in the social and power hierarchy and their institutional positions, the characteristics of the channels and technology through which ideas and practices flow, the nature of the ideas and the idea packages in which they are embedded, and the topography of the terrain in which these transfers take place.

Vernacularizers take the ideas and practices of one group and present them in terms that another group will accept. This is not the work of a single person. Chains of actors stretch from the sites of the global production of human rights documents and ideas (in New York, Geneva and Vienna) to localities where ordinary people around the world adopt them. They wrestle with the dilemma of presenting transnational ideas in terms that resonate with local justice theories and at the same time are sufficiently different that they will challenge local inequalities and appeal to the imagining of the "new." (446)

My argument, put simply, is that (1) veganism (along with animal rights and animal liberation) has undergone and continues to undergo vernacularization, (2) the process of vernacularization has produced an abundance of veganism(s) as shown earlier, and (3) MSJ's emphasis on multiplicity and relationality theoretically allows the creative flow of different veganism(s) to constructively and critically engage local and non-local justice theories, free from the confines of any singular worldview, the aim of these engagements being to dismantle or transform unjust institutions across all scales and relations.

The MSJ framework shifts the terms of the debate and turns the conversation from a rather philosophical one about universal or contextual morality and ethics to a more political one about the interacting forces between the global and the local. Effectively, vegans working through the MSJ framework can deprioritize answering the question of how to get other communities/movements to care more about the lives of individual animals (i.e., to not consume and kill them) and prioritize reimagining how vegans and veganism(s) might contest power across multiple fronts and scales of injustices as part of broader justice movements in relational terms.

I propose that the Gramscian concept of hegemony is more fitting than universalism as a focus when discussing the relations between the power differentials among different veganism(s) and all of the positions and entities that veganism(s) seek to resist. Italian Marxist philosopher Antonio Gramsci theorized the concept of hegemony as a form of "ideological superiority" that is "attained through the myriad ways in which the institutions of civil society operate to shape, directly or indirectly, the cognitive and affective structures whereby [people] perceive and evaluate problematic social reality" (Femia 1987, 24). A common distinction made between forms of social control compares hegemony (obtained through consent) to domination (obtained through force); whereas domination is essentially realized "through the coercive machinery of the state," hegemony involves "intellectual and moral leadership" exercised through various "educational, religious and associational institutions" throughout civil society (Femia 1987, 24). Applying hegemony to understanding veganism(s) allows us to consider what form of veganism has come to be uncritically accepted/tolerated by mainstream animal movements and broader societies due to its popularization by various dominant social, political, and economic institutions, while other forms of veganism are excluded.

Interestingly, in his chapter in *Ecofeminism*, Twine himself briefly notes that "hegemonic *and* counter-hegemonic values are increasingly transcultural—for example, cultural forms, practices, and identities inspire new socialities (such as the international animal advocacy, feminist, or Black Lives Matter movement) which transcend conventional state boundaries" (2022, 231, emphasis in original). In my opinion, in not foregrounding hegemony as a concept with which to think through veganism and sticking to the debate about universalism, ecofeminists missed an opportunity to investigate how veganism and animal advocacy have actually been transforming on the ground culturally, intellectually, and ideologically. For instance, vegan organizations such as Food Empower Project and Chilis on Wheels that were founded by women of color and that dedicate their efforts to challenging all types of systemic injustices occurring within and in relation to our colonial-capitalist food systems—including food insecurity, lack of accessibility of healthy foods, exploitation of migrant workers, ecological harms, and violence against nonhuman animals—demonstrate counter-hegemonic veganism(s) in action (Food Empowerment Project n.d.; Chilis on Wheels n.d.).

Based on the very parameters set out for MSJ, it would appear that hegemonic forms of veganism that align with oppressive and destructive ideologies and trends, such as those overly focused on consumption and depoliticizing veganism, would always be met with resistance and rejection within MSJ by vegans and nonvegans alike. However, by choosing to apply and amplify veganism as an indispensable tool within a counter-hegemonic toolkit, as many vegans embedded in communities or networks of resistance have already been doing, we may very well elevate the vegan commitment to justice for all animals to an integral place within MSJ through radical articulations beyond Western or Global North conceptions of animal rights and liberation.

CHAPTER FOUR

Veganism as a(n) (Overlooked) Component of Anarchafeminism?

Nathan Poirier

Movements or activities concerning the role of food in social justice and/or in resistance efforts are not an uncommon part of anarchism. Growing one's own food may seem mundane, but for communities that partake in it, it is an expression of resistance to external and dominating forms of illegitimate authority (White 2018; Thomas and Figueroa-Helland 2021; Awry 2023). Curiously, writings that combine anarchism and feminism frequently leave out veganism. Chiara Bottici's 2021 book *Anarchafeminism* represents the first systematic and holistic theorization of the convergence of anarchism and feminism. While the book is wide in its scope, veganism is conspicuously absent, at least by name or in reference to diet. In loving solidarity with this pioneering work, I build on Chiara's admittedly (and necessarily) incomplete book to argue that anarchafeminism should explicitly include veganism as—and into—its liberatory praxis. This essay will draw together anarchism, feminism, and veganism to illustrate how veganism could be included within anarchafeminism by using eco-Black-feminist theory. I position veganism as a logical and helpful addition to anarchafeminism, given its quest to oppose all forms of domination. In addition, I take cues from Black radicals and intellectuals involved in food movements—that is, those contributing to the collective body of thought and knowledge in this realm, according to Patricia Hill Collins (2022)—to offer an interpretation of veganism that highlights how veganism could be viewed by anarchafeminism as a form of rejection of current hierarchical, authoritarian, and deadly systems.

For ease in writing as well as reading this essay, I use the term "veganarchafeminism" to refer to the convergence of veganism with Chiara's anarchafeminism. Although I do not wish to coin this term or popularize its usage, I find it a useful shorthand for the present purpose of referring to a theory of anti-oppression that explicitly combines anarchism, feminism, and veganism. The goal of this essay is not to promote veganism per se, even though I support and practice it, but rather to highlight the role of veganism with(in) Chiara's anarchafeminism.

In referring to Chiara specifically, I also respect the naming convention they use in *Anarchafeminism*. Chiara discusses the patrilineal nature of citational practices, which use exclusively surnames for in-text references. Surnames, of course, are generally passed down through male members of the family, and so, in an effort to resist patriarchy wherever it arises, Chiara alternates between surnames, first names, and whole names (first and last together). Out of admiration for Chiara, *Anarchafeminism*/anarchafeminism, and this practice, I follow their lead by never referring to anyone by last name only. Also, while Chiara spends some time discussing and is sensitive to pronoun use, Chiara never gives pronouns for themself. Because of this, I use the pronouns they/their/them to refer to Chiara.

I see the present project as akin to what Marquis Bey (2020b) does in *The Problem of the Negro as a Problem for Gender*. Marquis's task is to highlight how Nahum Chander's book, *The Problem of the Negro as a Problem for Thought*, overlooks clear applications and extensions to gender. Marquis uses various dimensions of Nahum Chandler's book to show how gender would/should also be included by virtue of the theory used by Nahum. The methodology is similar here for veganism with(in) *Anarchafeminism*. Like Marquis, I view my intervention and addition to anarchafeminism not as a critique of Chiara but as a means of pushing Chiara's thought a little bit further towards where it would logically go. That *Anarchafeminism* prompted this thought and effort should be taken as a great credit to the value of Chiara's work.

ANARCHISM AND FEMINISM . . . AND VEGANISM?

Anarchist writings on feminism frequently do not include veganism. In classical anarchist thought, there is very little in the way of feminism, let alone veganism. Although Peter Kropotkin and Murray Bookchin derived much of their anarchist view from observing nature and possessed a certain reverence for nonhuman animals, neither had a particularly vegan discourse. Neither Emma Goldman nor Voltarine de Cleyre nor Lucy Parsons promoted veganism. Martha Acklesberg's (2004) coverage of Mujeres Libres, an anarchist women's organization, contains no mention of interspecies solidarity. Even the special issue of *Perspectives on Anarchist Theory* (2016) on anarchafeminism does not mention veganism, although the essays therein do make a number of other connections across *human* issues. Marquis Bey's (2020a) work on anarcho-Blackness, while thoroughly suffused with Black, trans, feminist perspectives, does not bring in nonhumans directly. Chapters in anarchist handbooks or similar collections also do not invoke veganism in discussions of anarchism and feminism (Jeppesen 2019; Kinna 2018). In sum, veganism is conspicuously absent from much of anarchist theory, at least explicitly (I'll return to this point shortly).

There are, of course, exceptions. Among classical anarchists, Elisée Reclus promoted vegetarianism (but not veganism; see "On Vegetarianism" in John Clark and Camille Martin [2013]) and feminism as part of an anarchist praxis. But he did not bring all three together directly. This is done by Simon Springer (2016), who nevertheless does not focus on the three domains' intersection and combination per se. Elsewhere, in *Women, Destruction and the Avant-Garde: A Paradigm for Animal Liberation*, Kim Socha (2011) states:

> Proper contemplation of anarchist traditions leads to concern for animals. Can a society whose abiding objective is freedom from violence, hierarchy, and oppression confine, slaughter, dominate, eat and wear other sentient creatures? Social anarchist vegans of the avant-garde [animal liberation movement] must say "no" without compromise. (15)

But Kim's focus is not on anarchism, which is barely mentioned past the introduction. The collection by Anthony Nocella, Richard White, and Erika Cudworth (2015) also combines veganism, anarchism, and feminism to various degrees but does not integrate them into a combined theory.

Select works do adequately combine feminism, anarchism, and veganism. All three are named directly in the title of Ophélie Véron and Richard White's (2021) chapter on anarchist political ecology. Brian Dominick's (1997) fairly popular underground pamphlet also highlights veganism and feminism both as necessary components of each other. No doubt there are others. The present essay could have built on such efforts, either summarizing works that combine anarchism, feminism, and veganism or synthesizing existing theories to create a veganarchafeminism. But the above-mentioned works often are short or distinctively lack at least one component. The goal is to show how veganism folds into and emerges out of Chiara's already holistic conception of anarchafeminism. I feel this is a more productive task as Chiara already provides an open and expansive theoretical framework that does *not exclude* veganism as a possibility. I view such a goal as parallel to Chiara's response to their own observation that feminist works rarely embrace anarchism.

ANARCHAFEMINISM AND ANARCHAFEMINISM

Chiara's book *Anarchafeminism* provides a theorization of the convergence of anarchism and feminism. The book is claimed to be the first of its kind. It represents a systematic treatment of anarchism and feminism with an exceedingly wide scope. Chiara builds their version of anarchafeminism initially from intersectionality. They note how the concept of intersectionality was founded on the intersection of race and gender but is by no means limited to that. Other categories are frequently added to the analytic: class, sexuality, disability, religion, age, and so on. Chiara notes that, over time, those studying interlocking oppressions have strung together longer and longer lists of various oppressions in publication titles and rhetoric, but that any list is "necessarily incomplete, while at the same time being necessarily closed" (2021, 40). This is one limitation Chiara identifies with intersectionality.

A second limitation could be added, which is that intersectionality as a concept is often anthropocentric. Take, for example, Combahee River Collective's famous quotation: "If Black women were free, it would mean that everyone else would have to be free since our freedom would necessitate the destruction of all the systems of oppression" (1977, n.p.). Similarly, bell hooks (1984) asserts that Black men are oppressed by racism but benefit from sexism, while Black women are oppressed by both racism and sexism but are exploiters of none. This is not entirely true as Black women frequently exploit nonhuman animals for food and clothing and in other ways that are often but not always outside of their control. Thus, the freedom of Black women will likely not necessitate the freedom of all as long as nonhuman animals are still oppressed—and this will likely remain the case if "our freedom" encompasses humans only.

Therefore, a wider theory is needed; Chiara's anarchafeminism provides a usable framework as it approaches (but does not claim to be) a theory of everything, given its focus on dismantling all oppressions. Chiara bases their theory in the philosophy of transindividuality, which asserts that people are made up of "others," are in constant flux, and are relational. While we may understand ourselves as discrete entities, we each house billions of small living organisms, such as bacteria, inside our bodies. We are the product of our relations with others, living and nonliving. Our cells multiply and die out at periodic intervals, leaving us with a completely different cellular makeup and, in a way, an entirely different physical constitution. We are constantly changing. We are not static or discrete entities. Yet, we are "individual" in that anyone's individual constitution at a given time is unique. Therefore, we are simultaneously unique and relational. Despite the scope of *Anarchafeminism*, Chiara admits that their book, as any single work (just like any single list of interlocking oppressions), is necessarily not all-encompassing. Thus, anarchafeminism is also in flux, and it is to this flux that I wish to humbly add veganism. In particular, while Chiara covers the environment to a large extent, nonhumans themselves are largely left out. They are not ignored, but they themselves are also not deeply engaged with. Besides scattered mentions of nonhuman animals, only one page is devoted to a dedicated discussion of animal rights.

Chiara's most focused discussion of nonhuman animals is in refer- ence to the *scala naturae*, which posits a hierarchy of beings. Chiara gives several slightly different iterations of the *scala naturae*, one of which being man > woman > slave > animal > plant > inanimate matter. Chiara's critique of the *scala naturae*, a recurring theme throughout *Anar- chafeminism*, scrutinizes its emphasis on a hierarchy that is presumed to be static. Chiara disavows the entire "natural scale," thus implying, and leaving room open for, animal liberation. In fact, in the sentence that points the most toward veganarchafeminism, Chiara explicitly declares: "we [. . .] fight for animal, plant, and even mineral libera- tion" (295). In discussing animal ethics, they critique humanist animal ethics because it reaffirms the *scala naturae* (152). Chiara uses anarchist ecofeminism in their critique of humanist animal ethics; however, the ecofeminists cited are not of the vegan variety. Rejecting the *scala natu- rae* and embracing anarchist ecofeminism, Chiara proclaims, can create conditions for all living creatures to be liberated from both capitalist exploitation and an androcentric politics of domination. Nonetheless, explicit veganism is absent.

Adding in Veganism Using Eco-Black-Feminist Theory

I believe veganism is a rather straightforward addition to Chiara's anarchafeminism. I will illustrate this using theory that resonates with Chiara's own, starting with vegan ecofeminist theory. As promi- nent vegan ecofeminist Carol Adams (1994) asserts, neither women nor animals are "acceptable" victims. In general, there are parallels between the situation of women and that of "food animals" in that both groups can be viewed as commodities, fragmented into parts and consumed, albeit in different and specific ways. Intersectionality can play a role in revealing this similarity. As much as Black women find themselves at the intersection of race and gender, female animals occupy the intersection of gender (female) and species (nonhuman). Female animals make up the majority of farmed animals because of their femaleness, because they provide eggs and milk and possess reproductive capabilities. Extending Carol's argument, Lori Gruen (2004, 286) insists that the structures of all oppressions are linked, so opposition to any other form of domination should imply opposition to speciesism by being vegan (while Lori uses the term "vegetarian," it is clear she is referring to veganism). Animals are beings with whom women can empathize because of their common oppression under a racist, capitalist patriarchy. Once we empathize with animals, they stop being seen as food. Later on, Kim Socha remarks: "To acknowledge the *reality* of women was to give up the pleasure that woman brought [men] as her superiors. In kind, to acknowledge the reality of animals is to give up the pleasure that comes from eating them" (2011, 46).

Likewise, Catherine Bailey (2007) views vegetarianism as resistance to classist, racist, heterosexist, and colonialist systems of power, systems frequently underlined by speciesism. Veganism gets to the roots of entangled oppressions because, even if centered on nonhuman animals, it is fundamentally against exploitation in general. Turning to Black feminism, Patricia Hill Collins (2022) emphasizes that the power of self-definition lies in its potential to resist and replace control. By rejecting controlling images of themselves and articulating their standpoints, Black women challenge the privilege of those who typically get to define others. Feminist veganism holds similar appeal by rejecting the sexual politics of meat and reclaiming veganism as an act of resistance against patriarchy.

Helping bring all of this together into a veganarchafeminism is Adrienne Rich's (1980) concept of compulsory heterosexuality—the expectation that men be attracted to women and vice versa. Under compulsory heterosexuality, all other sexual orientations are viewed as abhorrent and deviant, and rejecting it can be seen as resistance. Building directly on this, Marti Kheel (2004) argues that in the West, the societal norm of meat-eating bears resemblance to the norm of heterosexuality. She sees both norms as "compulsory." Quoting Adrienne Rich, Marti professes that heterosexuality is hardly a choice but rather something that is "imposed, managed, organized, propagandized and maintained by force" in order to secure males' right of access to women. Marti sees meat-eating as analogous to heterosexuality in that meat-eating is also "imposed, managed, organized, propagandized and maintained by force"—both uphold "male-dominated society's rightful access to nonhuman animals" (2004, 329). Through compulsory heterosexuality and meat-eating, women and animals are both reduced to an existence of serving others. Women's body parts are fetishized and so are animals'; women's bodies are symbolically consumed by men (through sex, marriage, or the "male gaze"), and animals' bodies are literally consumed. If meat-eating is hardly a choice, feminist vegans see veganism as an empowering *choice* that challenges and disrupts multiple dimensions of the status quo. But this is not a choice in the neoliberal sense. The veganarchafeminist choice is intentional and deeply political, part of an overarching philosophy aimed at resisting all oppressions and dismantling all hierarchies. Veganism thus empowers individuals by creating a sense of self-definition and agency, affirming their power, worth, and ability to make change.

Toward Veganarchafeminism

With this framework of Black feminism, vegan ecofeminism, and feminist theory, heterosexuality and meat-eating can both be viewed as imposed and maintained by force. I have talked about veganism as a diet, but because of its wide focus on exploitation in general, veganism cannot be reduced to simply not eating animal products. Indeed, vegan food is often grown by capitalist companies that exploit land and non/human laborers for profit. Therefore, alternative means of producing vegan food also constitute an integral component of resistance against exploitative systems. Many have recognized the potential for self-fulfillment and anti-capitalist resistance in growing one's own (vegan) food. K. Melchor Quick Hall and Gwyn Kirk (2021) assert the importance of "intergenerational family and community gardening as a response to the (food and economic) insecurities of the [COVID-19] pandemic" (9). Similarly, Aurora Levins Morales (2021), in reflecting on her return to Puerto Rico, states that "the sunflowers also reminded [her] of civil rights organizer Fannie Lou Hammer [. . .] who understood the power of food sovereignty for people working to get free" (93). Indeed, food sovereignty is a necessary step toward collective liberation for a people: "To free ourselves, we have to feed ourselves, body and soul [. . .]. What if we poured resources into the farming of food?" (Morales 2021, 94). And finally, beyond providing sustenance and nourishment, "planting food is an act of resistance" (95). The use of "planting" implies vegan food. Concerning the role of nonhuman animals in food justice, queer ecofeminist Greta Gaard states: "For too long, 'food justice' has been defined solely in terms of justice across human diversities, but authentic food justice cannot be practiced while simultaneously excluding those who count as 'food.' Food justice requires interspecies justice, which intersects with reproductive justice and queer justice alike" (2017, 132).

Of course, we must consume something. Eating only plant-derived foods is the best way to minimize impact on other beings: "Eating plants ensures humans consume less—fewer plants, and fewer animals—and ensures we cause less suffering [. . .] as well. It ensures we free up more land for all of life [. . .] to eat and thrive" (Gaard 2017, 40–41). These activists, intellectuals, and gardeners (not to draw a false distinction between these terms) bring up numerous ways in which growing our own (vegan) food can help us achieve total liberation—personal, collective, and planetary. It can help enable or enhance food sovereignty, nourishment beyond nutrients and the physical body, resistance against domination, food justice, and consistent anti-oppression work (Feliz and McNeill 2020; Rodrigues 2018).

Overall, I have positioned veganism as largely an individual choice in order to insert it into Chiara's anarchafeminism. The focus on individual choice here may seem somewhat unusual or ineffective in terms of building a mass movement for change. Some may also view veganism, as just discussed, as a "negative" act, one that emphasizes withdrawing oneself from exploitative practices, and not a "positive" act. The point of highlighting individuals is not to downplay social forces or systemic issues (which must be acknowledged and transformed) but to highlight how self-definition and self-empowerment are important for realizing collective change. Kim Socha emphasizes how "negative" actions—ones that involve *not* doing something—are also important forms of direct action: "[Torres's] stance echoes de Cleyre's conception of negative direct action, which is the refusal to participate in commonly accepted cultural practices. [. . .] A refusal to purchase and consume unethically manufactured animal products—which is all of them [. . .]—is a method of negative direct action as well" (2011, 17). Arguably, growing vegan food can be considered engaging in both positive direct action—just as vandalism, sabotage, and protest fall under this category—and negative direct action by avoiding animal products.

Another reason to focus on the individual is that it is individuals who act, even when they together form a collective. As Patricia Hill Collins (2022) writes, quoting Toni Cade Bambara: "Revolution begins with the self, in the self" (352). Thinking geographically, Cassidy Thomas and Leonardo Figueroa-Helland (2021) note how "anarchist (*and* indigenous) values have continued to exist and can flourish in the smallest spaces of resistance" (91). Therefore, within the small space occupied by the individual lies an enormous ability to feel and enact resistance. This includes the ability to control one's body and what one puts in it in solidarity with others. Feminist theory, perhaps especially Black feminist thought (Collins 2022), teaches us that the personal is political, that neither individual, nor group, nor institutional change is more important than the others. Collins shows how Black women often act with the wider community in mind, similar to Dean Spade's (2020) formulation of mutual aid. As an example, Cassidy and Leonardo (2021) point out how the larger social and systemic dimensions of "the modern-industrial mode of food production [are] underpinned by an intersection of hegemonic systems of power" (84). Personal decisions resist institutional injustices.

A connection between past, present, and future through land and food is discussed (and felt) by K. Melchor Quick Hall. She ruminates on the connection between liberation and land within Black history: "Black farmers, literally, fed the U.S. civil rights movement" (2021, 20). She further indicates how personal action can be part of a bigger movement, citing access to healthy and affordable food as a reason why "Black farmers are a critical part of any liberation struggle" (21). Malcolm Ferdinand (2022), speaking from a Caribbean perspective, also reiterates the historical importance of careful, symbiotic, sustainable land cultivation, as well as interspecies alliances, for runaway slaves. As it turns out, growing one's own food tends to lend itself to veganism because of the added difficulties of raising (not to mention killing and "processing") nonhuman animals, especially in more urban environments. Therefore, through support for and practice of veganism, the personal choice to be vegan is transformed into a political statement against a racist, capitalist patriarchy—and for the liberation, personal and collective, of all.

PERHAPS VEGANISM WAS THERE THE WHOLE TIME?

I want to suggest that one reason why veganism is not explicitly mentioned in *Anarchafeminism* may be that Chiara's entire theoretical framework essentially constitutes veganism itself. I wish to distance veganism from a mere diet; it is much more than a diet. It is the dietary component of veganism that I feel *Anarchafeminism* is missing. However, the framework Chiara provides encompasses critiques of structural inequalities, a radical and dynamic rejection of all dominating systems, a clear stance against external "authorities" such as the state, a positing of alternative ways of being, and a clear sense of collective struggle that takes nonhuman nature into account. Indeed, all of these are necessary components of a vegan praxis "without adjectives" (to reference Voltairine de Cleyre), of veganism as a radical, inclusive, holistic practice. With a reading of Nahum Chandler—specifically of his notion of paraontology—through Marquis Bey, one might say that Chiara's anarchafeminism dissolves the criteria for inclusion and exclusion (Bey 2020b, 14), automatically making space for and perhaps therefore *including* veganism. All I am saying is that anarchafeminism should also explicitly include support for a vegan diet as one (more) thing we can do within an anarchafeminist framework to help achieve liberation for all.

While a vegan diet may not be explicitly included, Chiara's anarchafeminism would likely refuse to exclude it. In other words, veganism—in all its vicissitudes—may be included by default and by implication, as is everything else. In such a reading, *Anarchafeminism* may already include (by not excluding) a vegan diet. This is similar to how Marquis Bey's anarchic "black trans feminism is not about black trans women": "The radical politics that black trans feminism names are not beholden to 'being' a presumed type of subject" (Bey 2022, 32). Marquis Bey situates their Black trans feminism within a space of total liberation from the outset, perhaps by definition, and does not impose criteria for inclusion, thereby always and already taking the liberation of "all" as literal and to its furthest reaches. At the same time, refusal to exclude is not necessarily equivalent to explicit inclusion. Not excluding is not necessarily the same as welcoming. Heather Hurwitz (2021) notes the limits of the "we are the 99%" framing of Occupy Wall Street due to this sort of lack of specificity. She states that the 99% framing "indicated that nearly everyone was included—but no one specifically" (71). Numerous oversights and a lack of cohesion resulted from this framing. However, in a footnote in *Anarchafeminism*, Chiara critiques the book *Feminism for the 99%* (Arruzza, Bhattacharya, and Fraser 2019) by saying that anarchafeminism "would go even further and argue for a liberation of 100 percent of us" (86). The specific context here refers to women, but this notion could be taken in the context of *Anarchafeminism* on the whole to apply to all beings and entities.

Also, anarchists are frequently hostile toward veganism and vegans towards anarchy. That tension and schism is the crux of Brian Dominick's 1997 pamphlet which tried to unite vegans and anarchists given their many ideological similarities. It is why I believe this chapter—a call for explicit inclusion of a vegan diet within anarchafeminism—is important. The anarchist credo "no gods, no masters" seems to almost not apply to nonhuman animals. Just as Chiara asserts that anarchism is not anarchy if it is not feminist and Marquis Bey (2020a) asserts that anarchism is not anarchy if it does not reckon with (anti-)Blackness, one can absolutely question if anarchy can even exist if it is not also for animal liberation and therefore dietary veganism—practiced, as always, to the best of one's ability (see Springer 2021). Conversely, veganism is incomplete if it is not also anarchist. Many self-identified vegans are perfectly happy to buy fake-meat products from corporations that may or may not also profit from animal-food products or "food" animal production; are frequently comfortable with purchasing animal-free products from companies with exploitative labor practices; or promote a racist (and speciesist) system of "law and order" to punish those who (directly) harm (certain) animals in certain ways (Marceau 2019). The overlooking of other marginalized groups within vegan communities is the reason for Julia Feliz's intervention and promotion of consistent anti-oppression (Feliz and McNeill 2020). I assert that anarchism is essentially veganism and veganism is essentially anarchism, at least in theory and ideally in practice. With all this said, Chiara's anarchafeminism is so expansive that I would have been satisfied with one sentence promoting a vegan diet. One promotional mention of this simultaneously negative and positive direct action would have crystalized all of the wider theorization and scattered mentions of nonhuman animals and their liberation.

The phenomenon identified in this paper is found elsewhere. Literature on movements (e.g., degrowth, veganism, anarchism) or sectors of society (e.g., childfree, radical activists) too often focuses on a topic as a whole and shows the diversity represented within it. For instance, Shelly Volsche (2020) presents a typology of the childfree (being childfree is voluntary and can be contrasted with being "childless," which typically refers to a biological inability to procreate). One type is the "hedonist," who eschews children in order to consume conspicuously. Though it is important to realize that such a position exists, I think it would be more helpful overall to instead focus on how being voluntarily childfree fits with degrowth philosophy. Another example: The book *Food for Degrowth* (Nelson and Edwards 2020) contains no mention of veganism. This is a striking absence for such a book. It would be nice to build a body of work that incorporates and integrates these various components, people, movements, and ideas so that those of one persuasion can be introduced to and see the value of other persuasions in a context that relates to them. In treating each school of thought individually as Shelly Volsche (2020) and Anitra Nelson and Ferne Edwards (2020) have done, one risks accidentally legitimizing an unsustainable behavior (conspicuous consumption) while promoting a sustainable one (being childfree). Such an integration is what I have attempted in this paper. Incidentally, being childfree is another component that could be incorporated into anarchafeminism, though that would require either much more space for the present chapter or a separate work.

So, there are at least two parts to my conclusion. One is that a vegan diet is overlooked in *Anarchafeminism*, and I have shown how it can be added. The other is that I have allowed that dietary veganism is potentially already implicitly present and I am merely making it explicit. Either way, I feel that it is possible to read *Anarchafeminism* and miss connections to veganism, especially if a reader is anthropocentrically inclined. It is all too common for social justice work to focus solely or primarily on the human element, as evidenced by Combahee River Collective's famous statement, cited earlier, or by the complete lack of mention of nonhumans in Dean Spade's (2020) conceptualization of mutual aid. I worry that someone could read *Anarchafeminism* and believe they support anarchism or intersectional liberation while still eating animals or supporting or being indifferent toward the consumption of animals. My goal is to make clear that veganism and anarchafeminism necessarily go hand in hand, each implying the other, and should always and everywhere be striven toward in a simultaneous practice of veganarchafeminism.

Even the addition of a vegan diet would not complete Chiara's anarchafeminism, which would be impossible as there is no theory of everything and anarchafeminism is designed to be always unfolding. But I would love to continue to see *Anarchafeminism* expanded upon and advanced further, perhaps by multiple authors in a future edited volume.

CHAPTER FIVE

Interbeing: A Spiritual Insight on the Suffering of Nonhuman Animals

Lucrezia Barucca

You are a fragment of the universe.
I recollect the words of my father from the living room of my current apartment. White walls, a creaky wooden floor, and large windows that welcome the gentle light of a mid-autumn afternoon. The air is oxygenated by the majestic—at times subtle—presence of plants, advocates of this harmony. The silence of the other rooms accompanies the quiet vacuity of this environment. In this space of stillness, as my thoughts begin to flow, I start writing. I dream of roaming in the expansive space of my soul, which breathes in from the humble place of my body and then moves about, vibrating until it touches the surrounding walls. It all happens in the *hic et nunc* of this deep intimacy of breaths, this fair exchange of oxygen and carbon dioxide. This room offers itself as a meeting place of apparent, individual existences, of which mine is the only human's. With a sheet of paper in my hands, waiting for words, I contemplate and reflect upon this entanglement of lives, of which I am part and parcel.

> If you are a poet, you will see clearly that there is a cloud floating in this sheet of paper. Without a cloud, there will be no rain; without rain, the trees cannot grow; and without trees, we cannot make paper. The cloud is essential for the paper to exist. If the cloud is not here, the sheet of paper cannot be here either. [. . .] If we look

into this sheet of paper even more deeply, we can see the sunshine in it. Without sunshine, the forest cannot grow. In fact, nothing can grow without sunshine. And so, we know that the sunshine is also in this sheet of paper. [. . .] We cannot point out one thing that is not here—time, space, the earth, the rain, the minerals in the soil, the sunshine, the cloud, the river, the heat. Everything co-exists with this sheet of paper. (Thich 1991, 95–96)

It is thanks to an insight into a simple sheet of paper that one can understand the meaning of the *interbeing*, suggests Thích Nhất Hạnh, a Vietnamese Buddhist monk who encouraged the spread of engaged Buddhism in the past century (1987, 127–30). Indeed, despite this new verb, *inter-be*, not yet being in the dictionary, one can grasp its significance by simply observing the surrounding expressions of existence, both living (e.g., a person, a plant) and nonliving (e.g., a sheet of paper), both sentient and insentient. According to Thich: "[Everything] is full of the whole cosmos, while at the same time it is empty of a separate self-existence. [A thing] cannot exist by itself alone" (2017, 11–12). Concerning the sheet of paper, he claims that it *inter-is* with the cloud, the rain, the sunshine, the forest (they *inter-are*), as well as with the logger, his parents, and his daily bread, thus also the wheat. What he means is that "everything depends for its existence on everything else," that "everything *inter-is* with everything else," since "to be is to *inter-be*" (Holst 2021, 17). All lives and expressions of existence can therefore be seen "in the network of interdependent relations" (Thich 1991, 70), envisioned in the *Flower Garland Sutra*, according to the metaphor of the Jewel Net of Indra:

[. . .] a beautiful net which stretches out infinitely in all directions. Every node of this net has a bright and shiny jewel placed in it. Since the net is infinite in all directions, it contains infinitely many jewels. Each one of the jewels in the net reflects all the other jewels, and each one of the jewels is reflected in all the other jewels, so that the jewels reflect each other infinitely. [. . .] [Each] one of the jewels depends for its existence on all the other jewels and each one of the jewels contains all the other jewels. If any one of the jewels was missing, none of the other jewels would still be what it is. Each jewel is vital to the existence of all the other jewels. (Holst 2021, 21)

The Jewel Net of Indra is not only an insight into *interbeing* but also a metaphor of the whole cosmos, wherein all elements are empty of self-being and full of everything at the same time. Indeed, what Thích Nhất Hạnh understood as the manifestation of the *interbeing* was already embodied in the ancient Buddhist principle of *Pratītyasamutpāda*. The term has seen many translations into English, whereof "interdependent co-arising" seems the most appropriate (to me). However, *Pratītyasamutpāda* may also be explained as a "co-evolutionary interrelated world based on co-dependency, built upon dynamic cause and effect to create aggregate conditions" (Murray 2012, 26). An understanding of this principle is portrayed in the South Korean film *Why Has Bodhi Dharma Left for the East?* (Yong-Kyun 1989), whose beginning goes: "Forever and ever, all is originally empty. There is no beginning and no end. The thing which neither comes into being nor perishes!" This remark is then followed by a series of speechless scenes of different human activities. In fact, the peculiarity of these scenes is that of depicting the implications of such activities. The technique is looking closely at the involved nonhumans—objects or animals—so as to show their viewpoints. Nonhumans become the protagonists of the setting, because in reality they are. Thus, their significance and feelings come to light. This sequence of the film exposes that everything is entangled and happens synchronously, that nothing has a life of its own as a result of the unity of things. It is in this characterization of "the universe as a continuous succession of action, reaction, and effect within a state of dynamic flux and transformation" that the Buddhist doctrine identifies the origin of suffering, which "arises and [. . .] ceases as a matter of natural interdependence" (Murray 2012, 31), implying that suffering was on Earth even before the appearance of humanity. That is indeed the First Noble Truth of Buddhism, that life entails suffering: "This is suffering. Life is suffering. *Everything* is suffering" (Thich 1998; 2010, 59). Pain, sorrow, distress, and disease come together in the Pāli term *dukkha* (Sanskrit: *duḥkha*), which stands for all sorts of sufferings.

Almost two years ago, I got close to this research on suffering owing to a sense of heartache that I used to refer to as *Weltschmerz* (in the modern sense of the word), by which I literally meant a *world-pain* that I felt within and everywhere. As painful as it was, I could not do without it. At the same time, my suffering concerned that of nonhuman animals in particular. That is how I learned of the first of the Great Sayings (*Mahāvākyas*) of the *Upanishads*: *tat tvam asi*, which means "you are that," "that you are," or "you are it." This mantra is explained in the following extract of the *Chandogya Upanishad* in which Uddalaka is speaking to his son, Śvetaketu:

> [6.2.1] In the beginning, son, this world was simply what is exis-tent—one only, without a second. [6.2.3] And it thought to itself: "Let me become many. Let me propagate myself." [6.8.3] It cannot be without a root. [6.8.4] [Look] to the existent as the root. The existent, my son, is the root of all these creatures—the existent is their resting place, the existent is their foundation. [7] The finest essence here—that constitutes the self of this whole world; that is the truth; that is the self [*ātman*]. And that's how you are [*tat tvam asi*], Śvetaketu. (Olivelle 2008, 152)

In other words, Uddalaka's speech to his son describes the principle of *interdependent co-arising*. However, compared to the previous examples, the subject addressed is neither a sheet of paper nor a jewel net. It is a person. That finest essence, that truth, that self is Śvetaketu, is you, is me, is each of us, is everyone. When I read that *tat tvam asi*, it was as if Uddalaka was talking to me. His words spoke to me. It felt like my sense of suffering would become rightful and legitimate, because I could see a correlation.

I was very sensitive as a child, and throughout my life, I had carried within me that sensitivity that was currently at its peak. I would sense the emotions of others as if they were mine, chiefly the emotions of those who suffered, in particular nonhuman animals. As a human being, I was especially aware that their suffering was intrinsically related to the causal system of human decisions—thoughts and deeds—imposed on their lives. Facing their suffering, I kept repeating "that essence is you," "you are that essence," so that their pain would belong to me. Unable to alleviate it, I could at least share it. Instead of being a witness, I would thus become victim of their own suffering, together with them. However, almost one year ago, I encountered a spiritual leader to whom I opened up: "As I acknowledge all the suffering going on in the world right now,

I just feel like silencing it all. I would wish not to be aware of it, so that it would not pervade me and make me feel so helpless." The key is your attitude to compassion, he suggested. The suffering of others must be recognized and witnessed, however not embraced within us. The idea was that although there exists a collective suffering that all individuals share and to which they all belong, each one needs to experience their own *dukkha*, according to their personal lifepath. In fact, it is precisely by experiencing our own suffering that we can understand its entanglements and go through them.

What I mean here is that we cannot feel responsible for the whole *Weltschmerz* within the narrowness of our individual essence. The key is to acknowledge our belongingness to the *world-pain* as fragments of a broken vase (originally integral), with each fragment being uniquely interconnected with the others. Each connection thus represents a specific interrelation of mutual interdependence, and each specific interrelation is a node of the net whereby everyone contains and enhances the value of all the other fragments of the vase. Consequently, each fragment is responsible for its particular connection, which has to be recreated in order to solve part of the suffering of the whole. In fact, however aware of the *dukkha* happening on the other side of the vase we may be, the only way to truly amend it is by helping our own interdependent relations. What this entails is an engagement toward easing the pain in our apparent vicinity. This does not mean being uncaring of those seemingly distant; it is about pursuing the right connection to and attitude toward suffering, thus addressing the *world-pain* or *vase-pain* that we are able to help ease. Only then will we be allowed to relieve an ever-increasing pain. It is a knock-on effect. You heal a fragment, and this healing thrives.

One should think that every fragment could take part in this healing process. And so, that "continuous succession of action, reaction, and effect within a state of dynamic flux and transformation" may be understood and welcomed into each existence. It follows from this reflection that each fragment has the task of sensing, acknowledging, accepting, witnessing, enlightening, and, finally, alleviating its neighbor's suffering, to which it belongs and which belongs to it. However, while accomplishing this task, we must bear in mind the source of suffering, as well as its magnitude and vastness. Only then will we be able to tell why the suffering we can endure is so little compared to that we can sense. Once on the frequency of acceptance, we will know not only how to witness pain, but also how to help it. This means to live in accordance with the morals of *tat tvam asi*, I concluded.

These findings on the managing of pain did not cut out—but, in fact, almost strengthened—the question of its possible sharing. While it is not possible to hold all *Weltschmerz* within the narrowness of our individual essence, we still have to manage a considerable amount of suffering on which we depend and for which we are accountable, at least to some extent. There is a fundamental connection between the idea of *interbeing* and the imperative that we, as individual essences entangled with the whole cosmos, experience life and suffering. In fact, if we are because everything is, even our experience of life and suffering is because others' experiences of life and sufferings are:

> The fact is that this sheet of paper is made up only of "non-paper" elements. And if we return these non-paper elements to their sources, then there can be no paper at all [. . .]. As thin as this sheet of paper is, it contains everything in the universe in it. (Thich 1991, 96)

As previously claimed, the sheet of paper depends for its existence on the cloud, the rain, the sunshine, the forest, the logger, and so on. In other words, there exists an endless chain of elements and relations behind its making. Also, all of its components are other than paper. This means that any sheet of paper is unavoidably related to an invisible network of apparently foreign elements (e.g., the wheat) that are reasonably hard to detect but still relevant. In short, it is about *interbeing* once again. Now, if we apply this reasoning to the existence of suffering, we might find similar answers. We could thus state that

> this *experience of suffering* is made up only of "non-*suffering*" elements. And if we return these non-*suffering* elements to their sources, then there can be no *suffering* at all [. . .]. As *little* as this *suffering* is, it contains everything in the universe in it. (Thich 1991, 97)

This excerpt offers some possible food for thought concerning the components and also the causes of suffering. What can we understand by "non-*suffering*" elements? Clearly, they can be directly related determining factors (e.g., animals, the act of distancing a calf from his mother) or apparently foreign ones (e.g., the economic need for a job and thus the decision to work in a slaughterhouse; or a family day at the sea, when a father decides to teach his son how to fish). Those "non-*suffering*" elements could thus be understood as experiences of joy, pleasure, happiness (e.g., the sensations of a father sharing his childhood memories with his son), justice, welfare (e.g., a stable economic situation), as well as other experiences of suffering (e.g., a child injuring himself with a fishhook; or the psycho-physical pain of working in a slaughterhouse).

Finally, this means that any specific experience of suffering is caused by and inextricably linked with any other kind of experience, which can be of the same sort or completely different, even opposite. According to this, the most pleasant experience can *inter-be* with the most painful and vice versa.

> Let us look at wealth and poverty. The affluent society and the deprived society inter-are. The wealth of one society is made of the poverty of the other. "This is like this, because that is like that." Wealth is made of non-wealth elements, and poverty is made by non-poverty elements. It is exactly the same as with the sheet of paper. So we must be careful not to imprison ourselves in concepts. The truth is that everything contains everything else. We cannot just be, we can only inter-be. We are responsible for everything that happens around us. (Thich 1991, 98)

As a result, my concern about the suffering of others was greater than ever, for it could still depend on or be caused by any of my own experiences. Moreover, all these reasonings strengthened even the interdependence of life and suffering, whereby the experience of life itself implied the experience of suffering and vice versa (as already stated, "life is suffering"). Following this line of thought, the existence of suffering became somehow necessary since its absence would imply the absence of life. Accordingly, life and suffering *inter-were*.

It is at this point in my research on suffering and pursuit of a right attitude toward it that my encounter with the Russian writer and anarcho-pacifist Leo Tolstoy took place. Indeed, one late evening, I found myself reading a nearly unknown essay he published in his seventies titled "The First Step." Nowadays considered a manifesto of animal rights and justice, "The First Step" has nevertheless remained a minor work of Tolstoy's, originally conceived as a preface to *The Ethics of Diet: A Catena of Authorities Deprecatory of the Practice of Flesh-Eating* by Howard Williams. Tolstoy had received a copy of *The Ethics of Diet* as a gift and asked his daughters to translate it into Russian for him. Sometimes referred to as "the original history of vegetarianism," the book advocates "abstinence from animal food" as "the first act of [. . .] a moral life" by suggesting "all mankind in the persons of its best representatives during all the conscious life of humanity" (Tolstoy 1911, 91–92). Williams chronicles the views of all those who had been critical of the "practice of flesh-eating," from Buddha, Pythagoras, Empedocles, and Plato up to his time. It is evident that reading *The Ethics of Diet* had a major impact on Tolstoy's life, as the following lines reveal:

> [. . .] when reading that excellent book, *The Ethics of Diet*, I had wished to visit a slaughter-house, in order to see with my own eyes the truth of the matter brought in question when vegetarianism is discussed. But at first I felt ashamed to do so, as one is always ashamed of going to look at suffering which one knows is about to take place, but cannot avert; and so I kept putting off my visit. [. . .] One Friday I decided to go to Tula, and meeting a meek, kind acquaintance of mine, I invited him to accompany me. "Yes, I have heard that the arrangements are good, and have been wishing to go and see it; but if they are slaughtering, I will not go in." "Why not? That is just what I wanted to see! If we eat flesh meat, it must be killed." "No, no, I cannot." It is worth while to remark that this man is a sportsman, and himself kills [animals] and birds. So we went to the slaughter-house. (Tolstoy 1900, 50–52)

What is described here is a strong inner feeling of pursuit: the pursuit of the experience of suffering. Tolstoy's desire to visit a slaughter-house marked a crucial turning point in the life of the author, whose past beliefs would then be completely overturned. Indeed, Tolstoy had already witnessed the bitter deaths of a significant number of nonhuman animals at the hands of humans even before his visit to the slaughter-house of Tula. We could even say that he was used to looking death in the face, since this was an integral part of one of his passions: hunting.

According to Tolstoy, hunting is for a man a healthy distraction from his daily work, its monotony and conventionalism, as well as a good chance to spend some time outdoors. He thus defines hunting as a dialogue between man and nature, whereby "man can identify with nature." Additionally, he admits: "I was a passionate hunter for a long period of my life. In fact, hunting was a very serious business to me" (Tolstoj 2020, 59, translation mine). A few hunting episodes can even be found in his writings, such as the account of his childhood memo-ries in the chapter "The Hunt" in *Childhood* (1852), Nicholas Rostov's wolf hunt in *War and Peace* (2016), and his bear-hunt expedition of 1858 that became the short story *The Bear Hunt* (1872), translated by Nathan Haskell Dole with the title *Desire Stronger than Necessity* in 1888. However passionate about this practice, Tolstoy would completely renounce it later in life, depicting it as cruel, bloody, murderous, needless, inhumane, and unjustifiable, worthy of men without a conscience. Recollecting all those episodes of witnessed animal suffering, he could finally recognize hunt-ing as "consistent moral suicide" (Tolstoj 2020, 71, translation mine).

Nevertheless, condemning his past was not enough. That is why, on "a warm day of June," he found himself at the entrance of Tula's slaughterhouse:

> That day about a hundred head of cattle were slaughtered. I was about to enter one of the "chambers," but stopped short at the door [. . .] because blood was flowing on the floor and dripping from above. [. . .] One suspended carcass was being taken down, another was being moved toward the door, a third, a slaughtered ox, was lying with its white legs raised, while a butcher with his strong hand was ripping up its tight-stretched hide. Through the door opposite to the one at which I was standing, a big, red, well-fed ox was led in. Two men were dragging it, and hardly had it entered when I saw a butcher raise a knife above its neck and stab it. The ox, as if all four

legs had suddenly given way, fell heavily upon its belly, immediately turned over on one side, and began to work its legs and all its hind quarters. Another butcher at once threw himself upon the ox [. . .], caught its horns, twisted its head down to the ground, while another butcher cut its throat with a knife. From beneath the head there flowed a stream of blackish red blood, which a besmeared boy caught in a tin basin. All the time this was going on, the ox kept incessantly twitching its head as if trying to get up, and waved its four legs in the air. The basin was quickly filling, but the ox still lived, and, its stomach heaving heavily, both hind and fore legs worked so violently that the butchers held aloof. [. . .] When the blood ceased to flow, the butcher raised the animal's head and began to skin it. The ox continued to writhe. The head, stripped of its skin, showed red with white veins, and kept the position given it by the butcher; on both sides hung the skin. Still the animal did not cease to writhe. Then another butcher caught hold of one of the legs, broke it, and cut it off. In the remaining legs and the stomach the convulsions still continued. The other legs were cut off and thrown aside, together with those of other oxen belonging to the same owner. Then the carcass was dragged away and hung up, and here the convulsions ceased. (Tolstoy 1900, 54–55)

I believe this description to be one of the cruelest and most revolting a novelist could ever write, however necessary it may have been. As Donovan (2009) corroborates, it is "possibly the most vivid and horrifying description [. . .] of animal slaughter ever written" (44). In those lines, Tolstoy recounts the ox's entire experience of suffering without sparing any the details, without filtering any of the most painful particulars. The author reports the scene in a way that is as real as his witnessing it. In doing so, he allows the reader to almost share his experience, the most shocking detail of which is the mechanical nature of the course of events. In the abattoir of Tula, slaughter is routine, as is suffering, and the butchers are accustomed to both. They never fail a shot, and if that ever happens, they are ready to shoot again in a never-ending sequence of violence and suffering. In Upton Sinclair's (1906) words, it is as if Tolstoy was watching "a slaughtering-machine" running in the most "cold-blooded, impersonal way, without a pretence at apology, without the homage of a tear" (48–49). A few pages later, Tolstoy writes:

> After me there entered a man, apparently an ex-soldier, bringing in a young yearling ram, black with a white mark on its neck, with its legs tied. This animal he placed upon one of the tables, as if upon a bed. [. . .] The live ram was lying as quietly as the dead inflated one, except that it was briskly wagging its short little tail, and its sides were heaving more quickly than usual. The soldier pressed down its uplifted head gently, without effort; the butcher, still continuing the conversation, grasped with his left hand the head of the ram and cut its throat. The ram quivered, and the little tail stiffened and ceased to wave. The fellow, while waiting for the blood to flow, began to relight his cigarette, which had gone out. The blood flowed, and the ram began to writhe. The conversation continued without the slightest interruption. (Tolstoy 1900, 57)

As previously discussed, any experience of suffering is caused by and inextricably linked with any other kind of experience. In these lines, it is clear that Tolstoy's butchers, as well as the ex-soldier, are simply indifferent in the face of pain and agony. Does this mean that there is no trace of *interbeing* in the abattoir of Tula? Could we instead claim that the nonhuman animals there and their slaughterers *inter-are*?

According to Porcher (2011), the relationship between workers and animals in the meat industry (she mainly talks about pork production as "an archetype of animal production") can be considered a case of "shared suffering." She explains that one could observe a "transmission of suffering" from the human to the animal and vice versa, since their living conditions and illnesses are linked. Finally, she defines suffering as "a shared pathology," which is physical, mental, and even moral (the last referring mainly to the ethical conflict experienced by workers, that is, "suffering from making another being suffer") (3–17). These considerations show that nonhuman animals and their slaughterers *inter-are*, however hard to believe that is.

In the same vein, Tolstoy's moral fable "Esarhaddon, King of Assyria" prompts reflection on some unthinkable entanglements of lives. In the story, a bloody king named Esarhaddon is visited by an old man at night, just when Esarhaddon is thinking about how to execute rival king Lailie, who has been confined in a cage since the conquest of his kingdom. The old man warns Esarhaddon, "You cannot destroy his life." The exchange continues thus:

"Yes," answered the King. "But I cannot make up my mind how to do it."

"But you are Lailie," said the old man.

"That's not true," replied the King. "Lailie is Lailie, and I am I."

"You and Lailie are one," said the old man. "You only imagine you are not Lailie, and that Lailie is not you." (Tolstoy 2021, n.p.)

King Esarhaddon, unable to understand what the old man means, is asked to enter a font full of water. Once under the water, he feels no longer like himself but like someone else: he finds himself in the body and living the life of his rival, King Lailie, at first, then of a she-ass in the company of her ass-colt. Esarhaddon experiences the sufferings of both, being aware of having caused them himself. Stepping out of the water font, he exclaims, "Oh, how terribly I have suffered! And for how long!" The old man continues:

"Do you now understand [. . .] that Lailie is you, and the warriors you put to death were you also? And not the warriors only, but the animals which you slew when hunting and ate at your feasts, were also you. You thought life dwelt in you alone, but I have drawn aside the veil of delusion, and have let you see that by doing evil to others you have done it to yourself also. Life is one in them all, and yours is but a portion of this same common life. And only in that one part of life that is yours, can you make life better or worse—increasing or decreasing it. You can only improve life in yourself by destroying the barriers that divide your life from that of others, and by considering others as yourself, and loving them. By so doing you increase your share of life. You injure your life when you think of it as the only life, and try to add to its welfare at the expense of other lives. By so doing you only lessen it. To destroy the life that dwells in others is beyond your power. The life of those you have slain has vanished from your eyes, but is not destroyed. You thought to lengthen your own life and to shorten theirs, but you cannot do this. Life knows neither time nor space. The life of a moment, and the life of a thousand years: your life, and the life of all the visible and invisible beings in the world, are equal. To destroy life, or to alter it, is impossible; for life is the one thing that exists. All else, but seems to us to be." (Tolstoy 2021, n.p.)

In this moral fable, Tolstoy shows clearly that "all life is one"—that all lives *inter-are*—and concludes that "when men wish to harm others, they really do evil to themselves."

Moreover, we find out that he does include nonhuman animals, describing Esarhaddon's sensation embodying the she-ass, the colt's mother, as a "glad feeling of simultaneous life in himself and in his offspring" (Tolstoy 2021, n.p.). Turgenev would describe this human–nonhuman relationship as "organic intimacy," especially while observing Tolstoy's kinship with animals:

> [Tolstoy] translated the animal's feelings to those around him. "I could have listened forever," Turgenev later said, "He had got inside the very soul of the poor beast and taken me with him. I could not refrain from remarking, 'I say, Leo Nikolayevich, beyond any doubt, you must have been a horse once yourself.'" (cited in Donovan 2009, 46)

Finally, Tolstoy's personal journey would prove extremely emblematic, encompassing a strong inner evolution from causing and witnessing suffering and evil to choosing good and peace. In fact, if he used to practice hunting and killing animals himself, eventually, he would not even be able to kill a fly. He was finally able to grasp what he described as "that sense of infection with another's feeling, compelling us to joy in another's gladness, to sorrow at another's grief, and to mingle souls with one another" (Donovan 2009, 49). Indeed, he would agree with the following excerpt from *Karma*, a Buddhist fairy tale that he translated into Russian:

> To consider yourself a separate being is a mistake, and one who directs his mind to fulfil the will of this particular being, follows a false light that would lead him into the abyss of sin. We think of ourselves as

individual beings because the veil of Maya dazzles our eyes and prevents us from seeing our unity with the souls of other beings. Few know this truth. Let the following words will be your talisman: "One who harms others, does evil to himself. One who helps others, does good to himself. Stop regarding yourself as a separate being—and you will get on the path of truth, [where you will] understand the value of the all-encompassing love for all living things." (Tolstoy 1902, 6)

The law of love is thus recognized by Tolstoy as the only law of human existence.

In *Letter to a Hindu* (1908), Tolstoy further draws a clear line between the use of violence and the teaching of love, claiming that to permit the former is to deny the latter. Consequently, he would reject violence in all its forms and toward any living creature, defining this choice as a form of abstention from a social disease:

> If we have understood that we are ill because some people use violence to others, [. . .] that [we] suffer from the violence done by some to others, it is already impossible to improve the position by continuing the old violence or by introducing a new kind. As the sick man suffering from alcoholism has but one way to be cured— by refraining from intoxicants which are the cause of his illness; so there is only one way to free men from the evil arrangement of society, and that is, to refrain from violence, the cause of the suffering, from personal violence, from preaching violence, and from in any way justifying violence. (Tolstoy 1900b)

The answer to the issue of suffering is, at bottom, intrinsic to its very nature. There exists a *natural, vital* suffering that is essential to life and all its manifestations. The source of this suffering is incredibly vast, as it is the font of life. One could do nothing but accept it as part of existence, experiencing it and pursuing the right attitude toward it. Afterward, there is an *unnecessary* suffering, caused by violence and lack of love. We have a better chance of eradicating this kind of suffering—if only we understood that in the end, we are all fragments of an entangled universe.

CHAPTER SIX

Animal Liberation under Capitalist Realism

Richard Giles

As the climate crisis continues seemingly unabated, "there is no ethical consumption under capitalism" has become a rallying cry for both action and inaction. A poisonous all-or-nothing political ideation has taken hold, and in accordance so has a sense of doom and despair about the prospects of existence on a battered planet. I posit that this worrying state of affairs stems from the fallout of capitalist realism, whose coinage was popularized by Mark Fisher and which refers to "the widespread sense that not only is capitalism the only viable political and economic system, but also that it is now impossible even to *imagine* a coherent alternative to it" (2010, 2). While Fisher did not come up with the concept, his work was dedicated to explaining it in as plain terms as possible, and toward the end of his life, he began trying to theorize ways out of it, though his suicide prevented the completion of his thoughts. The concept of capitalist realism has become considerably popular amongst many groups, but animal liberationists have yet to engage with it in Fisherian terms. I argue that capitalist realism is of considerable importance for animal liberationists; moreover, by engaging with it vis-à-vis animal rights, one can also identify the possibility that this sense of realism can exist outside of capitalism, creating an impetus for theorists and activists to both engage with animal activism under capitalist realism and conceptualize other forms of said realism. This chapter will briefly summarize Fisher's work, offer commentary on the animal condition under capitalist realism, and theorize the existence of various forms of realism.

CAPITALIST REALISM

Though the phrase "it is easier to imagine the end of the world than it is to imagine the end of capitalism" is often attributed to Slavoj Zizek, Frederic Jameson (2003) can be considered its originator. The sentiment expressed herein is one that Fisher built on throughout the entirety of his career. This chapter sets aside his K-Punk blog for no reason other than space and begins with his 2010 book *Capitalist Realism*, published toward the end of the Global Financial Crisis, a time of great ambiguity for both Fisher and the world at large. Beginning the book with an assessment of the film *Children of Men*, Fisher presents an understanding of the film as an extension of our current democratic predicament rather than a post-apocalyptic alternative to our world. Past and present are detached from one another with no feeling of continuity; the state exists, but only to serve the interests of capitalists, who wish the state did not exist; and political action makes no sense without a coherent target or a valid vision of what is to come after revolution. Fisher's assessment is, admittedly, one that oscillates between Marxist-materialist and postmodern-cultural, bouncing from specific incidents during the Global Financial Crisis to the immaterial question of whether there will ever be another cultural rupture. As individual life is presented as a hollowed-out consumer/spectator dynamic, culture becomes nothing but monetized preservationism, and, as a result, Gilles Deleuze and Félix Guattari's argument becomes retroactively true. Capitalism, throughout all of human history and society, lurked in the darkness, awaiting the opportunity to fill in the gaps of an unraveling existence and eventually become a Fukuyamian end point where history is essentially finished, with no new global struggles emerging. Fisher presents Kurt Cobain as the MTV generation's symbol of such a predicament—an artist who knew everything he did would be a cliché before he could even make it a cliché.

The bitter irony of Fisher's work is that he crystallized the concept of capitalist realism when Occupy Wall Street emerged and collapsed in record time. Fisher's examples of capitalist realism in action feel almost quaint in comparison to its manifestations today. *Wall-E*'s representation of "capitalism's widespread dissemination of anti-capitalism" (Fisher 2012, 10) arrived well before the rise in social media's impact, notably on how media would come to be written, critiqued, and disseminated in new forms. His discussion of teaching as simultaneously entertainment and authoritarian dictatorship feels hopeful when considering the state of modern public education, wherein teachers lament their inability to enforce rules and no longer have the energy to entertain, a combination that is likely contributing to the increasing rate of burnout within the profession. *Heat*—Michael Mann's 1995 crime/drama film—represents Los Angeles as nothing more than repetitive branded sprawl, a "world without landmarks." The reduction of landscapes to such repetitive branded sprawl has certainly not been rendered irrelevant but remains the defining feature of today's urbanization, at least as it is understood by Frederic Jameson in his 1991 book, *Postmodernism, or the Cultural Logic of Late Capitalism*. Stalin's valuation of symbolic achievement over actual achievement is more prominent in the modern neoliberal workplace that is continually forced into the everyday life of workers; capitalism subsumes not just the critiques against it but also the practices of what some believe is the only way out of capitalism. Fisher's critique of capitalist realism, like other theories—such as Erika Cudworth's (2005) theory of anthroparchy and Gary Steiner's (2013) theory of cosmopolitan veganism—finds itself attempting to overcome the postmodern rupture, moving away from general relativism and the subsequent inability to "find the center," but without returning to the more naïve, hopeful appeals to a modernist sense of inevitable progress that defined anti-capitalism prior to the neoliberalization of capitalism. Yet, trying to feel any sense of hope after reading *Capitalist Realism* is futile: the problems Fisher identifies remain widespread and rampant. Infantilization, atomization, bureaucratization, and marketization continue apace, with no real end in sight—save, maybe, for societal collapse occurring alongside climate change. Capitalist realism, in a sense, has become more inescapable than it was in the first decade of the new millennium: the new freedom conceptualized in blogging has more or less vanished, replaced by private social media firms; Occupy Wall Street has disappeared, and other movements like environmentalism and Black Lives Matter are dissipating due to the types of issues Fisher predicted in his controversial yet prophetic 2013 essay, "Exiting the Vampire Castle."

Even as this grim state of affairs unfolded, Fisher was thinking of ways out of capitalist realism: "It's well past time for the left to cease limiting its ambitions to the establishing of a big state. [. . .] [T]he goal of a genuinely new left should not be to take over the state but to subordinate the state to the general will." The irony of this quote is that sentences later, Fisher reconciles his idea—which has an undeniably anarchist edge to it—with more conventional Marxism by declaring that "against the postmodernist suspicion of grand narratives, we need to reassert that, far from being isolated, contingent problems, these are all the effects of a single systemic cause: Capital" (2010, 77). Fisher's examples of living up to this ideal, such as teachers' unions abandoning strikes so as not to hurt students, have not necessarily been accepted by the left, which he accuses of being stuck in old debates on "Kronstadt or the New Economic Policy" (78). How does one understand Fisher as a Marxist when he, frankly, espouses solutions that seem inherently non-Marxist?

The answer, unfortunately, has never been made truly clear. Fisher continued engaging with capitalist realism after 2010, though sometimes in different contexts. *Ghosts of My Life* (2014) and *The Weird and the Eerie* (2017) engage with capitalist realism in new terms like "hauntology" (the haunting of postmodern culture by the ghosts of modernism and desired future) and "the Weird" (the oddities of art that expose the strangeness of arbitrary social forces). His suicide on January 13, 2017, rendered his plans for *Acid Communism* moot, but he left behind both the introduction to the book and five lectures compiled for *Postcapitalist Desire,* which can at least provide some clues as to what he was thinking: "The libidinal attractions of consumer capitalism" must "be met with a counterlibido, not simply an anti-libidinal dampening" (Fisher 2020, Introduction). Postcapitalist desire, then, becomes this counterlibido, driving us toward whatever "acid communism" would have looked like. How to develop this desire, when Fisher even recognizes that one's consciousness of their material existence cannot be presumed to be self-evident, is obviously of tremendous difficulty. Matt Colquhoun, the editor of *Postcapitalist Desire*, interprets Fisher's final lecture as an attempt to develop a new praxis for "left-acceleration," a way to move accelerationism out of "the destruction of the old without the creation of the new," to generate a new history that does not just resurrect images of a dead past, attempting to parade them around anew (Fisher 2020, Introduction). In the introduction to *Acid Communism*, Fisher surprises his long-time readers by arguing that to develop this counterlibido, we need to return to the ethos of the 1970s, rereading and reinterpreting it for its potential: "Where the new culture was not being driven by those from working-class backgrounds, it seemed that it was being led by class renegades such as Pink Floyd, young people from bourgeois families who had rejected their own class destinies and identified 'downwards,' or outwards. They wanted to do anything but go into business and banking: fields whose subsequent libidinization would have boggled the expanded minds of the Sixties" (Fisher 2018, 854). If metaphysical questions could be mainstreamed in the sixties and seventies, Fisher seems to believe that it's possible to see that happen again: "I have a lot of problems with the term community, largely because of the way it's been easily appropriated by the right. But, also, because it implies an in and out. Some are in the community and some are out of it. I had a slogan once: 'care without community.' Isn't that what we want? Where you can give people the care regardless of whether they belong to the community" (Christman 2020). It is difficult to comprehend that Fisher presented this idea—somehow full of what can be interpreted only as naivety—just weeks before taking his own life.

The Animal Condition under Capitalist Realism

If the human condition is one of hopeless malaise and despair, it does not seem like a stretch to declare that under capitalist realism, animals are in a similar, if not worse, predicament. Corinne Painter (2016) has this unique way to characterize the difference between human and animal under capitalism: The human laborer is obligated to choose among, usually, a few bad options—starving, participating in meaningless work, or exhaustingly attempting to break out of the confines of the lower classes with low chances of success. Animals do not get to choose any of these options; depending on human desires and demands, they will be commodified, objectified, and rendered unable to act on the basis of any perceivable agency. Capitalist realism acts like a carnival of cruelty, forcing participation in its system while simultaneously depending on human free will and agency to make the working classes choose the option most beneficial to the system itself. The animal is not able to exercise even this remote, limited agency. Meat animals are born into animal agriculture, their fate predetermined by the demands of consumers and the market; animals used for scientific research will have their lives subject to the whims of scientific demand, the rat race of publication, and the need to justify the existence of such research in the first place; animals kept as pets are bred to be purchased, traded, and discarded, with their ability to express their agency essentially rendered null from the beginning. Though Eeva Puumala's (2013) ontological framework of the body may help identify the role of the body in attempting to regain agential status in situations in which the subject in question has no legal status or ability to regain agency through legal action, at this current historical juncture, the animal may scream in desperation, attempt to flee its situation, or exhaust itself in protest—its inability to exercise agency leaves it unable to choose even among a few menial, existentially draining options. The animal condition under capitalist realism is a material nightmare.

Immaterially, the animal fares no better. As John Berger (2009) famously postulates, the animal is disappearing even as it exists materially: the zoo animal is a monument to its own disappearance, its own erasure as a living, thinking, feeling being. Berger further argues that even with the increase in the number of pets (and, generally, the number of animals in existence), they are so far removed from both their own nature and nature in general that they are being erased from the human consciousness. Then there is the 7 percent of American adults who believe that chocolate milk comes from brown cows (Kalvapalle 2017); an admittedly extreme example, it still highlights how removed from human thought the animal has become. Those who hold such a belief demonstrate an inability to think of animals as living beings, instead relying on childhood narratives and imagination to attempt to form some understanding of the animal in the absence of one founded on any sort of animal dignity and presence. Though this dissonance can be found in how human beings think of one another—especially in the internet age, in which groups and cultures are understood through increasingly fractured, quasi-ironic imagery and labels—the animal, as a concept and as an existence, can be taken to signify its own hollowed emptiness.

However, there is a problem in the distance, one that goes beyond Painter's (2016) critique of Marxism as not sufficient to understand the animal condition. Foster and Clark (2018), in citing Marx's commentary on animals, present Marx as a liberationist, but all of Marx's examples of care for animals are within the context of animal welfare. He critiques the capitalist treatment of animals as excessive, inhumane, and unnecessary, but he never goes so far as to question why animals are being used in such ways in the first place. There were proponents of animal rights well before the onset of what we may understand as modern capitalism: Porphyry of Tyre and al-Ma'arri critiqued meat-eating, and other uses of animals, centuries before Marx was even born. I ask readers to consider the following scenario: Suppose that, somehow, the revolution happens the day after you read this chapter, and the day after that, we get a sense of what will take the place of capitalism. Maybe it is traditional Leninism, maybe it is anarchism, maybe it is acid communism. Can you envision these new systems putting an end to animal exploitation, by virtue of their arrival? Can you envision the end of animal exploitation, pending certain conditions? Or can you, like me, not envision the end of animal exploitation by virtue of the implementation of any of these systems? It is here where we must critique Fisher's theory for a moment, in order to consider a wider set of possibilities.

_____ REALISM?

Fisher, fairly, accuses capital of being the force that continually oppresses the working class, whatever form such a class may take. The generation of infinitely growing capital, held mostly by an increasingly excessive bourgeois class, drives capitalist realism to its all-consuming state. Yet, Fisher is not a strict, orthodox Marxist; his work recognizes how capitalism infiltrated Leninism and Stalinism, while simultaneously learning from their interpretations of Marxist theory. There is more than enough cultural theory, as well as engagement with how capitalism so greatly impacts the chemical experience of mental health, to indicate more underlying nuance than is sometimes recognized. Fisher may have been open to, at the very least, the recognition that while capital is a driving force, it may not explain every instance of oppression at every given time. Take, for example, the recent U.S. Supreme Court ruling on abortion. Many felt that it was not in the interest of capital to revoke *Roe v. Wade*, yet the ideological forces at the Supreme Court prevailed over capital's demands and (dis)interest. Ideology triumphed over capital. Capital may be an all-consuming force, but in an era of post-ironic politics and post-postmodern malaise, it sometimes seems as if capital is not quite quick enough to be the reason for every social, personal, or cultural ill. There seems to be something—"human nature," "subconscious trickery," or "cosmic surrendering"—that can sometimes clash with the explanations of the dialectical materialists.

When it comes to the animal, can capital be blamed for every instance of animal objectification and thereby oppression? Let us consider animals raised in localized, non-industrial contexts for eventual slaughter. Imagine, for a moment, that a community vows to use local agriculture to resist the logics of capitalism. The community will reject monoculture; it will pay fair wages to workers; it will be organic; and the animals will be able to roam in idealistic pasture. Maybe it will even, somehow, resist the logic of property ownership and provide food for everyone through communal means and the logic of the public commons. While an animal in this community may not be subject to a comparable demand of capital vis-à-vis an animal raised in an industrial system—fattened as quickly as possible, pumped full of antibiotics—if it is eventually killed and then sold, one cannot avoid the reality that the animal has still been rendered a commodified object. Now, imagine that someone rejects buying a piece of a dead animal and instead ventures into nature, rifle (or bow and arrow) in hand, in order to kill an animal so as to consume it. The animal may not be sold and, consequently, may not be inherently a victim of the capitalist system. But that does not protect the animal from objectification or even offer commentary on this objectification. And what of the animals in laboratory research? Though plenty of researchers use animals to test drugs, a considerable amount of animal research is aimed specifically at testing scientific hypotheses. Capital, then, is important not for creating new forms of profit but for maintaining funding for more research to confirm more hypotheses, for maintaining a self-insulated system. Scientific research involving animals has been a routine failure and remains hardly profitable for anyone except researchers, yet this reality is often not understood in such terms; instead, researchers reference the mission to advance science to justify their oppressive efforts.

Because Fisher did not give us much to work with in figuring out what acid communism would look like, some imagination is needed here. Say, tomorrow, we enter acid communism, and the general will is what the state bends to, accepting its fate. What does that mean for animals? The general will here is that of the people, the discontents of nature (Zizek 2008), the classes that have been chewed up, spat out, and rendered lost at sea by capitalist realism. Despite the promises of Fisher's notion of "care without community"—which I will return to later—his discourse provides no comfort for those who view oppression as going beyond the functions and results of capital. If we accept that the animal world is impacted by oppression in ways that don't have to do with just capital, then a new system of acid communism, even if it stops reiterating the Kronstadt debates of yore, does not guarantee that animals are suddenly going to be made participants instead of subjects. Human exceptionalism retains its ever-present functionality in such a vision; if the animal is to become a part of this new world, the integration would have to be explicit.

It is this notion that leads me to wonder if there might be something along the lines of carnist realism, speciesist realism, humanist realism, anthropocentric realism, and so on—systems that function alongside capitalist realism, sometimes interrelating and sometimes remaining separate. Or, is it possible that capitalist realism was misidentified as the end-all, be-all of realism, meaning that there is some sort of realism that transcends even the all-encompassing nature of capitalist realism? Of my proposals here, both raise considerable concerns. As for the former, some more traditional leftists may be concerned by the "distraction" of such realisms—concerned that it is possible for capitalist realism, in its nigh-capitalist competition with other realisms, to become diluted, thus more ineffective. Meanwhile, the latter proposal makes it seem as if I am preparing to dismiss Fisher's concept outright, serving the interests of capital by making the mistake of the postmodernists in questioning the grand narrative of capital's control over our lives, throwing us into the dark, cold ocean without a metanarrative to which we can attach ourselves. I do not want either concern to truly come to fruition; it is here where I will lay out the possibilities of each option.

When it comes to identifying other forms of realism, I argue that there is value in both engaging with capitalist realism and questioning whether there is a realism beyond capitalism that maintains control over animal life. Many activists and critical animal studies scholars are well aware of the feeling of helplessness that can come with attempting to convince people to consider the animal as more than an abstract object. "Like pulling teeth" is an under-description of this endeavor to convince others that humans' use of animals for food, clothing, entertainment, and so on stems from a general feeling of superiority that can be questioned, interrogated, and rendered irrelevant to our discussions of how actually to treat the animal other. It is sometimes difficult for people to even accept that animals feel, or that they may not want to die: narratives of "self-sacrificing" animals play into long-standing visions of the great chain of being and human domination of the natural world. The original phrase "it is easier to imagine the end of the world than it is to imagine the end of capitalism" can be edited to read "it is easier to imagine the end of the world than it is to imagine the end of anthropocentrism" and it would ring just as true, especially when one has exercised every line of argumentation to get others to consider animals differently, only for inaction and disregard to still prevail. Piazza (2015) argues that Joy's proposal of the three Ns—to describe the cultural framing of meat-eating as **n**ecessary, **n**atural, and **n**ormal—can be expanded to include a fourth N: when all else fails, meat-eating is rationalized by virtue of being **n**ice, which invokes a subjective feeling that transcends all questions of necessity, naturalness, and normalcy. How does one overcome such a rationalization? How is one to not become the enemy in demanding that people think beyond what pleasures them? Any form of such realism is felt by both critic and perpetrator: the perpetrator cannot imagine a world without an objectified animal, subjected to violence at human hands; the critic comes to a point where they cannot imagine a day when 100 percent of humanity gets on board with treating animals differently. Cultured meat represents this realism in action; support for a product that may not even result in the preservation of animal life (Melzener et al. 2021; Giles 2022) implies a (not-so-)subtle acceptance that the way toward a vegan, liberationist world cannot be envisioned and, therefore, mitigation of carnist, speciesist excesses is the best alternative. Even those who still believe in a post-carnist, post-speciesist, post-humanist world tend to acknowledge that it will not happen in their lifetimes, often contributing to frustration with the prospects of activism and advocacy, as well as to burnout. When it comes to the animal condition, it is genuinely easier to imagine the world coming to an end—in the near future, given climate change—than it is to imagine an entrenched, thousands-year-old multicultural practice being stopped.

Yet, there is another daunting aspect to this matter—what if there are not multiple forms of realism, and instead we are attempting to identify a singular realism that cannot be spoken of with any ease? In his final lecture, Fisher, in engaging with Lyotard's *Libidinal Economy*, reveals that capitalism's ability to neutralize all opposition—to swallow it whole and spew it back out—leaves no space for building resistance: "And, after all, aren't there some aspects of capitalism we want to keep? Is it possible, or even desirable, to oppose it *tout court*?" (Billet 2021). Fisher's work occupies a space alongside Zizek's contrarian views on how "there is no ethical consumption under capitalism" and Land's new-wave fascist accelerationism, becoming a go-to reference for those who are tired of the whole thing, who have thrown their hands up in frustration with the entirety of both capitalism and the anti-capitalist project. But Fisher, I argue, was uncomfortable with his concepts diving into such territory; capital may be the root cause of our woes, but Fisher's criticism of leftism's ease of appropriation points to a certain tension with leftism at large. The notion of "care without community" is, arguably, the best demonstration of this tension in action, with Fisher, as Christman (2020) notes, caring about what has yet to be imagined—a world in which we care without the confines of community, without the ins and outs that tend to define even the most radical of anti-capitalist projects. In an era when manifestos of the coming revolution seem to be little more than either fantasies of revenge and revolutionary slaughter or declarations of a life of excess self-absorption, Fisher's undefined, yet desirable, future not only seems to align itself with going "against the logic of the guillotine" (CrimethInc. 2019) but also pre-emptively imagines a problem that exists beyond capitalism. Suffering, violence, revenge, a lack of care and compassion for others—these issues seem to be what Fisher worries could continue on with humanity, even if we finally figure out what acid communism is and how it can overcome the elements of capitalism we do not want to keep.

It is here where engaging with this realism beyond capitalism is of value for animal liberation activists. We are often accused of not seeing the real issues when we advocate for animals, even though there are many of us who are no more fans of capitalism than we are of violence toward animals. Where we are having considerable trouble is how to create a consciousness conducive to "care without community"; making the case for why humans of any sort should care for animals is extremely difficult in an age of such realism. Harris (2022), discussing the concept of there being "no ethical consumption under capitalism," demonstrates this point succinctly thus: "If we are engaged in a collective liberation project, then we can end the debates about the individual ethics of consumption and instead begin to develop a strategic, shared analysis of our movement's needs. [. . .] [W]e shouldn't take that Hawaiian vacation, not because it's unethical by whatever philosophical standard, but because it undermines the struggle of Kānaka Maoli organizers who are in a specific and urgent fight for the future of their nation, which is part of the world struggle." In Harris's continuation of Fisher's rejection of complete hopelessness, we still find an in and an out—the humans of various stripes are in, while the animals and natural world are out, unidentifiable by their specific struggles. If we are to lead people to care for animals, we are trapped between making pleas for a general care and advocating specific, case-by-case care, which becomes exhausting. But, more important, Harris fails to see that individual ethics still play a role in developing a consciousness that can reject the notion of there being "no ethical consumption under capitalism." A collective-liberation project is composed of individuals who still choose whether or not to care, regardless of what community they see themselves as a part of; that is what makes Fisher's (lack of) vision for postcapitalist desire so radical. How do we create a libido that desires that people care? And should we really presume that we can do so only by eschewing individual ethics—which many proclaim themselves ready to do today—for a collective vision, instead of having both parts working alongside one another in tandem? Maybe Fisher had a point that some parts of capitalism remain desirable; maybe we should not completely destroy individualism that can lead one to critique others for actions that are unethical, undesirable, and so on. The monster lurking in the shadows of Fisher's concept of capitalist realism is a discomfort with shaking off responsibility, whether individually or collectively. Christman (2020) argues that Fisher cared—but he cared at a distance, avoiding sentimentality too carefully. Had Fisher been more comfortable with such sentimentality, we may not have had to do so much digging to question whether capitalist realism is the end point or but one (important) system in a series of many.

Concluding Remarks

I proposed this chapter—as I will probably propose many pieces of writing in the future—out of a sense of frustration. Colquhoun, Christman, and Billet all seem to be aware of how Fisher's work can be misinterpreted, misused, and stripped of all its contents in order to become a hollow way of saying "meh." Harris (2022) argues that the phrase "there is no ethical consumption under capitalism" has become exculpatory: "There is also no particularly *un*ethical consumption under capitalism. [. . .] [T]here's a certain truth there, especially in an era in which consumption can no longer support the world socialist project in a direct way [. . .] but it's suspect that the Marxist line Americans have been quickest to adopt is the one that excuses them to buy stuff and, by extension, be assholes." Though animal liberation literature and theory may not frequently engage with Fisher, we leftist animal liberationists are all too familiar with our fellow leftists' dismissal of our arguments, desires, and sentiments. Either "our consumption is unethical too" or "the world will end before the working class gives up meat, so we should do something better with our time." Frankly, I find it more frustrating to talk with dismissive leftists than with just about anyone else about animal liberation these days; it has become an exercise in tedious repetition. The nonleftist carnists and speciesists of today keep at least a few more rationalizations in rotation.

Engaging with the ghosts of Fisher's thoughts and writings will be important for animal activism as we go into what is an increasingly dire future. In many ways, we have been asking questions similar to Fisher's, even if the focus is different. The questions "Can we do things differently?" and "Do we want to do things differently?" plague anticapitalists and post-humanists alike. Can we completely shed ourselves of anthropocentrism? Or will we have to maintain some sense of human superiority to lead people to believe that it is possible to change our treatment of and relationship with animals, so as to avoid solipsistic, Gnostic sentiments of cosmic (natural) order? Though there are sometimes clearer answers—the animal liberationist wants no remnants of meat-eating left in a post-carnist world, whereas pieces of capitalism may remain even in a world that has shed capitalist realism—the questions of how to create "postcapitalist and post-speciesist desires" arise from a similar desire to overcome the Fukuyamian end of history. The driving force underneath all of these questions, as I have argued, is the desire to create care without community, whatever that may actually mean and whatever that may actually look like.

Of course, it is one thing to say that we must go down this path, and it is another to present it as an easy task. Complementing animal liberation philosophy with Fisher's theories means not just critiquing Fisher but also trying to stress to leftists, the working class—whoever will listen— that better treatment of animals is worth fighting for. It is a process that involves our potentially staring in the face of a future in which we cannot argue that everything is desirable, and it is a process that will involve our trying to create desire at a time when even basic care seems nonexistent—we are already trying to do so when many seem ready to accept the end of the world. We need to find a way to make the case that a system of nonviolence toward animals is both imaginable and desirable; it is not enough to merely make the case that current practices are wrong and, therefore, their abolition will lead us to better ways of living. This prospect means that we, much like Fisher, have to accept that "a thing is ruined when it starts to exist" (Christman 2020). Whatever world we envision in which animal and human live more peacefully will be ruined by virtue of never being perfect, much as acid communism, even by our just speaking it into imagination, is ruined by the ghosts of communism and the entrapments of capitalism. That is where the irony of Fisher's work becomes poetic: he tried to be cool in proposing a postcapitalist world, only for its actualities to make it unpalatable before it could even be conceptualized. Much like the punk music he celebrated, what is cool becomes uncool—but losing sight of such energy entirely becomes misery. There may be opportunities for animal liberation, should it pick up where Fisher most unfortunately left off.

CHAPTER SEVEN

Black Anarchy through Urban Agriculture as a Potential Alternative and Resistance to State-Regulated Cell-Based Meat

Nathan Poirier

INTRODUCTION

Food technology presents an exciting, trendy, and lucrative opportunity for start-ups and investors. In the rapidly evolving field of cell-based meat production, cells are biopsied from an animal and grown in a mix of nutrients so that they can grow into meat without the need for farming (Swartz and Bomkamp n.d.). This technology has garnered interest from wealthy investors, celebrities, animal protection organizations, and even the meat industry (Shapiro 2018). Proponents of cell-based meat frequently assert that such products can significantly make up for the negative consequences and shortcomings of traditional meat production, being more efficient to produce, healthier to consume, and better for farmed animal welfare, as they eliminate the need to intensively house and slaughter animals.

On August 23, 2018, cell-based meat company Memphis Meats (MM) and the North American Meat Institute (NAMI) wrote a joint letter to then-U.S. president Donald Trump, urging for combined United States Department of Agriculture (USDA) and Food and Drug Administration (FDA) oversight of cell-based products. In October 2018, the USDA and FDA held a joint public meeting (see Evans and Johnson 2021) that seemingly led to the two agencies establishing, in March 2019, shared regulations in alignment with the request of MM and NAMI. NAMI is a national lobby group for North American meat processors. MM (which changed its name to Upside Foods but is referred to as MM in this chapter because this is the name used in the letter under study) is a cellular-meat company founded by cardiologist Uma Valeti in 2015. It is the first company dedicated to creating cellular-meat products, producing the first cellular meatball, chicken, and duck (https://upsidefoods. com/about). This chapter presents a critical discourse analysis of the joint document sent to Trump.

This letter is an important cultural artifact to study as it calls into question whether such a regulatory pathway would challenge or promote existing ideologies and institutions that uphold inequality and injustice. Would it help or hinder those beyond just the corporate players involved? Being federal regulation, it is also important because it would oversee the supply of all cell-based meat in the United States and apply to the entire population, including Black communities and, by extension, Black anarchists. Are these groups okay with this? Would they see this as being in line with their own liberation struggles, a hindrance to their struggles, or something else? This chapter is the first to interrogate cell-based meat from an anarchist perspective.

The chapter parallels and complements a previous publication by Evans and Johnson (2021) on the joint FDA and USDA meeting on cellular-meat regulation that resulted from the MM-NAMI letter. Evans and Johnson analyzed the complete manuscript from this landmark two-day meeting and concluded that discourses from this meeting supported existing state regulatory frameworks and instrumental uses of nonhuman animals, such as meat consumption. Additionally, they noted that discourses concerning intrinsically more sustainable alternatives to cell-based meat (i.e., veganism) were absent, as was discussion about the ability or inability of state-regulated cell-based meat to address social inequalities that give rise to food insecurity and public health issues related to diet (2021, 88). The present chapter adds to Evans and Johnson's discussion by analyzing the letter that preceded this joint meeting. Importantly, since the FDA-USDA meeting happened *after* the MM-NAMI letter, the similarities between my findings and Evans and Johnson's indicate that the shortcomings of the joint letter extended to the subsequent meeting and thus are likely to exist in practice too.

LITERATURE REVIEW

The joint letter from Valeti of MM and Barry Carpenter of NAMI to (then-)President Trump is analyzed predominantly through a Black studies lens, borrowing particularly from the Black radical tradition (Robinson 2021), Black geographies (McKittrick 2006), and Black anarchism (Bagby-Williams and Suekama 2022). Literature on urban agriculture and veganism of color is used supplementarily. This approach is a response to Evans and Johnson's suggestion to connect the interests of marginalized humans and nonhumans within exploitative, capitalist food systems.

Bagby-Williams and Suekama (2022) position Black anarchism as a component of the long Black radical tradition of resistance to colonialism, slavery, and marginalization. As explained by Cedric Robinson (2021), the Black radical tradition critiques and makes up for the overlooking of race in Marxist thought. Black anarchism is a highly varied and highly diffuse praxis that has its ultimate origin in African colonization and the Atlantic slave trade and its more recent origin in contemporary mass incarceration. Sam Mbah and I.E. Igariwey's *African Anarchism* (2007) shows that numerous pre-colonial African societies exhibited many anarchic characteristics and were, for all intents and purposes, essentially or literally anarchist and distinctly African. In the classic 1979 text *Anarchism and the Black Revolution* (2022), Loreanzo Kom'boa Ervin explains his journey to anarchism through imprisonment and frustration with "radical" Black activism, particularly with how groups like the Black Panthers became reformist, followed leaders, and capitulated to state interests. William C. Anderson is yet another scholar who discusses how traditional African anarchism was carried over to the United States via the slave trade as a necessary basis for Black survival under white supremacy. Anderson's *The Nation on No Map* (2021) and Samudzi and Anderson's *As Black as Resistance* (2018) both provide heavy criticisms of the U.S. nation-state and U.S. nationalism and citizenship. Anderson's book also critiques "leaders," especially the rich, celebrities, and politicians.

Marquis Bey's (2020) anarcho-Blackness goes a step further than "traditional" Black anarchism yet could also be read as a form of Black anarchism. Uninterested in anarchism per se, Bey focuses on revolutionary ways of life. Perhaps somewhat akin to Saul Newman's (2016) post-anarchism, Bey's anarcho-Blackness is thoroughly infused with Black, queer, trans/feminist theory, all things Newman's formulation lacks. Black anarchism, as a form of Black resistance, is anti-capitalist out of a recognition of the violence capitalism, in conjunction with the state, has wrought not just on Africans and the Black diaspora but on all people of color, the poor, and non-males. Yet *Black* anarchism is distinctively rooted in Black history and present circumstances (which, in turn, are rooted in Black history and colonialism).

Geography and anarchism have historical links to European anarchism (Springer 2016) as well as to Black anarchism (Anderson 2021). In fact, Black anarchism emerged largely within the context of mass incarceration, which can be characterized by a lack or constriction of space. Katherine McKittrick (2006) describes Black geographies as the locations where "the imperative of a perspective of struggle takes place" (6)—in other words, the places where confrontation and autonomy happen. Just as "traditional" (white, European) anarchism largely displaced race from its purview, "traditional geographies did, and arguably do, *require* black displacement, black placelessness, black labor, and a black population that submissively stays 'in place'" (9). In this context, urban agriculture emerges as a site of contestation, autonomy, and survival, a distinctly geographical phenomenon. Urban agriculture takes place predominantly in large urban landscapes referred to as "post-industrial" cities. It also tends to be practiced by majority-Black populations. The places of urban agriculture include neighborhoods, community lots, backyards, and vacant properties undergoing reconfigurations of space: "To put it another way, social practices create landscapes and contribute to how we organize, build, and imagine our surroundings" (McKittrick 2006, xiv).

As Samudzi and Anderson (2018) make clear, Black identity is intimately tied to land. From its origins in Africa to colonialism and slavery in the Western Hemisphere, "blackness has come to symbolize a kind of rootlessness" (Samudzi and Anderson 2018, 22–23). These conditions have tended to favor nationalist-based cultural identities, fusing aspects of geographical presents with temporal and geographical pasts. Yet, the United States has been particularly brutal in its treatment of African American and Black communities; this is where Black anarchism and federal regulation of cell-based meat intersect. As Evans and Johnson comment, the United States "is the jurisdiction where factory-style, intensive animal agriculture was first developed, where meat consumption per capita is relatively high and often the highest and where many, if not most, of the cell-cultured companies are based" (2021, 82). Thus, this chapter has chosen the United States as the central area of focus. It is further noted that Ervin, Anderson, and Bey all write primarily (but not entirely) from a U.S. perspective, and MM and NAMI are both headquartered in the United States (Berkeley, California, and Washington, DC, respectively). Lastly, Detroit, Michigan, is highlighted as a prime example of the potential of urban agriculture.

Commentaries on the MM and NAMI partnership in the literature on cell-based meat (see Purdy 2020, 176–77) tend to be general, descriptive, and brief, summarizing the content of the joint letter or providing details of national (U.S. or otherwise) food regulation. No one has analyzed the letter itself and connected it to a social movement for liberation as the present chapter seeks to do, specifically with respect to Black anarchism. Moreover, as Evans and Johnson (2021, 84) ask in their study, "Do the discourses offer solutions?" And since the discourses of the FDA-USDA public meeting did not, this chapter presents urban agriculture as an alternative to state-regulated cell-based meat, in line with Black anarchist theory. Indeed, urban agriculture addresses community-based needs by resisting systemic inequality pertaining to food access, security, and sovereignty, and by providing mutual aid. In contrast to the globalized, privatized, and capitalist food systems in which cell-based meat is emerging (Evans and Johnson 2021), urban agriculture tends to be based on local, public use of open and abandoned spaces.

ANALYZING THE LETTER

This chapter employs critical discourse analysis (CDA) to analyze the MM-NAMI joint letter. CDA seeks to find and interrogate examples of power in cultural artifacts, offering explanations of why and how discourses work by analyzing relations between discourse, cultural items, and power (Machin and Mayr 2012). Importantly, CDA also looks for what is *not* said as an indication of what is taken to be important and what is hidden, unknown, or contradictory to the available discourse. CDA is intentionally and explicitly political and normative; as such, applications of CDA should be accompanied by a sense of solidarity with marginalized groups. As a mode of analysis, CDA is at its strongest when used to study shorter tracts of text because it looks at minute details to examine how they communicate certain messages.

To begin, I will describe the overall structure of the joint MM-NAMI letter, along with the major discursive themes. Then, I will discuss some general implications of the text and provide additional context and wider commentary in relation to relevant literature as previously summarized. For simplicity, Valeti and Carpenter are referred to as "the authors" (of the letter).

It is important for a researcher to be clear on their positionality. Thus, I declare mine here: I follow a vegan lifestyle, which is a lifestyle through which one aims to minimize one's negative influence on others as far as is practicable and possible, within one's abilities. Social and geographical locations play a role in determining the feasibility and extent, as well as the meaning, of one's veganism (Hodge et al. 2022; Brueck 2019). Veganism includes abstaining from animal-based foods and other animal-derived products (clothing, cleaning products, etc.). To me, it also entails being anarchist. As such, I am skeptical of the ability of capitalism, corporations, or the elites to foster non/human liberation. From this standpoint, I see cell-based meat as unnecessary for addressing environmental, animal welfare, and human health problems as veganism can already address those issues—and is generally possible through means such as urban agriculture.

A CRITICAL READING OF THE TEXT

The entire letter is just under two pages in length. Overall, it appeals to the authority and structure of the White House, the FDA, and the

USDA. It praises the U.S. food system, the U.S. system of regulations, and the country as a whole. The authors use respectful language and present themselves as humble and subservient to the wiser, more powerful, and more capable federal agencies. The authors use the honorific "Mr. President" in their opening salutation to denote respect for the recipient. In the first paragraph, the authors "respectfully request" federal regulation of cell-based meat and poultry products. Once again, the use of "respectfully" places the authors in a humble position, one that recognizes the higher authority of the president. Regardless, this is likely a strategic move to flatter a person in charge.

The authors go on to reference "the existing comprehensive system that ensures U.S. consumers enjoy the safest and most affordable food in the world." Much of this clause praises federal institutions and suggests U.S. supremacy. Calling the existing regulatory system "comprehensive" indicates belief in and support of current federal regulatory structures. The authors also give no evidence or clarification to support their statement that U.S. consumers "enjoy the safest and most affordable food in the world"; meanwhile, both claims of "safest" and "most affordable" could be debated based on different interpretations of these terms. Such a statement also overlooks the fact that the U.S. food system may be the most environmentally destructive given its heavy reliance on animal-based and heavily processed food products. Further, U.S. food products may be the "safest" regarding, say, disease control and contaminant inspection, yet the country is a world leader in obesity and other chronic health conditions that are linked to food consumption patterns, especially among people of color (Harper 2009; Rodrigues 2018). Thus, safety and affordability are ambiguous concepts, used here in a particular way to elicit favorable action—but favorable for whom? The authors position the United States in relation to the world; their comparison is no longer relative but absolute. They are asserting U.S. supremacy.

The authors describe themselves as "leaders and partners in meeting the world's protein needs." The use of "leaders" emphasizes their own authority. As we'll discuss later, this ignores the pioneering work of grassroots community food movements to supply their *own* food and meet their *own* needs. But where does this presumed leadership come from? With whose consent is it exercised? Under what criteria? The discourse here indicates that both animal- and cell-based food products are "meeting the world's protein needs." Notice the present tense, implying that these companies are addressing the need or demand for (animal) protein as we speak. But whose demand and under what pretenses?

Reference to the "world's" protein needs suggests that U.S. companies have a global influence, further carrying underlying tones of U.S. supremacy. Why do these companies care about protein needs outside the United Staes? Why are there protein needs issues (actual or at least perceived) in other countries? Some of this likely has to do with the system of imperialism and colonialism, connected to capitalism, whereby the United States exploits others for its own gain. It is also noteworthy that the authors refer to the world's "protein" needs, focusing not on food, nutrition, or even meat or animal products but on one macronutrient. Thus, all protein sources are condensed into an undifferentiated category. This move obscures the fact that some protein sources are healthier to consume than others, more efficient or ethical to produce, or more accessible to certain populations. There are large (and silent) discrepancies here.

The authors go on to say that "large-scale production methods, small-scale farming, and cell-based meat and poultry production methods will all play a role" in upholding the demand for protein worldwide. In unequivocal terms, the authors state that they "know" that these sectors are necessary. There is no hedging here: these three sectors "will all play a role." No indication is given as to what role each will play or why all three are even necessary. Presumably, the answers to these questions reside within the authority of the authors. Because they are world leaders, they know this to be true and either know or are capable of discerning how these three sectors should relate to each other and why each is necessary. This could also be a ploy to appeal to conservative U.S. values of farming and meat consumption—values that are deeply rooted in and glorified throughout U.S. (whitewashed) religion, history, culture, and politics. Indeed, the authors state that cell-based meat products are "the latest in a long history of innovation in American agriculture." In using "latest" and "long history," the authors have faith that such technological innovation will or should continue. No mention is made of technological treadmills and their effects, which dispropor-tionately fall on communities of color (Pellow 2018).

The phrase "feed the world" is vague: Exactly how do the authors and their companies aim to carry out this plan? Do they have in mind a well-balanced diet, a diet of sufficient calories, or a diet of sufficient protein only? Also, why do they presume that they need to feed the rest of the world? Why is the rest of the world perceived as not capable of feed-ing itself? Why are even U.S. citizens not perceived as able to feed them-selves? Perhaps because the authors see themselves as "uncompromising on product safety and [cognizant of] the importance of consumer trans-parency." So food safety and transparency are key values. But again, it is not clarified what safety and transparency mean to the authors or how the authors interpret the federal government's upholding of these values. Perhaps more insightful is the authors' support of "a fair and competi-tive marketplace that lets consumers decide what food products make sense for them and their families." The positioning of merely providing choices clashes with the authors' desire to feed the world. If consumers throughout the world choose not to buy their companies' products, will MM and NAMI accept that? What about consumers choosing to grow their own food? What if people resist this structure and wish to substitute it with their own?

The authors request that the USDA regulate these products "after pre-market safety has been established with the FDA." Such a regula-tory scheme would presumably "ensure food products are safe, whole-some, and properly labeled." Yet again, safety occurs without clarifica-tion as to how, this time along with "wholesome" and "proper" labeling. The authors ultimately defer to federal organizations: "We nonetheless understand that decisions regarding a regulatory framework must be made with the input of all stakeholders." However, it is unclear whom "all stakeholders" entails. For instance, to what extent do consumers—and if so, which consumers—have a stake and a role in designing how their food is regulated?

In the second-to-last paragraph, the authors write: "The United States is currently the world leader in protein production, including cell-based meats. But we will not maintain that position without regulatory clarity." Again, U.S. supremacy is implied, but there is no reason given as to why specifically cell-based products will help secure this dominance, especially when many other sources of protein exist and are readily available. The authors end by thanking the president for his "thoughtful" consideration of this "crucial" issue. But why is this issue so crucial? Could it be because animal agriculture has been so destructive to the planet that an alternative is needed? Could it be that the United States is a world leader in resource use and environmental destruction? Could it be that the United State's involvement in neoliberalism, imperialism, and fascism and its catering to the self-interest of elites have created crises of health, safety, and "scarcity" for its own and the world's inhabitants?

INTERPRETATION AND DISCUSSION WITHIN THE CONTEXT OF BLACK ANARCHISM

The MM-NAMI letter leaves out many details about cell-based and traditional meat, and the rhetoric seems to be closely aligned with that of the meat industry, not with food sovereignty, food justice, or food security. These findings are congruent with those of Evans and Johnson (2021). The letter makes no mention of the (many) downsides of animal agriculture. Further, its discourse implies that the only potential problem with animal agriculture is that, on its own, it will not be able to meet the world's growing demand for "protein," and this is why cell-based meat production should be a federally regulated industry. This, however, ignores that one of the central pillars of scholarship on cell-based meat is the fact that cell-based meat is emerging precisely in response to the ills of factory farming. In the letter are also frequent, if indirect, nods to U.S. supremacy, setting up a "structural opposition" (Machin and Mayr 2012, 41) between the United States and the rest of the world and subtly promoting nationalism and patriotism. This discourse does not pay attention to community-level needs.

Safety aspects of cell-based meat seem to be overemphasized given the suppression of discussion about health or the necessity of these products. Paralleling the results of Evans and Johnson (2021, 87), the narrow focus on safety evidenced in the letter means that it leaves out issues of public health and food justice while reifying state-led regulation. This discourse does not leave room for local food governance, which urban agriculture could provide. Moreover, despite the authors' attention to labeling, food labels often communicate more about marketing than about actual health or ethical issues concerning food products (Harper 2009).

This joint letter, along with the partnership it represents, emphasizes capitalism, the free market, self-appointed leaders, the centralized authority of the White House, the FDA, and the USDA, and U.S. supremacy. Needless to say, it therefore goes against many of the tenets of Black anarchism. In stark contrast to U.S. supremacy and patriotism, Anderson's (2021; Samudzi and Anderson 2018) vehement refutation of U.S. hegemony advocates direct resistance against it and even de facto non-citizenship. As Anderson writes, "The United States does not *have* problems, the United States *is* the problem" (2021, 4). Indeed, Black anarchism does not recognize the authority of national organizations composed of people out of touch with what happens on the streets of Black and poor neighborhoods—people who Anderson would even say do not care about what happens on the streets or about the health and safety of Black populations because it is not their business to care. Such a top-down approach does not address systemic inequality in food systems, nor does it address local conditions in neighborhoods that are poorer and food-insecure, often due to national or multinational governance schemes. It is the business of the FDA and USDA to support the United States, a country that has always been antithetical to Black persons and is fundamentally and inextricably premised on anti-Blackness. To Black anarchism, the moment one appeals to the state is the moment one's back is turned on the people.

MM and NAMI's request for federal support addressed to Trump is an appeal to the white masculine authority of "America with a capital 'Merica.'" This appeal to authority is reminiscent of Marquis Bey's letter to a sheriff, pleading for action on a case of police brutality against a Black woman. As Bey reflects: "Why did I say 'please'? Why did I 'request'? Why am I asking?" (2019, 121). Indeed, why would anyone appeal to the powers that be for help? Why not demand, as Bey laments that they should have done, and provide no option, with dire consequences in case of non-compliance? I do not believe Black anarchism would make requests. Similarly, the respect shown toward and praise heaped on Trump and U.S. history by the letter's authors fly in the face of Black existence and well-being (Anderson 2021). Given Trump's and the United State's history and treatment of marginalized communities and people, any respect toward either entity, as MM and NAMI showed, is out of line.

Meanwhile, Ervin (2022), whose Black anarchism is focused on the masses as composed of individuals, might ask what Black people, people of color, the poor, women, and others can do for themselves in their own communities. Large capitalist corporations are not the answer. This is obviously contrary to the vision of national regulation expressed in the MM-NAMI letter. Ervin also imagines social organization as consisting of a federation of relatively small local communities, each operating largely autonomously. That is, communities would take care of themselves without larger regulatory bodies' oversight. Urban agriculture, which is overwhelmingly plant-based, then seems much more in line with Black anarchism. Both Ervin and Anderson mention food as one specific aspect of community autonomy. Ervin also specifically promotes Black communal farms as a means to end hunger and malnutrition. It is interesting to note that the MM-NAMI letter never indicates concern about world hunger or malnutrition, only about food safety and labeling, as well as protein needs. Food's being "safe" does not mean that the hungry will receive it, nor is it guaranteed to be nourishing. As Ervin (2022) cautions, "we should not be tricked into surrendering grassroots people's power to dictators who pose as our friends or leaders" (55). The authors from MM and NAMI specifically describe themselves as "leaders." I think Black anarchism would see this joint letter as authoritarianism in disguise.

Worldwide, there is increased interest in urban greening as a strategy to address long-term social and economic challenges from abandoned properties, often found in older, post-industrial cities. Urban agriculture projects repurpose vacant properties into multifunctional and sustainable spaces, provide an opportunity for urban dwellers to reconnect with food production, improve food access, and promote a sense of community through gardening. Thus, urban agriculture fits with anarcho-Blackness (Bey 2020a), representing care for oneself and one's community and a rejection of state authorities. Urban agriculture also provides food that is healthy, safe, and affordable, achieving the same ends that MM and NAMI supposedly strive toward but by more appropriate means. This theme continually appears in Black radical thought and is very place-dependent (White 2018; Reese 2019). bell hooks reminds us that some 90 percent of Black people were involved in farming before the great migration to the Northern U.S. (hooks 2009). Others have advocated urban agriculture more explicitly: New Afrikan anarchist Kuwasi Balagoon (cited in Black Rose Federation 2016) states that we should "turn vacant lots into gardens," and Ashanti Alson (cited in Pellow 2014, 110) says that "we need to see [community gardens] as resistance." To help make matters concrete, it is estimated that in Detroit, Michigan, for example, there are approximately 100,000 vacant lots, totaling 23 square miles, potentially available for gardening. Already, there are 1,400 existing gardens. The use of all available space could provide 75 percent of Detroiters' vegetable demand and 40 percent of fruit demand (Swenson 2022).

There are two opposing currents in Detroit. On its part, the city has been trying to bring in large-scale firms from outside, with a focus on development and profit-driven businesses. The other current is community-led, focused on grassroots efforts aimed at food security, sovereignty, self-sufficiency, and empowerment, and is historically linked to past civil rights and agriculture movements in Detroit and the South (White 2018). Currently, the city of Detroit is implementing a plan that will gradually cut off municipal services to the most destitute neighborhoods, then relocate the people living there and replace those areas with large urban gardens. This clashes with the grassroots approach's preference for smaller, personally owned gardens scattered throughout the city, near residents' current homes. Detroit's community-focused urban agriculture is tied to an interconnectedness with nature rather than control of or dominion over it, with anti-racism and anti-capitalism integrated into its practice (White 2018). Urban agriculture is a form of resistance because farming and the resulting food security, in addition to community mutual aid through sharing food and space, become steps toward self-determination and self-reliance. Therefore, and perhaps most important, urban agriculture is an example of autonomy, prefiguration, and direct action—the imagining and creation of alternate realities in the present, for and by the individuals most affected and neglected by systemic inequality.

That urban agriculture tends to be largely plant gardening means it also has the potential to contribute toward Black liberation and the liberation of other peoples of color. A. Breeze Harper (2009) contends that a diet of heavily processed foods, especially animal products, is a major contributor to poor health conditions among African Americans. As Harper points out, this is the fault not of individuals but of the corporations that produce and market unhealthy foods while, importantly, constraining the availability of healthy ones. Harper promotes veganism as a way to decolonize the diets of Black people, diets that they can be said to have inherited from their ancestors and that were dictated by slave masters during the slavery era. Likewise, Rodriguez (2018) sees local, veganic gardening as resistance to policies invented by the state to suppress communities' autonomous solutions to hunger. This points to how urban (veganic) agriculture, but not a federally regulated cell-based meat industry, can and does align with the Black radical tradition and Black anarchist praxis. Within Black anarchism, the goal is not to win over the elites but to eliminate their power, so a partnership between two "leaders" in providing the world with protein (read: "elite corporations and executives") would be rejected.

I think it is important to interpret urban agriculture and Black anarchism through Stibbe's (2017) "positive discourse analysis" (PDA). PDA goes beyond exposing problems signaled by language to locate discourses on which to base society while, importantly, remaining critical. Critiquing negative discourse is only a "first step"—or even a "useless" one if there is no positive alternative to point to (Stibbe 2017). Indeed, urban agriculture could be posited as a positive discourse, as could Black anarchism, as it creates the conditions for liberation. Urban agriculture aligns with Black anarchists' ecological philosophy, which consists of feeding oneself and one's community with healthy, accessible, safe food while taking care of the land in a way that benefits all beings. Urban agriculture is also positive in the sense that it is creative: it is an active process of creating relationships and sustaining life. It presents an alternative to top-down, hierarchical, homogenous, external food regimes while simultaneously exposing the problems of industrial and state-managed agriculture. It is truly a vision on which to base societies and one that is already a reality (if not yet realized to its full potential) in many "post-industrial" cities like Detroit. As we face rising inflation, a precarious environment, and an increasingly powerful and evasive global elite, urban agriculture is a way for us to take back our health, community, public spaces, and even lives.

Looking Forward to Collective Liberation

This chapter is not meant as an argument of what I think Black anarchists should do or eat. I support urban agriculture because it is an existing community project in many post-industrial cities, in some cases with a rich history—in Detroit, it is linked historically and ideologically with Southern Black farming organizations, as mentioned earlier (White 2018). At the same time, many Detroit residents are against growing their own food, feeling too direct a connection to forced farming under slavery. As a racial and geographic outsider, I understand and respect their sentiment. For this reason, I make no normative claims. Rather, to try to see a radical Black perspective on cell-based meat, I have applied principles of Black anarchism to the MM-NAMI joint letter to Trump. Particularly, this chapter argues that the approach proposed by MM and NAMI—federally regulated cell-based meat—clashes with Black anarchism. However, Black anarchism may very well accept non-capitalist, locally produced, cell-based meat (if it were possible). To find out, we would need to talk to Black communities. As Black people are among the most oppressed in the United States, such a viewpoint "from below" is important. The present analysis has found that the joint letter to Trump emphasizes uncritical techno-scientific innovation, free-market capitalism, a reliance on elites, and U.S. supremacy. Black anarchism uncompromisingly rejects all of these—but does support urban agriculture.

This chapter has focused specifically on a Black anarchist perspective of cell-based meat. This is not the only or necessarily the best viewpoint through which to examine the subject, however, though surely an important one. A fuller take would require multiple voices in ongoing conversation—including Indigenous voices, as the cell-based meat industry that MM and NAMI are advocating for, as anything happening in the United States, is playing out over land stolen from Indigenous peoples. Indeed, Black anarchists in the United States would agree, readily acknowledging their complex and varied relation(s) with Indigenous people and the land (King 2019). Indigenous communities, many of which have started amazing food/farming projects, such as Ramona Farms, White Earth Land Recovery Project, The Sioux Chef, and Red Lake Nation Foods, would certainly have much to add to the subject at hand. These projects aren't all urban, but they are small-scale and focused on growing traditional produce and protecting native seeds. And they bear resemblance to urban agriculture in that one of the goals is to reclaim traditional food ways that were destroyed by colonization.

To make further connections with this book's theme of coexistence, we might think about the impact that urban gardening could have on city wildlife, pollinators, and migratory birds. Our world would be so much better for humans and nonhumans alike if we just started doing something as simple as transforming vacant lots into gardens.

So, to answer my original question of whether cellular-meat companies joining hands with the meat industry would support or challenge existing ideology and institutions, support or challenge social justice efforts, it does not seem like such a partnership would foster liberation for marginalized peoples, nonhuman animals, or the environment. Ervin, Anderson, and Bey all are anti-capitalist because capitalist structures (re) create racial, class, and gender hierarchies. In closing, I take a page from Anderson (2021), who says this about Black people in elite positions:

> The people occupying these high positions in white society are safety valves to quell Black uprising and complaints. We are all supposed to be happy because "one of us" made it. However, what does any of this matter if *where* they're making it is a place that needs to be completely torn down? (61)

Echoing Anderson, I ask: What does it matter if cell-based meat is regulated in white, cis-heteropatriarchal, colonial society (i.e., it "makes it") if its being there supports a system that needs to be completely torn down?

CHAPTER EIGHT

The Kurdish Diet and Vegetarianism: A Journey of Rediscovering Wild Food Plants

Jihan Mohammed

One day, when I was on the phone with my mother, who lives thousands of miles away in Iraqi Kurdistan, I mentioned I had transitioned to vegetarianism. There was a pause. Then, the first thing she said to me was, "Who has indoctrinated you?" Five years later, I called her to ask if she could send some dried wild food plants with a close family member who was travelling from my hometown of Dohuk to Nashville, Tennessee, where I now live. The same plants that my generation and younger generations despise because of their strong aroma and taste. That was a much more interesting phone call with my mother. We talked all about plants. She instructed me on how to cook them; she shared some secret recipes that she swears by and some memories from when she was young and foraged for those wild plants with her family and friends. She never verbalized it, but I know my mother was happy after that phone call. Not once did she mention meat or why I should eat it again.

In this brief chapter, I share my journey as a Muslim Kurd who transitioned to vegetarianism five years ago. I will discuss the mixed reactions of my Kurdish Muslim community, from seniors who struggle to understand vegetarianism and veganism from a religious standpoint to Gen Zers who are more understanding and supportive. My goal is to further complicate the debate about religion and animals with perspectives from the intersection of ethnicity and class. I start the chapter with a discussion of Islamic ethics and laws pertaining to animals. I then address some of the concerns Muslim Kurdish omnivores have about transitioning to a plant-based diet and argue that they perceive vegetarianism and veganism as forms of Western neocolonialism that put into question the ethics of Kurdish food, religion, and culture. I conclude the chapter with a discussion of how the traditional Kurdish cuisine is actually vegan- and vegetarian-friendly. Historically, the Kurds had limited access to meat and ate plant-based food more often compared to today. Nonetheless, industrialization and the globalization of meat production have changed our cuisine.

Religion

Animals, including insects, are mentioned in over two hundred Qur'ānic verses. Allah SWT (Subhanahu Wa Ta'ala, which translates to "Glory to Him, the Exalted") says: "Do they not see that We single-handedly created for them, among other things, cattle which are under their control? And We have subjected these [animals] to them, so they may ride some and eat others" (Qur'ān 36:71–72). In another Qur'ānic verse, Allah (SWT) says:

> And the camels and cattle We have appointed for you as among the symbols of Allah; for you therein is good. So mention the name of Allah upon them when lined up [for sacrifice]; and when they are [lifeless] on their sides, then eat from them and feed the needy and the beggar. Thus have We subjected them to you that you may be grateful. Neither their flesh reaches Allah nor their blood; it is your piety that reaches Him. He has subjected these animals (to you) that you may magnify Allah for the guidance He has bestowed upon you. Give glad tidings, (O Prophet), to those who do good. (Qur'ān 22:36–37)

These Qur'ānic verses point out that animals are created by God. Some of them are created to be domesticated and used by man, and others to be eaten and consumed. Sheep, goats, and cattle are commonly domesticated for their meat, wool, and skin, while pack animals such as donkeys, horses, and camels are commonly used for transportation. Additionally, in Islam there are many instances when animal sacrifices are ordained or encouraged. For example, during Eid al-Adha, Muslims—those who can afford it—are recommended to sacrifice sheep, goats, and cows. Here, *Adha* literally means "sacrifice" in Arabic. Allah (SWT) says:

> Then when the boy reached the age to work with him, Abraham said, "O my dear son! I have seen in a dream that I 'must' sacrifice you. So tell me what you think." He replied, "O my dear father! Do as you are commanded. Allah willing, you will find me steadfast." Then when they submitted to Allah's Will, and Abraham laid him on the side of his forehead for sacrifice, We called out to him, "O Abraham! You have already fulfilled the vision." Indeed, this is how We reward the good-doers. That was truly a revealing test. And We ransomed his son with a great sacrifice. (Qur'ān 37:102–107)

This is the Qur'ānic version of Prophet Ibrahim's—Abraham in the Book of Genesis—story in which he receives the shocking command from God to sacrifice his son. As a devoted servant of God, he agrees to obey God and takes his son to Mount Moriah to slaughter him. The story ends with God accepting his devotion and a ram being substituted as sacrifice. Thus, the act of sacrificing animals commemorates Prophet Ibrahim's devotion to God. After an animal is sacrificed, one third of the meat goes to the family; one third goes to relatives, friends, and neighbors; and one third goes to the needy and poor.

The major point of contention between Muslims and vegans and vegetarians is that practices surrounding meat consumption—*halal* slaughter—are signifiers of Muslim identity. Veganism and vegetarianism seem to challenge the primacy of this religious identity (Ali 2015). Just like the Judeo-Christian beliefs that came under fire due to criticism by Lynn White Jr. (1967), Islamic animal ethics, too, has come under fire, specifically when it comes to religious slaughter. Western advocates of nonhuman-animal rights have characterized religions including Islam as anthropocentric. In defense of their religion, Muslims insist that Islam is highly attentive to the well-being of nonhumans (Bousquet 1958; Rahman 2017). For example, there are stringent laws governing their treatment, rearing, and breeding, as well as the pre- and post-slaughter process. Like other Abrahamic religions, Islam requires Muslims to treat animals with kindness. Harming animals physically or psychologically, or killing them without a justifiable reason, is one of the major sins (Rahman 2017). Another example is the protections extended to aged and diseased animals. Muslims are required to spend time and money on these animals even if no more benefit can be gained from them (al-Dīn 2000). Tlili describes this approach as apologetic. This is why Muslims, including Muslim scholars (see, for example, Al-Shaykhalī 2006; Al-Qarāla 2009), argue that Islam treats nonhuman creatures better compared to other faiths. They insist that Islam predates the "West" by many centuries in advocating for animals' well-being. I agree with Tlili that this approach sounds apologetic. However, I am afraid that from an animal rights standpoint, the Islamic tradition is not entirely innocent or free of problematic views and practices, specifically surrounding killing animals for food, which I believe will remain a major point of contention. Furthermore, Ottuh and Idjakpo (2021) argue that the West tends to romanticize and idealize older, indigenous cultures and religions. The authors are concerned that this romanticization would prevent us from asking critical questions on animal ethics. I want to extend this discussion by arguing that Muslim scholars and Muslim omnivores, too, tend to idealize Islamic teachings and laws pertaining to nonhuman animals. Like Ottuh and Idjakpo, I am concerned that this attitude of theirs would prevent vegan and vegetarian Muslims from asking them critical questions, therefore precluding the chance of productive dialogue.

Nonetheless, I also understand the cultural and political anxieties underlying this apologetic approach. Muslims have good reasons to be wary of Western animal advocacy. After centuries of colonialism and imperialism, the West continues to use justifications based on religion, gender, and, more recently, animal ethics to dehumanize racialized others (Tlili 2018, 2). Part of the concern is that animal advocacy has been used as a pretext to inflict physical and social violence on Muslims. See, for example, the number of animal rights campaigns in Europe that recently have been denounced as smear campaigns against Jews and Muslims (Bergeaud-Blackler 2016).

Now, is religiosity strictly correlated with opposition to veganism and vegetarianism? Anecdotally, I have noticed that Muslim Kurdish omnivores have different degrees of religiosity. There are those who are devoted Muslims, who follow Islam's teaching strictly in their everyday lives, and there are those who are less religious, who barely pray, for example. The latter category interests me the most. Often, conversations around veganism and vegetarianism start on non-religious bases. When these omnivores struggle to address some concern vegans and vegetarians have, they use the religion card to cope with guilt and discomfort; they state that God alone determines what is lawful or unlawful, what can or cannot be eaten. In fact, Muslims are required to eat what is lawful, wholesome, pure, nutritious, and safe; they are prohibited from eating anything that is impure or harmful (Farouk et al. 2015). There is a specific verse often referenced by Muslim Kurdish omnivores that suggests that humans should not attribute to themselves the authority to proclaim things either lawful or unlawful according to their own wishes. Allah (SWT) says: "Believers! Do not hold as unlawful the good things which Allah has made lawful to you, and do not exceed the bounds of right. Allah does not love those who transgress the bounds of right" (Qur'ān 5:87). Muslim Kurdish omnivores argue that vegans and vegetarians transgress God's rules. This is a debate I have had multiple times with fellow Kurds who have brought religion into the equation. On their part, they struggle to understand how I can question the *ethics* of viewing animals in terms of their serviceability to humans. In their minds, only God can determine that. On my part, I struggle to understand how animal slaughter is not a form of extreme violence committed against nonhumans. I struggle to understand how Allah (SWT), who is attributed in Islam as the Compassionate and Merciful, would condemn someone who is vegan or vegetarian. How is advocating that we stop exploiting animals—including killing and sacrificing them—not an act of compassion? In fact, nowhere in the Qur'ān or Hadith is it suggested that abstaining from eating animals is sinful. So why would my fellow Kurdish Muslims paint me as less of a Muslim?

This brings up another issue often misunderstood by my fellow Muslim Kurds: that of animals' supposed inferiority. "Are animals inferior to humans?" is a complicated question that Sara Tlili (2012) tackles in her book. There is no explicit statement in the Qur'ān in favor of human domination over nonhumans, in contrast to the Book of Genesis in the Old Testament. Nonetheless, Tlili argues that Qur'ānic verses could be interpreted in a way that grants humans special status or superiority over animals. This could explain why some Muslim Kurds believe that animals do not have feelings or emotions. One of the simplistic explanations I have heard for this is that God created them without feelings and emotions. More important, Muslim Kurds insist that *halal* slaughter is the least painful slaughter method. For me, slaughter using any method, *halal* or not, results in the death of another being and is an act I cannot comprehend.

As mentioned, Qur'ānic verses convey the idea that everything on earth and in heaven is created by God and is serviceable to humans (Tlili 2012, 74). This conceptualization of animals and of their serviceability (their various destined uses) often implies their inferiority. This is how the average Muslim, growing up, perceived animals: animals are less than humans, and their ability to reason, use logic, or control their sexual desires is limited (for a discussion on animal inferiority and human domination in relation to Islam, see Tlili 2012; 2018). These views are not shared by Muslim scholars and theologians. For example, Iranian ethicist and theologian Seyyed Hassan Eslami argues that all animals are intelligent to some degree and can exercise reasoning skills. The disconnect between the normative and empirical dimensions of Islam is an issue indeed. If the religion has the best teachings about animals, it means little if these teachings are not heeded or are misunderstood and misinterpreted: recent studies suggest that Muslims' treatment of nonhuman animals has in fact deteriorated (Stilt 2017, 5).

ETHNIC IDENTITY

What does it mean to be Kurdish and vegetarian? The first concern Kurdish omnivores have is health. Many believe plants cannot provide all the nutrients required by humans and thus vegans and vegetarians are malnourished. As most readers are aware, these arguments have been largely debunked. The second concern, on which I want to focus, is identity. Ali (2015) argues that the choice to consume or avoid meat conveys social identity and affiliation. In religions such as Islam, refusal of meat is strictly equated with criticism of others' eating habits, ethics, piety, and purity. Muslim Kurds, for example, abstain from eating non-*halal* or impure meat. Thus, consumption of Kurdish dishes that are *halal*-meat–based is a signifier of the Muslim Kurdish identity. Now, refusing those dishes also demarcates a distinctive identity. More important, in adopting an identity label such as "vegetarian" or "vegan," one faces the problem of competing identities, loyalties, and norms. Being Muslim Kurdish and a vegan or vegetarian means being a critic of one's ancestors' eating habits, ethics, piety, and purity. It means having one's religiosity and Kurdish authenticity—whatever that means—questioned. Sadly, it means even having one's sanity questioned—typically by Kurdish seniors and millennials.

These types of contentious debates emerge during social gatherings at which food is shared and celebrated. These moments are central to the Kurdish culture—important for strengthening one's existing bonds with family members, friends, and loved ones. Nonetheless, in my experience, it is on these occasions that vegans and vegetarians are picked on, humiliated, and ridiculed. Just two weeks prior to my writing this draft (in September 2023), I had been labeled "mentally unstable," "crazy," and "not a true Muslim" at such an event. I could clearly sense the disappointment and concern for my mental state in the eyes of the people around me, as if they were grieving the loss of a beloved member of the community to Western secular ideologies. With that said, over the years I have learned some self-defense strategies and techniques, one of which is shifting the conversation to traditional vegan and vegetarian Kurdish dishes. Many Kurds think I must have given up so many traditional dishes. Once they learn that transitioning to vegetarianism has pushed me to rediscover tasty wild plants, their tone changes, and that is how we start a conversation, a definitely less contentious one.

Next, I provide a short historical overview of the consumption of meat and wild plants in Kurdish culture, with the aim of debunking the myth that going vegetarian means giving up one's Kurdish roots.

For centuries, my Kurdish ancestors lived as herders and farmers in the mountainous areas of Northern Iraq, also known as Iraqi Kurdistan (Bruinessen 1992). Throughout the twentieth century, Kurds relied on livestock and agriculture as their main source of income. Villagers in the mountains, where my parents and grandparents come from, owned land and worked on it. Many owned some land inherited from their fathers and grandfathers, but only a few kept animals, mainly sheep and goats, occasionally cattle, mules, donkeys, and horses. Due to political instability and sanctions, meat was scarce in general. Kurdish seniors like my parents and grandparents often recall how lucky those families were that could afford to slaughter a sheep or a goat for the cold days of winter or for the holy month of Ramadhan. They say that meat was consumed once a week or once a month, mostly on holy Fridays, on the Eids, or during social occasions such as weddings and funerals. According to Father Thomas Bois, a French orientalist who visited the Kurdish areas in the early twentieth century, meat was reserved just for guests (Bois 1966, 27). Typically, when an animal was slaughtered, some of the meat was consumed fresh; the rest, including intestines, was either dried or cured. As for eggs and dairy, villagers who did not keep domesticated animals typically exchanged crops or labor for milk or eggs. Thus, butter, cheese, and other dairy products such as *keşk*, made from strained yogurt, were consumed more regularly than meat. In terms of preserving meat, the old method of drying meat has been replaced by freezers. Today, meat is mainly frozen, sometimes cured. One popular Kurdish dish is *qalī*, which is meat cured in animal fat, then served as an entrée or added to other dishes, such as rice or soup, for flavor. I grew up eating eggs fried in the *qalī*'s fat. Another popular dish is *serû pe*, also known as *kepayeh*, which is made from sheep's stomach, intestines, legs, and head. The intestines are cleaned, stuffed with ground meat, rice, salt, and black pepper, then boiled in bone broth made out of the legs and head. In any case, because access to meat was historically limited in the region—it was the food of *aghas* and *shaikhs*, of nobles and princes—Kurds still perceive meat as a "rich people's" food, and eating meat still confers feelings of power and status despite its abundance on the market now.

With that said, I insist that traditional Kurdish cuisine is vegan- and vegetarian-friendly. My ancestors were herders and farmers. They mainly consumed crops and wild plants. They planted a wealth of native crops, such as rice, wheat, barley, corn, lentils, chickpeas, black-eyed peas, mung beans, onion, tomato, chard, cucumber, dill, mint, cilantro, thyme, parsley, celery, zucchini, okra, eggplant, potato, and more—not to mention that the climate and soil in Iraqi Kurdistan are suited to growing grapes, pomegranates, figs, pears, peaches, plums, apricots, watermelons, melons, apples, almonds, walnuts, and mulberries. Grains and legumes were essential, but so were dried fruits and nuts. In fact, one of the most delicious Kurdish traditional dishes is a soup of dried fruits known as *khuşav*. It consists of dried apricots, apples, plums, pears, and raisins, all boiled together to make a sweet-and-sour juice. For extra flavor, some people add walnuts, almonds, and wild pistachios (*Pistacia atlantica*). Kurdish seniors recall that they consumed fresh or dried fruits and nuts as snacks daily and served them to guests as well. Sadly, political instability, globalization, and rapid urbanization have changed some of these traditions. Today, healthy plant-based snacks have been replaced with sugary pastries, cookies, other junk food, and energy drinks.

Foraging is a Kurdish tradition that dates back centuries. According to Pieroni et al. (2019), Kurds tend to gather and consume a large number of wild plants, and spring tends to be the busiest season. These plants are consumed raw, cooked, or fried—typically cooked with rice or added to soups and salads. For storage, they are sealed and frozen or sun-dried. Kurdish seniors grew up foraging for wild plants themselves and thus enjoy eating them more than younger generations do. It is common in a Kurdish household to see the parents and grandparents cook and eat wild plants, while the children and grandchildren complain about the strong taste and smell, one common characteristic of these foods. The political events of the second half of the twentieth century explain these generational differences.

Up until the 1980s, many Kurds lived in the villages and rural areas, and the Kurdish economy relied mainly on agriculture. In the 1970s, the Iraqi central government implemented radical policies to acceler- ate urbanization, made possible by booming oil revenues. Part of the plan was also to suppress the Kurdish nationalist movement that was thriving and relying on the support of Kurds living in rural areas. One way to control the Kurdish movement was through forced urbanization. Saddam Hussein's ethnic persecution of the Kurds intensified in the 1970s and the 1980s. As a result, hundreds of thousands of people were reported killed, missing, or relocated from villages to resettlement camps near cities. More than five thousand villages were destroyed (Human Rights Watch 1995). My parents and grandparents were among the lucky few who survived this difficult period. In the late 1970s, their village, Bigdawda, and the surrounding ones were destroyed, and the people living there were forcibly relocated to resettlement camps. In 1980, my family moved to the city of Duhok, as did many others. These events destroyed the Kurdish agricultural sector (Leezenberg 2000; Natali 2007; Stansfield 2003). Some of the villages, including my parents', are still partially or completely abandoned. In 1992, the Kurds were able to form their own government; since then, they have lived semi-autonomously in northern Iraq. Nonetheless, the Kurdish government has failed to revive the agricultural sector and failed to protect Kurdish villages from continuous attacks from neighboring countries, mainly Turkey and Iran (Bechocha 2023; Sirwan 2022). In the past few years, several Kurdish villagers have been killed by Turkish bombardment of their villages. This political instability and the failure of the Kurdish government to invest in the agricultural sector are discouraging people from going back to their villages or foraging for wild plants (End Cross-Border Bombing Campaign 2022). These events, coupled with globalization and the global increase in meat consumption, have created generational differences in Kurds' eating habits. Many Kurdish seniors were born and raised in the villages. They grew up eating more plants and less meat. By contrast, millennials and younger Kurds were born and raised in the cities, where the consumption of meat and dairy is continuously on the rise. Hemin and Khasraw (2020) found that between 2009 and 2018, red meat consumption increased overall in the Kurdistan region. Today, cities across the region are dotted with the flashy LED signs of fast food restaurants.

After transitioning to vegetarianism, I started cooking some traditional dishes without meat. *Dolma*, for example, can easily be veganized: vegetables and rice are stuffed inside grape leaves and cooked with sour sumacade (sumac soaked in water). *Kubba* and *tirşik* or cracked-wheat dumplings, traditionally containing beef, onions, celery, and black pepper, can also be veganized by substituting eggplant, mushroom, or cauliflower for the meat, or simply omitting it. To many of my fellow Kurds, it comes as a surprise that I can still enjoy these dishes.

Furthermore, thanks to my dietary change, I have discovered how tasty wild plants are. Take, for example, the common purslane (*Portulaca oleracea*), which is typically steamed and added to yogurt to create an appetizer. Some people cook it with onions for a delicious breakfast entrée. Others make red soup from it. Similarly, in the spring, many Kurdish families cook common mallow (*Malva neglecta*) for breakfast, sometimes with the addition of eggs for extra flavor. The pack that my mother sent me contains a mix of three plants: *Allium ursinum*, *Allium calocephalum*, and *Allium akaka subsp* (special thanks to Professor Mijda B. M. Alsinayi at the University of Duhok for her help with translation). People typically cook these plants separately with rice. My mother cooks them together. Either way, they make a delicious entrée for lunch or dinner. Before going vegetarian, I hardly ate any wild plants, whereas now I am eager to try new ones and introduce them to my children.

In conclusion, understanding veganism and vegetarianism at the intersection of religion, ethnic identity, and class is a complicated task. As Foltz (2001) asserts, "ethical questions surrounding the use of animals for food are not raised in the legal literature of classical Islam, and, even today, any serious discourse on the viability of an 'Islamic' vegetarianism is difficult to find" (39). For Islamic scholar Mawil Izzi Dien, there is no such thing as Islamic vegetarianism. In his book *The Environmental Dimensions of Islam* (2000), he writes: "Muslims are not only prohibited from eating certain food, but also may not choose to prohibit themselves food that is allowed by Islam. [. . .] Vegetarianism is not allowed under the pretext of giving priority to the interest of animals because such decisions are God's prerogative" (146). Yet, for the more moderate Islamic scholar Hamza Yusuf, the Prophet was a "semi-vegetarian" because He and the post-prophetic Muslim figures like Umar ibn al-Khattab ate meat sparingly (Ali 2015, 272). For a seventy-year-old Kurdish senior like my mother and for my millennial friend, adopting a label such as "vegetarian" is contradictory to the primacy of the Muslim and Kurdish identity. But the fact of the matter is that all around the world, the number of Muslim vegans and vegetarians is growing. In the Muslim world, including the Kurdistan region, the number of nonprofits and other organizations fighting for the rights of animals is growing. Muslims and Kurds must acknowledge that. How do we move forward and accept this minority within our community? As Ali (2015) rightfully asks, how do we initiate a productive dialogue among parties that disagree about basic assumptions about God, human beings, animals, and the relations between them? Instead of hesitating to engage constructively in a conversation, instead of creating more division, how do we invite the other party to a dialogue that promotes critical reflection and refinement of presuppositions and arguments? Muslim Kurds ought to acknowledge and embrace their vegetarian and vegan counterparts. It is time we take small steps to move the conversation forward, even if, for now, that means agreeing to disagree.

CHAPTER NINE

On Total Liberty: Species Privilege and More-than-Human Autonomy

Amanda R. Williams and Paislee House

Whether it is to flap wings, grow in the direction of the sun, sprint across a territory, socialize with friends, or simply not be harmed, on some level, liberty is important to all living beings. Liberty is the state of being free and having the power to act as one pleases. The word is often used interchangeably with "freedom," but "freedom" means a total absence of restraint in fulfilling one's own desires. In this sense, one's freedom can infringe on the freedom of others. For example, we have the freedom to shoot someone, but that shooting would infringe on the other person's freedom to not be harmed. Liberty is not unbounded but rather a balancing act, the responsible exercise of one's freedom without depriving others of theirs. There is an old legal saying that captures this notion: "Your right to swing your arms ends just where the other man's nose begins." As human animals, we are dreadful at finding that balance and respecting the liberty of others, be it other humans or, especially, other species.

At this point in history, we humans have an unparalleled power over other species, granting us substantial privilege as a result. This species privilege, like any other social privilege, is made up of a spectrum of individual perks to which we have access. While all human animals possess species privilege to some degree, there are those of us who may not have as many particular privileges as the rest of us. For example, in a world dominated by white supremacism, people of color are often treated as lesser, which manifests in a variety of both institutional and interpersonal acts of discrimination. If we also consider the interconnected nature of oppressions, this complicates the systems of advantage and disadvantage related to race, gender, sexuality, ability, class, and other categories (Robinson 2017). Everyone possesses their own list of privileges, which afford them a level of advantage based on their unique identity and unique life circumstances (jones 2014). Irrespective of one's personalized list, the advantaged reality of *Homo sapiens* today is the consequence of an anthropocentric prioritization of human-animal life and liberty above, and to the detriment of, those of other species.

With billions of animals imprisoned in farms, laboratories, entertainment facilities, and our homes, our society is replete with examples of liberty deprivation and disrespect. Even companion animals—who are often treated to better conditions than are other captive animals—are still not afforded the same privileges of liberty as their human-animal keepers. More often than not, our companions are not allowed, among other things, to choose for themselves where they go or live or with whom they develop relationships. Meanwhile, farmed animals—the majority of whom exist in a factory-farm setting—who suffer an extreme form of confinement and are denied the opportunity to perform many of their most basic, natural behaviors, such as finding food, playing, raising children, living out a natural lifespan, or simply walking, flying, or swimming around. Indeed, what commonly comes to the fore for many people when they think about liberty is the ability to move one's body freely throughout the world—to generally go where one wants, when one wants, without restraints or barriers.

Apart from some human animals who are also forced to live in confinement (e.g., prisoners) or under egregiously exploitative conditions, we as a species have the ability to fulfill our whims, which is a cornerstone of our species privilege (again, defined as a system of advantage based on species that affords unearned preferential treatment and benefits to human animals while oppressing other animals). Although there are societal-level forces, such as culture, economic organization, oppression, national demarcation, and governmental regulation, that limit human animals in myriad ways, there is no other animal species limiting human liberty in a significant or authoritarian manner. If you want to walk outside to talk to your neighbor, hug your partner, investigate an interesting plant in the yard, or visit a new city, no one prohibits you from doing so. For many other animals, movement is specifically limited by the confines of human structures, such as roads, yards, buildings, walls, and fences.

Suppressing or eliminating the liberty of another causes them harm. For this reason, human animals should try to maximize the liberty of all living beings. Avoiding harmful actions is very much within our capacity, and as such, we have a moral obligation to do so. But it is not our moral obligations to other living beings that separates us from the rest of nature, as some claim (Lestel 2016). The opposite is true. Our capacity for morality is very much a part of our species' own nature, and even if we like to imagine ourselves as somehow outside of nature, we never can be. We are animals in nature, like any other, and using our human abilities to ensure no harm comes to others is a celebration of our animality and a demonstration of solidarity with all life on Earth.

This solidarity requires that we knock down the hierarchy that places human animals at the top and devalues all other lives, one that was instituted arbitrarily by human animals to privilege certain humans and otherize those deemed less than human, including both humans and other species (Nibert 2013). Hierarchical (and often binary) social constructs such as species (human/animal), race (white/nonwhite), class (rich/poor), gender (male/female), age (young/old), and ability (able/disabled) work to reduce groups to characteristics that are given more or less value and enable one group's domination of others. This is why total liberation—total liberty for all—is imperative. Total liberation requires an acknowledgement of the ways in which oppressions are interconnected and a stance against all oppressions, against the underlying hierarchy that supports them (Nocella et al. 2014). Stances favoring single-issue justice cannot deliver widespread liberation because they fail to attack the foundations of inequality and do not allow for different groups to work together for the good of all.

In everyday discourse, liberty is typically reserved for human animals and rarely applied to the more-than-human world. Even in the human realm, liberty can be complex in its application, confused by divergent philosophical approaches, political analyses, and individual interpretations. In the United States, liberty derives its meaning from the Declaration of Independence and is sometimes tied to state politics; other times, it is a staple buzzword in right-leaning, nationalist rhetoric. These things considered, it is important to look more critically at what liberty means and who gets to enjoy it. Many human animals around the globe are subject to governments as well as societal structures that can curtail liberty, with such limitations and violations of individuals' liberties by institutions being exacerbated as one moves further away from the groups that hold the most power. If one's beliefs deviate from the norm, politically or religiously, if one belongs to a minority group, a lower economic class, or a species other than *Homo sapiens*, one is at risk of having their liberties ignored or actively quashed to maintain oppressive hierarchies and unfair privilege.

No matter the level of access, liberty remains a cherished privilege of human animals. When surveyed, individuals consistently cite freedom of speech, the right to life, and the right to liberty as the top rights that should be protected (Bardon et al. 2018). In the United States specifically, liberty, as a constitutional right, has a strong cultural reverence; infringement on liberty, perceived or enacted, is a surefire way to set folks of all political affiliations ablaze. This is good and important, of course, as liberties throughout human history have often been hard-won. But the liberty of other species isn't treated with the same passion and reverence. Many human animals are unfazed by the fact that 1,758 other animals die every second for human consumption alone (Hussain 2021). No national protest occurs when a grizzly bear's home is demolished to make way for logging on public lands; indeed, none occurred in 1999 when more than four million fishes' lives in the White River of Indiana were abruptly ended by intentional chemical dumping by the Guide Corporation (Bowman 2019). Our species privilege is a blinder that allows us to ignore or accept as normal the massive violations of liberty endured by more-than-humans. This chapter will explore a few major liberty violations, their intersectional nature, and their implications.

KEEPING PETS FROM SELF-DETERMINATION

"What kind of love is based on ownership?" asks Aiyana Goodfellow (Goodfellow 2021, 14). A pet is defined by the Oxford English Dictionary as "an animal (typically one which is domestic or tame) kept for pleasure or companionship." To be a pet, at least in the United States, is to be a living piece of property owned by a human animal to satisfy the latter's interest in acquiring "pleasure or companionship" (some pets are also used for labor). Legally, a pet's "owner" can make any sort of decision on their behalf, short of only abuse (as defined by the law): where they go, with whom they interact, what they eat, what behavior is acceptable, when and why they get medical attention, when they are no longer part of the family, and even if they live or die. It is a uniquely human privilege to keep another being in this way and have complete control over every aspect of the relationship, a relationship that is most often involuntary for one of the participants.

Even under the best of conditions, petkeeping represents an unequal power dynamic between two individuals who both have an interest in autonomy. The owner–pet relationship can result in some positive effects, of course, but all relationships should always be subject to ethical inter-rogation so as to prioritize liberty and guard against coercion. More-over, petkeeping does not always exist under the best of conditions. With power come corruption and abuse. In addition to the many cruelties that can be perpetrated against pets by their "owners," companion animals have long been favored as research specimens for scientists and breed-ers alike. In another example of dominating behavior, we humans have been and still are selectively breeding (purposely designing) companion animals to conform to our own desires. Not only this, but some compan-ion animals are fated to suffer horribly in puppy mills or similar inten-sive breeding operations, which are not unlike dairy farms in that female animals are subjected to extreme sexual manipulation, in addition to crowded and unhealthy living conditions.

When we think of companion animals, *Felis catus* and *Canis lupus familiaris* are the first to come to mind. Both cats and dogs have a long, interactive history with human animals. Dogs were the first animal to be domesticated, but how exactly that came to be is a point of dissension among scholars. Moreover, the domestication of dogs likely does not have a single origin but multiple—meaning they were domesticated at multiple points in history, in different locations across the globe—with each origin story being distinctive (Handwerk 2018). What we know for certain is that ways of keeping dogs have changed over time. Early wolf and dog companions spent time with humans on their own terms, coming and going as they pleased and leading rich social lives of their own. Although in some parts of the world this is still the case, in the United States—the petkeeping capital of the world (Walden 2015)—we see companion animals kept increasingly in confinement, with monotony, long hours alone spent in boredom, and a lack of autonomy being defining characteristics of their experience. This model of petkeeping is spreading around the world as the petkeeping trend grows and associated industries expand.

It is indicative of our privilege that we think distorting what is natural to satisfy our whims—as is the case with petkeeping, zookeeping, farming, and all other practices that hold animals captive—is a positive thing, even when it comes at the expense of others. Many human animals will patronizingly argue that other animals benefit from these types of forced relations with humans: in exchange for their bondage and service to humans, other animals receive shelter, regular meals, and fresh water—that is, have their basic needs met, which might be less certain if they were free-living. But the speciesism in this line of thinking is obvious if we put ourselves in the paws of the animal other. Would we humans accept the trade-off of autonomy for reliable fulfilment of basic needs? If your decisions, your body, and your life were no longer your own but instead used to serve another animal's need for companionship, entertainment, research, or consumption, would you oblige in exchange for consistent meals and a roof over your head? That we are not willing to make this trade is a testament to our own arrogance and the warped notion of saviorism that leads us to believe our species is best suited to make decisions about the bodies and lives of other animals.

Modern dog-breeding began to take shape in the Victorian era. The exact number of dog breeds on record varies, but there are somewhere between two and three hundred different breeds today (The Kennel

Club n.d.). Dogs of many breeds have congenital health problems or live shorter-than-average lives because of breeding practices by human animals. For example, due to artificial selection, French Bulldogs cannot naturally copulate with one another and are prone to spine, back, and eye issues. For French Bulldogs to reproduce, a human animal must intervene and artificially inseminate the female because the male's hips are too slim, making it impossible for him to mount (Adams and Evans 2010). Indeed, the breed would no longer exist were it not for the sexual manipulation carried out by human animals. The intentional breeding of dogs today is driven by consumer demand for purebred pups. Despite the persistently large number of homeless dogs and dogs in shelters, many at risk of being killed for lack of space and resources, pet-obsessed human animals purchase 4 million dogs from breeders each year in the United States, 2.6 million of whom come from puppy mills (Humane Society of the United States 2021).Cats took a slightly different route to become the internet sensation and the compact, grumpy floofs that they are. Although a precise origin is unknown, it is generally agreed that the cats who live with humans today were first domesticated around 7,500 BC in the Near East, a geographical region that encompasses Western Asia, Turkey, and Egypt (Driscoll et al. 2007). Descendants of Old World wildcats, domestic cats retain an anatomy similar to those of other felid species and lack the common characteristics of other domesticated animals, such as floppy ears, curly tails, larger eyes, rounder foreheads, and shortened muzzles (Apps et al. 1987), with a few exceptions in less common breeds. Domestic cats also behave similarly to their wild counterparts, which has prompted many to question if they are truly domesticated. What is interesting is that even though cats have lived with humans for at least the last 10,000 years, there is no evidence of human interference with feline breeding until the last 1,600 years, which explains their minimally changed state (Newitz 2017). Even if our proactive interference with cat reproduction is a more recent phenomenon, our desire to commodify, control, and manipulate the bodies and lives of felines is expressed ubiquitously in the modern world. There are now numerous breeds of cats, and as many cats suffer from poor health outcomes due to common genetic diseases as dogs— often as a result of inbreeding, a common practice among breeders (VIJ

2019). Globally, feline companions are allowed far more independence than their canine counterparts, yet in the United States, the majority of cats are kept indoors (HSUS n.d.). One common consequence of feline captivity is obesity, which can result in a shortened lifespan, osteoarthritis, heart disease, cancer, and more (Downing and Williams 2021). Of all domestic cat companions in the United States, between 40 percent and 60 percent are considered obese (Cornell University College of Veterinary Medicine 2017). Other possible consequences of feline confinement include anxiety, boredom, depression, aggression, inappropriate soiling, excessive vocalizations, and feeding problems (Croney and Stella 2016). Of course, there are also contentious issues in regard to cats who live more autonomously. It is well established that free-roaming cats have a negative effect on bird populations. Some claim that cats are the number one human-caused threat to birds in the United States and Canada (Sizemore 2015). There are several ethical dilemmas presented in the world of petkeeping—from the commodification and use of animal bodies for human-centric purposes, the denial of autonomy, the compromised health and manipulated reproductive abilities of pets, and the killing of other animals for pet food, to the effect of pets' behavior and waste on the larger ecosystem. Although some writers have examined these issues, a meaningful critique of the practice of petkeeping in general has yet to be adopted into the popular discourse. Even animal liberation activists often neglect to include companion animals in their advocacy. But solidarity with more-than-humans can begin at home, with those who live in our yards and on our couches. Considering and respecting the liberty of those with whom we are in closest relationship can have a ripple effect on our interactions with all other living beings.

OBSTRUCTION OF MOVEMENT

A foundational liberty is the ability to move freely through space—to take one's legs, fins, wings, or wheels and produce motion to traverse the landscape, swim across bodies of water, or cut through the troposphere. Whoever you are, when your freedom of movement is restricted, there is bound to be frustration and conflict. Infamously, the issue of freedom of movement has created a conflict zone at the U.S.–Mexico border. There, movement is impeded by stretches of walls, fences, and roadways and by border guards. Human animals alone invented borders—arbitrary boundaries that create an "us" and a "them," concentrate power into fewer and fewer hands, and privatize that which belongs not to a single animal but to all living beings in that area of the planet. The anthropocentric imposition of borders has negative consequences for the liberty of human and other animals alike.

Migration—or movement from one place to another, permanently or temporarily—is a feature of so many species today and throughout history, a common denominator that bonds human animals with other animals. In the 200,000 years since the birth of *Homo sapiens*, we have migrated across the globe: current evidence suggests that we left Africa and went to Asia and Europe between 70,000 and 100,000 years ago and have since spread out all over the world (now also including Antarctica) (Rincon 2020). Although migration on this scale is not common among all animals, human animals are not the only species to inhabit all corners of the globe. Bears, for example, descended from common ancestors who spread across the globe and evolved into a variety of subspecies along the way; the same is true for subspecies of wolves. Other animals, such as camels, started on one continent and relocated entirely to others, ceasing to exist in their original habitat. Camels originated in North America. Then, one to three million years ago, the North American *Camelidae* family migrated via the new land link now known as Isthmus of Panama to South America, where its descendants (guanacos, llamas, alpacas) live today. Currently, the majority of camels are domesticated and live in North Africa and West Asia (Meyers 2000). Camels and their evolutionary cousins are just one example of how movement affects species. Many other animals used to enjoy such freedom to roam about and explore the land.

Though they are often inhibited, animals are still on the move nowadays. Permanent migrations are being forced by rapid changes to climate and habitat. It is estimated that half of all species of plants and animals on Earth are being displaced due to anthropogenic climate change (Welch 2017). Beautiful seasonal migrations also occur naturally each year, marking the temporary relocation of many species of birds, insects, fishes, and mammals from one area to another. Indeed, even some human animals migrate seasonally, from migrant farm workers who follow harvests to vacationers who winter in warmer areas. For many animals (the snowbirds being a notable exception), migration is essential for survival, and when it is disrupted, whether by climate destruction or landscape alteration, disastrous consequences follow.

Along the U.S.–Mexico border, migration is impeded by human-made constructions. Roughly 23 percent of the border is blocked by fencing, with the purpose of stopping the migration of humans from Central and South America (Department of Homeland Security 2021). Although the fence was designed primarily to keep human animals out of the United States, it also affects the movements of other animals who live in the border region. In 2005, Congress passed the REAL ID act, part of which allows the secretary of homeland security to waive local, state, and federal laws that could potentially slow the construction of "national security infrastructure" (HR 418 2005)—such pieces of legislation as the Endangered Species Act, the Migratory Bird Treaty Act, and the Wilderness Act. In other words, Congress made it permissible to disregard laws that protect other animals in order to create structures that restrict human movement, thereby jeopardizing both human and more-than-human liberty and putting lives and livelihoods at risk.

Take, for example, the Sonoran pronghorn, a mythic, antelope-looking creature with horns for eyebrows and an almost comically prominent white butt. The fastest land mammal in North America, they are known for their speed. As their name indicates, the pronghorn occupies and is endemic to the Sonoran Desert region of the United States and Mexico. They move throughout their range, crossing the border in search of food and mates. The pronghorn is considered an endangered species, with only about 160 individuals left in the United States and 240 in Mexico (Defenders of Wildlife 2022). With the increase in border surveillance, infrastructure, and vehicle traffic over the past hundred years or so, their movements have become increasingly limited. But the border is not the only human-made construction harming the pronghorn. Forty percent of the little habitat that the pronghorn has left is occupied by the Barry M. Goldwater Air Force Range (BMGR), which is an active U.S. military bombing range (Krausman et al. 2007). After a lawsuit brought by Defenders of Wildlife, a monitoring program was put in place to ensure there would be no accidental deaths of pronghorns from humans testing bombs and artillery nearby, but the BMGR still significantly hampers the pronghorn's ability to move throughout their own habitat. This example also illustrates how speciesism is intertwined with militarism.

Given the current human-caused disruptions within the Sonoran pronghorn's habitat, scientists do not believe the species can continue to exist without aid from federal wildlife officials. By "aid," they are referring to facilities for breeding pronghorns in captivity, which have been operational in Arizona since 2003 (Land Conservation Assistance Network 2017). Not only has the pronghorn's freedom of movement been hindered, but their freedom of reproduction has also been taken from them. Where will these captive-bred pronghorns be released? Right back into the heavily fragmented and permanently altered range where their predecessors struggled to survive. If the focus stays on the activities of the pronghorns instead of the activities of the human animals, it will continue to be a losing game for pronghorns and for many other animals who reside in the border region.

We cannot talk about liberty of movement, or of life for that matter, without addressing the widely held belief that some animals belong in a certain space and some do not. Nativism is an ideology that favors those considered to be native inhabitants of a place above those who are considered to be non-native. These labels are determined and applied by those in power and used as justification to infringe on the liberty of individuals designated non-native, immigrant, or invasive. In the human-animal realm, we see nativism play out in the policies concerning immigrants, as well as in the backlash and discrimination against them. The border region is so militarized and heavily guarded because the United States perceives immigrants from Central and South America as a threat. This kind of prejudice exists around the world and goes by many names, but the term "nativism" originated from mid-nineteenth-century U.S. political movements, particularly in response to discrimination against Catholic immigrants from Europe, who were seen as a threat to "native-born" Protestant Americans (Falvey Memorial Library 2022). Of course, these

Protestant "natives" were also immigrants in relation to the Indigenous population that had been living in North America long before them.

Nativism is political, and its strength waxes and wanes with the public perception of a disappearing harmony between the nation and the state (Friedman 2017). It is also influenced by the discriminatory ideologies of the day, especially racism and classism. Nativism usually manifests as majority ethnic nationalism, whereby those who consider themselves natives or the rightful settlers of a country swear to protect their demographic dominance. That is why those who wish to cross the southern U.S. border, who are largely people of color, are aggressively pushed back, demonized, and targeted with violence and deportation campaigns, while the mostly white immigrants coming from the north are rarely questioned (Murdza and Ewing 2021). Nativists devote a lot of time to defining and characterizing those they consider to be non-native, the "them" in the "us versus them" dichotomy. These characterizations are also influenced by popular values. Especially in right-wing populist politics, immigrants are portrayed as barbaric (rather than modern), godless (rather than God-fearing), lazy, promiscuous, and impure (Mudde and Kaltwasser 2017). Nativist ideology has historically rich ties to colonialism, racism, and speciesism. One need not look further than the dehumanization—or rather, animalization—of the other as a cornerstone of anti-immigrant discourse. As former and future president Donald Trump, known for his often nativist rhetoric, said about Mexican immigrants, pushing them away from the category of "human": "These aren't people. These are animals" (Gomez and Korte 2018). A similar prejudice against those considered non-native is applied to more-than-humans. There is no shortage of animosity toward so-called invasive species—living organisms who are introduced (often by human animals) into an ecosystem where they did not exist previously. You can visit almost any governmental or environmental organization's website that has something to say about invasive species, and it will likely be negative. In the authors' home state of Wisconsin, the Department of Natural Resources has identified Asian carp—a commonly targeted group of silvery, golden, or light brown fishes with large scales—as "invaders," a "threat to Wisconsin waters," and destroyers of the ecosystem who consume "plankton at an alarming rate" (Wisconsin DNR 2019). There is even a negative connotation in Merriam-Webster's definition of "invasive" or "non-native" organisms as those who "grow and disperse easily usually to the detriment of native species and ecosystems" (Merriam-Webster n.d.). Huge, well-coordinated campaigns to eliminate invasive species are commonplace, with governments and environmental agencies working together to prevent their proliferation and kill as many individuals as possible. Wisconsin has banned the sale, transport, possession, and introduction of Asian carp in the state. Anglers who catch one of these fishes are encouraged to kill them, then to "put the fish on ice and bring it [*sic*] to the local DNR office" (Wisconsin DNR 2019). But are there good reasons why the lives and liberties of these so-called invasive animals are any less valuable than those of their native neighbors? Why is the possibility of cohabitation seen as preposterous? The discourse around more-than-human immigrants is tainted by nativist, capitalist, and anthropocentric discrimination, leaving little room for individual liberty to be taken seriously.

In many instances, capitalist logic is applied to the perception of the issue of more-than-human immigration. Who is accepted or rejected in an ecosystem is often determined based on profitability. Honeybees, who are native to Europe and Africa, are a widely accepted and beloved invasive species in the Americas. *Apis mellifera* was first introduced by European settlers in the seventeenth century, and several other honeybee species were actively imported by beekeepers in the nineteenth and twentieth centuries (NatureMapping Foundation n.d.). Used heavily in food agriculture, these bees are shipped around to help pollinate plants for human consumption, even when native bee species are better at the task (Taylor 1981). Honeybees' population density creates competition for foraging and reduces the connectedness of plant–pollinator networks, thus putting native bees at risk (McAfee 2020). But the profitability of honeybees is undeniable, making them embraced by governments, industry, and hobbyists alike. In the United States alone, the honey industry grosses over $4 billion annually (Bee Health Collective 2020).

By contrast, invasive species who are not profitable or who pose a threat to profit are demonized and killed. Asian carp are considered a concern because "they can aggressively compete with native commercial and sport fish for food" (Wisconsin DNR 2019). However, Asian carp are known to improve water quality, control vegetation, consume disease-carrying snails, and reduce undesirable plankton like toxic blue-green algae (Kight 2012). The profit-driven lens often neglects the benefits that a particular species may provide to an ecosystem and always neglects the inherent value of each individual life. A similarly capitalist logic is alive in the discourse around human immigrants as well, with some immigrants viewed as more acceptable based on "merit," which is often measured using economic valuations such as the marketability of their skills or trades, their employment, education level, and financial standing (Bolter et al. 2019). Respect for individual liberty is a lesser priority, if a priority at all, under capitalism.

Many commonly held beliefs about invasive species are false or exaggerated. One of the most pervasive myths surrounding more-than-human immigrants is that they inevitably lead to biodiversity loss in ecosystems. More often, the opposite is true: the majority of foreign species have a neutral or positive impact on their environment (Thomas 2017). Schlaepfer, Sax, and Olden (2011) identify a variety of underappreciated roles played by invasive species: providing ecosystem services, reviving human-damaged regions, and generally helping ecosystems sustain some semblance of natural health, even as many struggle to survive. That a species reproduces speedily, taking up an ecological niche, does not always mean it is eliminating other species in the process (Cummings and Stanescu 2016).

Most often, when a native species is struggling, it is due to a variety of ecological factors, not just the activities of a single non-native species. But what if such a species does present a significant hazard to existing species in an ecosystem? Is this a sufficient justification for taking lives? We humans are guilty of the very crimes of which we accuse more-than-human immigrants—and on a much larger scale. Human overpopulation and overconsumption continue to deplete resources, drive countless species to extinction, and destabilize ecosystems. Yet, on the whole, we as a species are not systematically or even fatally punished for just existing and moving about this planet. Human-animals' liberty is consistently privileged above that of other species, including those forcibly moved from their native habitat into an unfamiliar environment by humans, then penalized for simply adapting.

It is also important to point out that ecosystems are not static. There is not a pristine, original version of any habitat, one that is completely unaltered by time or human intervention. Indeed, much conservation work has been done to achieve this fictionalized vision of the environment that has never existed and will never exist. Ecosystems change as time goes by, and so do the individuals who make up these ecosystems. Right now, rapid climate change is creating drastic shifts. More than 89 percent of the changes in ecosystems today are consistent with a response to human-caused climate change (UCAR 2022). Human animals further alter ecosystems through natural-resource use, land development, pollution, and wildlife management. A look at history will reveal that the Earth's ecosystems have been in flux for its entire existence. This change will go on via ecological succession—the process by which old species become rare or go instinct and new species enter ecosystems, creating a new community composition. Abandoned agricultural fields, left alone for years, can become meadows as new grass, flower, and shrub species move in.

The illusion of a kind of ecological pure state echoes the ethnic-nationalist sentiment that crops up in anti-immigrant discourse. The same nativist arguments used against human immigrants are then used against more-than-human immigrants. The combative language used to talk about immigrants makes ample references to the "threat of being overrun" by "hostile invaders who must be stopped," the "contamination of non-natives," and the "dangers of promiscuity and rapid reproduction." In reality, the harm caused by invasive species is rarely a biological fact but rather an ethical determination. As Claire Jean Kim (2015) points out, too often harm is defined by anthropocentric and capitalistic views of resource management, by a concern with utility "rather than moral concern for the animals themselves" (141). This means that the honeybee goes unchallenged but the Asian carp needs to be eliminated.

Let us toss out speciesist, nativist, and capitalistic views of nature and other animals. Let us no longer privilege some beings' lives and liberties above others' and work to transform our relationship with the more-than-human world into one of cohabitation and true egalitarianism. Human and other animals should be free to move through their environments as they wish, receiving support and respect wherever they go in place of discrimination and violence.

PATRIARCHY AND BODILY AUTONOMY

The preceding discussion of what goes on at the U.S.–Mexico border demonstrates how racism and speciesism can work together and thus how non/human liberty is tied. Even though liberty is one of the various privileges enjoyed by the human species that advantage us over other animals, it is not afforded to all of us in equal measures. Many working-class immigrants from Central and South America, for example, are not free to move their families from their hometowns to the United States without encountering severe pushback or violence, while wealthier, more well-connected immigrants, or immigrants from more highly valued, often majority-white countries, can exercise their freedom of movement to enter the United States without the same roadblocks.

Thus, while on the whole liberty is a species privilege of humans, how much liberty one is granted can be constrained by the workings of various systems of oppression, not only racism but also ableism, classism, sexism, and so on. For example, persons with disabilities are over-represented in confinement settings such as prisons and immigration detention centers; they may also face a deprivation of liberty in the form of involuntary institutionalization, which they are then given few legal avenues to challenge (Anjorin et al. 2019). In the same vein, the working class's liberty is limited by its lack of access to economic resources and opportunity, to quality education, housing, and other social support services that could enhance freedom, health, and choice in life. Finally, due to a lack of reproductive rights and sexual autonomy and due to persisting inequalities in the home, the workplace, the economy, and the culture at large, those who are not cisgender heterosexual men are prevented from exercising their liberty fully.

For decades, several radical feminists, ecofeminists, and animal activists have pondered the links between sexism and speciesism as well as means of maximizing liberty for both women and animals. In her book *New Woman, New Earth*, considered one of the first ecofeminist texts, Rosemary Radford Reuther (1975) wrote that women must come to realize that they will not be liberated, nor will the environment, as long as society is fundamentally organized around a logic of domination. More recently, in the last decade or so, Lori Gruen and Carol J. Adams have gained recognition as influential thinkers in this space. Their writings, like Reuther's, critique the fundamental hierarchies in society that serve to oppress both women and more-than-human animals (Adams and Gruen 2014). Relationships of domination, along with the objectification of sentient life and limitation of bodily autonomy, are central to both sexism and speciesism, and thus to both the feminist and anti-speciesist struggles.

A popular phrase in the feminist movement, which came out of the fight for reproductive rights and against limitations on access to abortion, is "my body, my choice." The idea is that women should be able to control what happens to—and make choices regarding—their own bodies. Those who enjoy such bodily autonomy can choose whether to get a tattoo, whether to enter a romantic relationship, or whether to become a parent. Feminists agree that to force any one of these choices on another individual is wrong and abusive. However, humans' treatment of other animals regularly involves a denial of bodily autonomy. Many farmed animals, animals in laboratories, and other captive animals are forcibly tattooed (branded) or tagged, are artificially inseminated and/or bred for human consumption or benefit. Violations of the same bodily autonomy that the women's movement seeks to protect so often go unchallenged or underchallenged when more-than-human animals are involved.

While the oppression of women and anyone who is not a cisgender heterosexual man in society is undeniably egregious, one is left to wonder why more-than-human animals, who are often treated as literal property and whose suffering can parallel that of women, receive little attention. It is not a contest to see who suffers more, however. Non/human oppressions are maintained by the same ideology of domination, the eradication of which would mean liberation for all. In 2022, the Supreme Court made the authoritarian decision to overturn *Roe v. Wade* and leave the question of the legality of and access to abortion up to individual states—a decision that many rightly saw as an extreme infringement on the liberty of people who can become pregnant. Now, with state governments in control of abortion laws, abortion has been made a criminal offense in some states. This means that some individuals would have to carry a pregnancy to term regardless of the situation or health risks—not unlike the animals who are called livestock.

The subjugation of women and that of more-than-human animals are entangled in several ways, one of which is via terminology: the word "husbandry" in "animal husbandry," another name for animal agriculture, comes from "husband." "Husband" is defined as "the male head of a household, the master of the house" and husbandry as "careful management" (Oxford English Dictionary n.d.). These definitions expose the historical link between maleness and control (or "management") of others, which pattrice jones (2014) pointed out in writing:

> First and foremost, all uses of animals in agriculture depend on sex. By becoming the "husbands" of farmed animals, men like GMC's farm manager arrogate to themselves the right to choose whether, when, and with whom the animals under their control will mate. Only by controlling every aspect of reproduction can people profit from the exploitation of animal bodies. [. . .] Not surprisingly, for an interaction among oppressions that literally goes back millennia, speciesism and sexism are so entangled that I personally tend to see them as two sides of the same coin—that coin being the profits (in terms of power and privilege as well as money) of controlling somebody else's body, including its reproductive capacities. (92)

Historically, cishet men have had the express privilege of controlling those deemed as their property or subordinates, whether that be human women and children or more-than-human animals.

The links between patriarchy and anthroparchy can be seen in society more broadly. Throughout history, through various means, from dowries to the withheld vote, cishet males have sought power via control of women and the female body. Today, the long-running debate on access to abortion as a reproductive right remains most divisive. Conservative legislators, backed by religiously affiliated interest groups, are continuously finding ways to restrict access to abortion while simultaneously limiting education on gender, sexuality, and safe-sex practices, including contraception. These politicians seek to undermine female bodily autonomy both by eliminating people's ability to choose abortion and, in many instances, by obscuring or inhibiting sex for purposes other than procreation Through the patriarchal lens, the female body is a breeding machine to which men can lay claim. Countless more-than-human animals—females in particular—are victims of the same form of reproductive control, sexually violated and forcibly impregnated repeatedly until they are no longer useful in this capacity. The very notion of human control and domination of more-than-human animals, diverse as they are, is patriarchal.

No industry exemplifies this anthroparchal and patriarchal domination quite as wholly as the dairy industry. Just like all other mammals, including humans, cows must become pregnant to lactate, or produce milk. This means that throughout her life, a dairy cow will be impregnated multiple times, often by way of artificial insemination by the farmer—that is, bestiality. She has no say in when or how often she becomes pregnant. She will also have no control over what becomes of her calf. In a more natural setting, a calf would nurse from their mother for eight to eleven months, but on a typical dairy farm, they would remain with their mother for only roughly three days before being taken away so that the milk meant for them can be harvested for human consumption (Kayouli et al. 1998). If you ever drive by a dairy farm and see igloo- or dog house–like outdoor structures, they are housing calves who have been separated from their mothers.

For the calves and their mothers, both viewed as objects of profit, liberty of choice and bodily autonomy are almost nonexistent. Dairy production, and animal husbandry more broadly, is the way it is because it is informed by the patriarchal idea that human animals, males in particular, have the right to dominate and control others. It is emblematic of an oppressive system that impacts human women and more-than-human animals alike; but while women have been combating it with some success, other animals are often excluded from the fight altogether.

As human animals, we benefit from varying degrees of liberty and privilege that allow us some room to challenge our current situations and fight for something better. The cow and her calf do not have the same means of contesting their object status and the resulting violence—although more-than-human animals do protest through vocalization and physical communication, and they do fight back by attempting to escape.

All individual non/humans deserve access to maximized liberty. It is time for us to imagine and work toward a society where everyone's liberty is respected, movement is uninhibited, no one owns the body of another, cohabitation is practiced earnestly, and the sound of a mother cow screaming after her stolen baby is never heard again. This requires us to actively embrace and practice total liberation, because in a world of linked oppressions, we must break all the chains to be free.

CHAPTER TEN

What Animal Liberation Activists Need to Know about Values: Debunking Three Common Myths

Mark Suchyta

INTRODUCTION

Animal liberation activists employ a variety of tactics to increase public awareness of the poor treatment of nonhuman animals in our society as well as to promote social and behavioral change to end their suffering. These tactics are diverse and range from the distribution of pamphlets (e.g., on college campuses, outside of circuses) to "direct action" strategies, such as undercover investigations exposing animal abuse on factory farms or in research laboratories (Munro 2005). Considering that these activities all require resources such as money and countless volunteer hours, it is important to examine how effective they are. For example, the U.S.-based organization Vegan Outreach is well known for distributing over a million leaflets promoting a plant-based diet each year on American college campuses (Camp 2014). Does this approach result in a significant number of people adopting a vegan lifestyle? Furthermore, animal liberation activism can take a toll on activists' mental health as such work can be traumatic and exhausting (Gorski, Lopresti-Goodman, and Rising 2019). This may especially be the case for those engaged in direct action tactics, which expose them to egregious suffering or even subject them to legal prosecution. Therefore, activists need to be mindful of how to best expend their energy and passion.

A growing number of studies are already asking some important questions about effectiveness (Cherry 2016; Fernández 2020; Jasper and Poulsen 1995; Wrenn 2013), and some animal advocacy organizations, such as The Humane League, have developed their own research departments to assess their tactics and messaging (The Humane League 2023). However, a shortcoming of the existing studies is that they tend to not consider the role of values, which social psychologists consider to be the building blocks of people's beliefs and, eventually, behaviors (Heberlein 2012). Accounting for values is crucial because it can inform animal liberation activists of what is important to their audience and thus give insights into how their messaging and activism can be most effective.

This chapter provides an accessible account of the implications of the social science literature on values for animal liberation activism. It seeks to break down the barrier between the academic community and the activist community, providing tools for activists to best connect to their audiences as well as to appeal to as many people as possible for the ultimate goal of fostering respect for nonhuman animals and ending their suffering. First, a brief overview of the concept of values and how they relate to people's beliefs, attitudes, and behaviors is presented. Then, for the remainder of the chapter, values research is drawn upon to debunk three common myths relative to animal liberation activism. The first myth is that animal liberation activists are concerned about only nonhuman animals and not humans. The second myth is that concerns for the environment and for nonhuman animals are not compatible. Finally, the third myth—and maybe the most important to address—is that simply providing people with information is enough to change their beliefs and attitudes.

WHAT ARE VALUES?

The terms "values," "beliefs," and "attitudes" are often used interchangeably, but for activists who are working to influence people's behaviors, it is useful to be clear as to what these terms really mean and how they are related to each other. In social psychology, the term "values" refers to the guiding principles in people's lives—they correspond with what is most important to an individual (Schwartz 1992; Steg 2016). Another way to think about values is that they are the lens through which one sees and interprets the world. People's values determine what they direct their attention to and how they evaluate what is going on in the world around them, as well as which actions they choose to take (Feather 1995; Rokeach 1973). Values are believed to develop largely during childhood based upon an individual's needs, traits, experiences, and culture (Steg 2016). It is important for activists to understand that once these values are formed, they tend to be quite stable and unlikely to change significantly. This is one explanation, as will be discussed later in this chapter, for why it can be so hard to change people's minds. However, this is not to say that values cannot change. Major events in one's life, as well as the process of maturation, can lead one to reconsider and reconfigure one's values (Feather 1995). Indeed, you, the reader, can think back to what brought you to the animal liberation movement and how that may have influenced your core values.

Among the fascinating findings from values research is that a set of common values can be observed across the world. While particular values may certainly be more prominent in some cultures than in others (e.g., in collectivist versus individualist cultures), the research suggests that many values can be observed to some extent across all cultures.

How are these values measured? The most widely used technique is to conduct a survey that presents study participants with a list of concepts. Each concept is associated with a specific value. Each participant is then asked to indicate to which extent each concept is a guiding principle in their life, typically on a numerical scale ranging from one ("not important at all") to seven ("extremely important"). Research by Milton Rokeach (1973), a pioneer in the field, initially identified thirty-six distinct values. More recent work by Shalom Schwartz (2012) emphasizes ten core values: self-direction, stimulation, hedonism, achievement, power, security, tradition, conformity, universalism, and benevolence. Every person has varying levels of these values, which together form their value orientation.

Values are very important to consider in the context of activism because they influence how people will perceive the information presented to them, whether they will see issues such as industrial animal agriculture as problematic (and for what reasons), as well as whether they feel behavioral change is warranted. In other words, values provide the foundation upon which specific beliefs, attitudes, and behaviors are situated (Schwartz 1992; Steg 2016). Some scholars refer to this as the "vertical structure" of cognition (Bem 1970; Heberlein 2012). The general idea is that values inform people's beliefs, which refer to what they think to be true about a particular person, practice, concept, and so on. For example, the statement "Animal agriculture is immoral" represents a belief. Then, attitudes are simply beliefs that have affective, or emotional, components, as exemplified by the statement "I hate industrial animal agriculture because it is immoral." Activists often seek to change people's beliefs, attitudes, and eventually behaviors. However, considering that beliefs and attitudes are simply applied reflections of values, it is critical that activists not overlook them.

Researchers have found that values are particularly important when people interpret situations with which they are not yet familiar (Kahneman 2011). Considering that the general public is often not very knowledgeable about common practices in industries that exploit nonhuman animals, this is important to note (Alonso, González-Montaña, and Lomillos 2020). Under such circumstances, people are likely to rely on their "gut instinct"—a colloquial way of saying that they rely entirely on their general values—to quickly develop a belief or attitude or to quickly decide to partake in a particular behavior.

In recent decades, research on values has been adopted into environmental science to understand how they correspond with concern for the environment and engagement in behaviors, including activism, that seek to protect the environment (often called "pro-environmental behaviors") (Dietz 2015; Stern, Dietz, and Guagnano 1998). Using a modified version of the list of values promoted by Schwartz (2012), researchers have identified six particular values that are relevant in understanding people's beliefs about and concern for the environment: traditionalism, humanistic altruism (i.e., concern for other humans), biospheric altruism (i.e., respect and concern for the Earth and its nonhuman inhabitants), openness to change, self-interest, and hedonism (Dietz 2015; Steg et al. 2014). Studies have generally found that individuals are particularly less likely to demonstrate high levels of concern for the environment or to partake in pro-environmental behaviors when they hold high levels of self-interest or hedonism. A likely explanation for this is that many pro-environmental behaviors can be seen as inconvenient or not particularly pleasurable. Therefore, if a person prioritizes the two said values relatively highly, they would be disinclined to engage in such behaviors. Meanwhile, people with higher levels of altruism, particularly biospheric altruism, are more likely to demonstrate concern for the environment as well as to partake in pro-environmental behaviors (Steg et al. 2014).

Recognizing the need to conduct similar research regarding how the public perceives animal rights issues, some scholars have proposed (and found empirical support for) a distinct "animal-concern" value that diverges from biospheric altruism (concern for the Earth), which concern for animals has previously been lumped into. The animal-concern value corresponds with such concepts as "treating animals with dignity and respect," "preventing cruelty towards other animals," and "companionship with other animals" (Dietz, Allen, and McCright 2017). A recent study of my own collected nationally representative online-survey data to examine whether a distinct animal-concern value could be observed among Americans by asking participants about the three concepts just mentioned, as well as how animal concern and other values would predict Americans' beliefs about farmed-animal well-being (Suchyta 2021). The study reaffirmed the presence of a distinct animal-concern value and also found that, taking into consideration various demographic variables (e.g., income, age, sex, race, education, diet, political orientation, and religious beliefs), Americans who demonstrated higher levels of the animal-concern value, compared to Americans who reported lower levels, were more likely to believe that farmed animals were less protected by farmers and laws. Moreover, those with higher levels of humanistic altruism, compared to those with lower levels, evaluated the well-being of farmed animals as worse—an interesting finding relevant to the first myth that this chapter will address.

MYTH 1: ANIMAL LIBERATION ACTIVISTS ARE
CONCERNED ABOUT ONLY NONHUMAN ANIMALS

Activists and scholars who focus on animal liberation have all been asked a question along the lines of: But why do you focus on animals when there are so many issues affecting humans? Indeed, both activists and organizations in the movement often must justify why their work matters and how helping nonhuman animals does not equate to ignoring human suffering. It is no surprise, therefore, that the issue is discussed by several authors in this book.

Many activists recognize that such a question is, at its core, speciesist, as it suggests that human concerns always trump nonhuman concerns (Noske 1997), but that is beside the point. More important, a quick review of the concept of total liberation, which encompasses all beings, human and nonhuman, can quickly dispel this myth (Pellow 2014), as can the existing research on values. For example, my own (Suchyta 2021) finding that Americans with higher levels of humanistic altruism demonstrated more concern for farmed-animal well-being serves as scientific evidence for what activists already know well—that this myth is indeed simply a myth. Other studies have produced similar findings. For example, Dietz, Allen, and McCright (2017), who conducted a survey of American adults using Amazon's Mechanical Turk interface, found that individuals who demonstrated higher levels of animal concern also tended to have higher levels of humanistic altruism as well as biospheric altruism. This result is significant because it suggests overlap between concern for nonhuman animals and concern for other humans.

In a mail-based survey of Ohio residents, Deemer and Lobao (2011) asked respondents several questions about their concern for other human beings as well as their concern for farmed-animal well-being. The researchers found a positive correlation between these concerns, even when considering several sociodemographic variables, including religious and political affiliation, income, and education. Taylor and Signal (2005) found similar results in a study of 194 undergraduate students. These findings seem sensible considering that many popular books on food-system issues highlight the mutual suffering of humans and nonhumans in the agricultural industry (e.g., Pollan 2006; Thompson 2015).

Overall, the evidence suggests that concern for humans and concern for nonhumans are two values frequently correlated with each other. This is notable for two reasons. First, it means that there is a scientifically informed rebuttal animal liberation activists can use when accused of ignoring human suffering to address nonhuman suffering. However, more important, it emphasizes the potential for collaboration between human rights and animal rights activists and organizations. It also suggests that people who hold deep concern for marginalized human groups may be receptive to calls for the liberation of nonhuman animals, so long as activists can communicate a clear connection between human and nonhuman suffering. As Deemer and Lobao (2011) note, both nonhuman animals and humans from historically marginalized groups can be thought of as "outgroups," subject to mistreatment and discrimination. This is certainly not to say that the two are the same, but their oppressions stem from some of the same ideologies and biases. For this reason, the framework of total liberation is potentially highly effective for social organization and change.

MYTH 2: CONCERNS FOR THE ENVIRONMENT AND FOR NONHUMAN ANIMALS ARE NOT COMPATIBLE

This myth may at first seem puzzling, as concern for the environment is often discussed alongside concern for at least certain animals, such as wildlife. However, it should be noted that many scholars are skeptical about the nature of this relationship. This is because these two forms of concern can often be at odds with each other. Philosophers emphasize how environmental ethics focuses on the stability and thriving of ecosystems and species, whereas frameworks such as that of animal liberation or animal rights tend to focus on the rights and well-being of individual animals (Campbell 2018). Again, these frameworks can at times clash. A commonly cited example involves invasive species: while adherents of animal rights philosophies emphasize the right of individual animals to live out their lives, regardless of their origin, those focused on ecosystem preservation may promote the eradication of such species due to their substantial negative impacts on the rest of the ecosystem and its inhabitants (Callicott 1980; Campbell 2018).

Yet, values research appears to debunk this second myth as well. Just as studies have found a correlation between concern for nonhumans and concern for humans, they have also found concern for the environment (i.e., biospheric altruism) to be highly correlated with concern for nonhuman animals. As previously noted, this is precisely what Dietz, Allen, and McCright (2017) found. Using a statistical analysis called regression, they also found that study participants with higher levels of animal concern were more likely to identify with the animal rights movement, but not necessarily with the environmental movement, compared to those with lower levels of animal concern. However, those with higher levels of biospheric altruism, compared to those with lower levels, were more likely to identify with both the environmental movement and the animal rights movement. I did not find such a relationship in my study, but it is notable that I did not observe lower levels of concern for farmed-animal well-being among those with higher levels of humanistic altruism (Suchyta 2021). Together, these findings emphasize that there are opportunities for alliances with environmental activists and organizations, and it is no surprise that many in the animal liberation movement, including several authors in this book, are also involved with environmental causes. Certainly, there may be occasional conflicts between animal rights and environmentalism, such as in the case of invasive species or ecosystem management, but activists should focus on the opportunities present to improve the lives of nonhuman animals—even including seemingly unlikely alliances with conservation groups that endorse activities such as hunting and fishing but whose goals sometimes align with ours (e.g., protection of wild animals and opposition to factory farming). While many animal liberation activists may scoff at the idea of being associated with groups that do not endorse veganism, doing so can result in missed opportunities to make impactful change and appeal to a broader audience—opportunities that the movement cannot afford to throw away.

MYTH 3: PROVIDING PEOPLE WITH INFORMATION IS SUFFICIENT TO CHANGE THEIR BELIEFS AND ATTITUDES

This final myth is arguably the most important to address. Activists across a variety of movements often assume that if they educate the public about how problematic an issue is, this will result in social change. In the case of animal liberation activism, this logic suggests that if activists continue to hand out more leaflets and release more undercover videos, they will get closer to animal liberation. Unfortunately, the research on values proves that this, too, is a myth. The point of this discussion, however, is not to discourage activism but to encourage activism that makes the most efficient use of resources, whether it be volunteer hours, finances, or blood, sweat, and tears.

A significant number of studies have examined the effectiveness of various strategies, such as the use of graphic imagery or leafleting, in convicting people to change to a plant-based diet (e.g., Cooney 2011; Fernández 2020; Greig 2017; Herzog and Golden 2009; Mika 2006). Findings from these studies are generally mixed in terms of what the best forms of activism are, but many of them conclude that more important than the actual messaging or tactics used are the characteristics of the target audience. This, of course, includes values.

Consider, for example, an interesting study by Whitley, Gunderson, and Charters (2018), who used Amazon's Mechanical Turk to conduct a survey that explored public support for policies promoting plant-based diets and the correlation between such support and various social characteristics, including gender, income, education, religious beliefs, political beliefs, and values. They also adopted an experimental design into their study, in which varying "rhetorical frames," or particular arguments for adopting a plant-based diet, were presented to the respondents to see if they altered respondents' receptiveness to policies promoting plant-based diets. There were three such frames, which corresponded with environmental protection, animal welfare, and public health. Surprisingly, the researchers found that the three frames did not generally influence people's support for plant-based policies; instead, the respondents' values, particularly altruism, as well as other demographic characteristics (e.g., gender, political views) were stronger predictors. In other words, the information presented to respondents did not matter so much, but their values did. Whitley, Gunderson, and Charters's findings echo those of scholars in the environmental sciences who have also emphasized how difficult it can be to convince people to engage in pro-environmental behaviors simply by presenting them with information (Heberlein 2012).

The key takeaway here is that providing information in itself is not enough to change people's beliefs, attitudes, and behaviors. If activists do not appeal directly to the values of the people they are trying to reach, then the information they are providing will likely be ignored or quickly forgotten. This also means that each type of information used by activists will be effective in catching the attention of those whose values that information resonates with. For example, a person who has a high degree of animal concern or biospheric altruism will be receptive to information about animal rights or environmental problems. They have probably always been conscious about such issues but may have just needed an opportunity to get more involved. These are the easiest people to reach. However, to pursue large-scale change, activists need to broadcast their message as far and wide as possible. This entails bringing into their circle those who may not share their value orientations.

Many people do not demonstrate high levels of animal concern or other altruistic values. How do activists approach them? Are they unreachable? Not necessarily, but activists would need to employ other strategies to be effective in such instances. For example, activists may ask themselves if there is an alternative argument for animal liberation that would appeal to these people by drawing upon the values that they hold most strongly.

In an ideal scenario, activists could use survey research, like in some of the studies discussed in this chapter, to find out exactly what the landscape of values they are facing is. This would allow activists and organizations to best tailor their messaging to their audiences. However, such an endeavor can be very costly and thus is not a realistic option for most. Other strategies to "read the room" include speaking to prominent "insiders" of the group one is trying to reach. Are there local leaders or activists, for example, who could help one understand what is important to members of the community and therefore how best to approach them to advocate for nonhuman animals?

Some activists may find that they can develop a good feel for this on their own. Sociologists use the term "sociological imagination" to refer to the ability to understand how personal characteristics and experiences converge with the culture and moment in history one is living in (Mills 1959). By understanding both what is important to people and what the major social issues are, activists can better communicate with their audiences. For example, if one is presenting at a college campus where there is an emphasis on human rights, then making connections between human and nonhuman rights may be particularly impactful, especially if one can present parallels between one's cause and ongoing human rights struggles.

When trying to reach a particularly broad audience, such as people across a nation, activists would be wise to appeal to widely held values in that society. For example, self-interest and certain aspects of humanistic altruism (e.g., social justice and equality) are prominent values in U.S. culture. Therefore, U.S. activists may well be most effective when they are able to emphasize the rights of individual animals, animal rights as a form of social justice, the legal protection of animal rights, and so on.

When all else fails, activists may choose to appeal to a wide variety of values. For example, many animal liberation activists emphasize "ethical veganism," which promotes a lifestyle that abstains from all animal use due to perceived moral obligations and respect owed to nonhuman animals as autonomous, thinking, feeling beings. This framing may resonate with people with high levels of animal concern and other forms of altruism but may not convince people with high levels of self-interest or hedonism. To appeal to the latter, activists would find other strategies to be more appropriate, such as emphasizing the health benefits of a plant-based diet. The effectiveness of appealing to numerous values is apparent even in this book, whose authors advocate the same general cause via a variety of arguments, which will be received by each reader differently based on their values.

The debunking of this third myth suggests that not only can activists be more effective by speaking to diverse values, but they also need to acknowledge that some people will never be convinced—that animal liberation is just not in alignment with their current value orientations. However, in realizing this, activists can more adeptly navigate the murky waters of values, beliefs, and attitudes.

CONCLUSION

The purpose of this chapter was to provide activists with a brief introduction to the social-psychological field of values as well as to demonstrate the implications of the current research on values for effective activism. In doing so, the chapter has attempted to debunk three common myths about animal liberation activism: that animal liberation activists are concerned about only nonhuman animals (and not humans), that concerns for the environment and nonhuman animals are not compatible, and that activists can facilitate changes in beliefs, attitudes, and behaviors simply by providing information about the suffering of nonhuman animals. In addressing this last myth, I sought not to discourage activists but to provide some useful advice on what activists should consider to be most effective.

Ultimately, the most important conclusion of this chapter is that values matter immensely in efforts to educate people about the suffering of nonhuman animals and promote social change. It is values that determine how activists' messaging is received, and a successful appeal to a wide range of values is bound to further the cause of liberating all animals, human and nonhuman.

CHAPTER ELEVEN

Humane Education: A Pathway to Compassionate Coexistence

Emily Tronetti and Macy Sutton

INTRODUCTION

"We live in a messy, complicated, frustrating, demanding world,
and it is impossible to do the right thing all of the time, however
we define it. Compassion is the glue that holds ecosystems, webs
of nature, and circles of life together. Compassion also holds us
together. We are an integral part of many beautiful, awe-inspiring,
and far-reaching webs of nature, and we all suffer when these
complex interrelationships are compromised."
—Bekoff 2014, 45–46

Unfortunately, these complex interrelationships have already been
compromised, and we don't have to look far to find examples of the
suffering Marc Bekoff describes. In the last fifty years, global wildlife
populations have declined by more than two thirds, largely due to
human-generated climate change and deforestation (Rott 2020). Further,
approximately eighty billion nonhuman animals are slaughtered for
human consumption each year (Ritchie, Rosado, and Roser 2019). This
statistic excludes the aquatic animals who are killed and processed into
food, whose deaths are measured only by their weight. This does not
take into account the billions of animals sacrificed for research or dying
of unnatural causes in captivity each year.

These numbers give us a glimpse of a hard but necessary truth:
humans are failing to coexist with other species on a global scale. And

yet, as we continue to descend into ecological crises, it is evident that statistics alone are not sufficient to cause behavioral change—especially away from normative practices. Time and again, we learn about the negative personal, societal, and ecological effects of animal exploitation but fail to take action, even when we know it's in our best interest. A radical shift in how we perceive and treat the more-than-human world is necessary (Bekoff 2014). According to Cornish et al. (2018), "education and awareness-raising play a pivotal role in increasing society's consideration of non-human animal welfare" (1). But we need more than animal welfare—we need total liberation. And we also need more than consideration. We need coexistence.

Coexistence is not a new construct, and there are numerous examples of humans coexisting with individual nonhuman species throughout history. Upon closer examination, though, we see that many of these references to coexistence are flawed. In some instances, humans "coexist" with one or more nonhuman species while continuing to oppress others. In other instances, the parties said to be coexisting are not benefiting equitably. For example, some claim that ranchers, wolves, and "livestock" are coexisting when ranchers use nonlethal means of deterring wolf predation. While there are certainly benefits to all three parties, the "livestock" are still considered property, being kept alive only temporarily and only for human profit.

This chapter is based on the belief that true coexistence is inclusive of all species and does not value some at the expense of others. However, many of us struggle to embody the compassion and reverence required for coexistence in our daily lives. One approach to education that aims to change this is humane education, which proposes the following:

> If [people's] reverence for the natural world, for animals, for the good in human beings, and for peace is cultivated and nurtured, they will likely make choices that reflect their reverence, which will, in turn, create a more compassionate and peaceful world. When we feel reverence, our lives are enriched, our experiences are touched with power and purpose, and our actions are permeated with respect. (Weil 2004, 26)

Humane education acknowledges and teaches about the interconnectedness of humans, other animals, and the natural world. Typically, humane education is geared toward children and youth, but there is significant potential for it to be integrated into adult education, including as part of the total liberation movement. Indeed, humane education can work in partnership with critical animal studies and other fields that have provided theoretical foundations to justify the need for interspecies coexistence. A widespread, collective effort is required to transform our systems and individual practices. These transformations call not only for education but also for healing. With this in mind, we recommend a trauma-informed, healing-centered approach to humane education. Through deepening empathy, teaching critical thinking, and inspiring compassionate action, this approach can help us learn new ways of being.

DEFINING HUMANE EDUCATION

Many people have questioned whether education is the answer to our global challenges. According to Zoe Weil (2009), co-founder of the Institute for Humane Education, education is key to solving complex problems. However, education in its current form is often lacking, and many adults are left out of educational systems entirely. Alternatively, humane education can be integrated into a variety of contexts and reach learners of all ages. Critical components of humane education include providing factual and comprehensive information; cultivating curiosity, creativity, and critical thinking skills; inspiring awe, respect, and responsibility; and encouraging, but not imposing, positive choices (Weil 2004). Humane education centers the well-being of individual humans and nonhumans as well as "entire ecosystems, species, [and] communities" (Weil 2004, 56).

This inclusivity necessitates teaching about interconnected oppressions and how we can dismantle systems that perpetuate inequity (McPhall 2020). The oppression of nonhuman animals exists in tandem with other forms of oppression, such as racism, ableism, and sexism (Ko and Ko 2017; Taylor 2017). Nonhuman-animal oppression is tied to speciesism, which, in its simplest sense, refers to discrimination based on species membership. Speciesism is demonstrated through inconsistencies in how we treat different species and variations in the value we ascribe to them (Dhont et al. 2020). One interpretation of speciesism, referred to as anthropocentrism, asserts that humans are intrinsically superior to other species and deserving of preferential treatment. It establishes a moral hierarchy with humans on top, often resulting in humans, caring for our own species at the expense or exclusion of other species (Bekoff 2014; Kopnina et al. 2018). Unlike traditional approaches to education, humane education recognizes speciesism and anthropocentrism as contributors to global suffering and aims to facilitate compassionate coexistence among all species.

Compassionate coexistence requires that we expand our perception of community to include the more-than-human world. This means deepening our understanding of other animals and nature and learning to cultivate mindfulness in our interactions with them. According to Bekoff (2014), "knowing about how their well-being and ours are closely tied together will help guide our decisions so we foster respect and coexistence" (132–33). Compassionate coexistence is far from simply existing in the same space. It's about being in community with, learning from, and respecting one another. Humane education can help foster this.

HUMANE EDUCATION AND TOTAL LIBERATION

Humane education and compassionate coexistence align well with other animal justice philosophies, including that of total liberation, which calls for the liberation of all oppressed humans, nonhuman animals, and ecosystems (Colling, Parson, and Arrigoni 2014). Indeed, total liberation is the goal of critical animal studies, a field that shares many principles with humane education. Critical animal studies examines the "exploitation and liberation of animals; the inclusion of animals in a broader emancipatory struggle; speciesism; and the principles and practices of animal advocacy, animal protection, and animal-related policies" (Pedersen 2010, 2). One way in which critical animal studies and humane education are similar is that both recognize how all manifestations of oppression have shared roots while being supportive of individual social justice movements. Both advocate critical thinking, dialogue, and action to dismantle the dominant systems that perpetuate oppression (Best et al. 2007).

Meanwhile, the most prominent difference between the two fields lies in how they define their goals. As previously mentioned, in critical animal studies, the goal is to achieve total liberation by whatever means necessary and feasible for those working toward it. In contrast, the goal of humane education is to, through education, minimize suffering perpetuated by individuals and systems. Humane education empowers people to make choices, based on accurate information, that do the most good and the least harm (a principle referred to as *MOGO*, short for "most good") but does not dictate what choices people should make (Weil 2004). In this way, humane education may be seen as more approachable or accessible and critical animal studies as more direct.

At least one scholar has presented a solution to the perceived shortfalls of each discipline. Olson (2019) proposes merging humane education and critical pedagogy into a new, more expansive subject: critical humane education. Olson suggests that this fusion would "allow students to engage in compassionate, dignified relationships with 'the other' while simultaneously stripping away the systems that enable othering in the first place" (37). We contend that critical animal studies and humane education already do this through their emphasis on systems, critical, and solution-oriented thinking. Each of these disciplines has different strengths, and we ultimately recommend a collaborative approach. By working together, practitioners of humane education and critical animal studies create more opportunities for people to reexamine their values, model compassionate choices, and educate their communities.

The Role of Humane Educators in Cultivating Coexistence

A humane educator is someone "who fosters respect and compassion for all, and helps people become problem solvers and changemakers for a better world" (Weil 2009, xiii). Humane education doesn't have to take place in a classroom. Indeed, our interactions with each other and our environments can be opportunities for learning and teaching (Irvine 2002). We must recognize these opportunities, however fleeting, when they present themselves and know how to make the most of them. For example, if a coworker or a peer makes a disparaging comment about someone based on their race, gender expression, or disability status, we can respond in multiple ways. A constructive approach would be to use this situation as an opportunity to inquire into the speaker's perspective while demonstrating and encouraging critical thinking, empathy, and respect.

Teachable moments arise at different times and in different ways, but skills such as critical thinking and empathy are applicable across contexts. When combined with a trauma-informed, healing-centered approach, humane education can facilitate for us renewed relationships with ourselves, other beings, and our shared world.

A Trauma-Informed, Healing-Centered Approach

It's vital that we, as members of the global community and educators in both traditional and nontraditional settings, recognize that those with whom we engage may have histories of trauma. Trauma can be experienced at the individual level as well as at the community or systems level. It arises from any physical, emotional, psychological, sexual, spiritual, or environmental event, experienced or witnessed, that causes distress. Responses to trauma include fatigue, fear, anger, depression, and anxiety—all of which can create deeper divisions within oneself and one's communities (jones 2007; Lyon et al. 2022). Because of this variability, it is practically impossible to know who may be triggered by what, which makes a humane education framework like MOGO all the more valuable—one that recognizes that our world is too complex for one-size-fits-all approaches, especially in response to trauma, and instead encourages inquiry, introspection, and informed choice-making (Weil 2009). One way to demonstrate a trauma-informed perspective is by choosing words with intention and compassion, knowing that they have the power to (re) traumatize.

A newer approach that evolved from trauma-informed theory and practice is referred to as *healing-centered* (Ginwright 2020; Lyon et al. 2022). Ginwright describes it as such:

A healing-centered approach views trauma not simply as an individual isolated experience, but rather highlights the ways in which trauma and healing are experienced collectively. The term healing-centered engagement expands how we think about responses to trauma and offers a more holistic approach to fostering well-being. (2020, para. 10)

Given humane education's focus on tackling systemic oppression and promoting collective well-being, it's uniquely suited to adopt a healing-centered approach. One strategy that humane educators can use to express healing-centeredness is to demonstrate active listening, which makes it clear to people that they are being heard, seen, and understood. This communication style also helps build connection, recognition, and emotional support, all of which are necessary for healing trauma (jones 2007).

Another strategy is to create and maintain reflective spaces, whether physical or virtual, that are both safe and brave—spaces that allow for uncomfortable feelings and emotions (Brookfield and Hess 2021). This type of environment can help individuals from diverse backgrounds acknowledge, challenge, and move past trauma and cognitive biases, such as speciesism and anthropocentrism (jones 2007). To optimize such spaces for humane education, participation in dialogue ought to be encouraged but not required. This strategy allows individuals to address feelings of cognitive dissonance in ways that meet their particular needs (Brookfield and Hess 2021).

Lastly, mindfulness techniques have the potential to promote individual and collective healing and are something we can incorporate into our daily lives and share with others. As defined by mindfulness researcher Jon Kabat-Zinn (2013), "mindfulness is cultivated by paying close attention to your moment-to-moment experience while, as best you can, not getting caught up in your ideas and opinions, likes and dislikes" (21). The benefits of a mindfulness practice include decreased depression, decreased negative biases, decreased pain, improved sleep, improved executive functioning, and improved stress response (Kabat-Zinn 2013). In line with the objectives of humane education, mindfulness allows us to be more perceptive of and receptive to what, why, and how others, including nonhuman animals, are communicating. As such, mindfulness, as part of a healing-centered approach, can be integrated into humane education.

Teaching Critical Thinking

The relationships we humans have with other animals are complex. We each have nonhumans for whom we care deeply, with whom we share our homes and even our beds (Menor-Campos et al. 2019). Nonetheless, most species on our shared planet experience suffering, exploitation, even extinction as a result of their forced relationships with humankind. As discussed previously, human–nonhuman relationships have long been shaped by speciesism and anthropocentrism, ideologies that interlock with the many other systems of oppression embedded within our society (Saari 2018; Spanjol 2020). These biases detach us from our animality and reinforce the "otherness" of nonhuman species (Saari 2018), which then allows us to more easily commodify and exploit nonhumans (Lupinacci and Happel-Parkins 2016). Humane education teaches us how to recognize and dismantle these biases in ourselves and others, aiming for a much-needed paradigm shift in how we relate to other beings (Saari 2018; Spanjol 2020).

Saari (2018) argues that education can "challenge the dominant narratives of human–animal relations in society" (3). Humane education tackles this objective by prioritizing critical thinking and reflection (Rumford 2018; Weil 2016). Critical thinking is described by Brookfield (2011) as a social learning process in which we recognize how our assumptions influence our thinking and behavior, thereby determining the validity of those assumptions and examining them from various perspectives in order to take informed action. Use of critical thinking skills forms an important part of the mission of humane education and is encouraged throughout as a means to advance personal and systemic changes that reduce suffering across species (Rumford 2018; Weil 2016).

As we interact with others through our work and activism and in our day-to-day lives, there are subtle yet powerful ways we can promote these crucial critical thinking skills. Taking into account a trauma-informed, healing-centered approach, we seek to build trust as an essential first step. This includes empathizing with our (co-)learners and making it clear that the conversation is a judgment-free space where they will not be shamed or criticized for their assumptions or beliefs (Philpotts, Dillon, and Rooney 2019). Then, educator and learner can get curious together. We can gently prompt our learners to think about their thinking, to question their assumptions (Maynes 2015; Spanjol 2020). We can ask them to tell us more about what their beliefs are and why these beliefs are important. It's also helpful to discuss how and why humans develop biases in the first place, to examine the role of norms and dominant systems in shaping beliefs (Spanjol 2020). In partnership with our learners, we can critically reflect on how our beliefs and behaviors impact ourselves and other beings. This process requires vulnerability on the part of the humane educator—a vulnerability that helps create a space where people feel safe to share and ask questions as they engage in their own critical thinking process (Rumford 2018).

According to Brookfield (2013), "thinking critically lies at the heart of acting powerfully" (35). By promoting critical thinking through a humane education lens, we inspire people to act powerfully for a better world. However, to achieve compassionate coexistence, we must focus on empathy as well. Critical thinking and empathy combined empower all of us to create positive change within ourselves, within our communities, and within systems.

Deepening Empathy

Humane education strives to foster empathy to help people understand how their behavior influences the experiences of others (Rumford 2018; Young, Khalil, and Wharton 2018). Empathy has been defined as an emotional state induced by recognizing, understanding, and caring about another's perspectives and experiences (Young, Khalil, and Wharton 2018). Gruen's (2015) relationship-centered concept of entangled empathy integrates emotion with cognition and requires that we be "responsive and responsible in [. . .] relationships by attending to another's needs, interests, desires, vulnerabilities, hopes, and sensitivities" (10). Empathizing with another, human or otherwise, must include recognition of and respect for their agency and autonomy (Gruen 2015). Unfortunately, this is often lacking in our relationships with other animals, especially domesticated animals, whom we tend to view as mere resources for our consumption rather than as individuals with their own preferences, experiences, and relationships (Taylor 2017). Humane education encourages a form of empathy that acknowledges other animals, including domesticated ones, "as vital participants in and contributors to our shared world" (Taylor 2017, 207). To attain such empathy, we must learn to listen to the unique perspectives of members of species other than our own.

While they are commonly referred to as "the voiceless," nonhuman animals are communicating with us all of the time (jones 2021). Gruen (2015) discusses how entangled empathy means resisting our assumptions about what another being is feeling and, instead, taking the time to understand what their perspectives and experiences might actually be like. This might entail observing an individual animal and researching their species-typical behaviors to gain insight into their personality. Indeed, empathy should be an active rather than a passive process, and though complex, it is a skill that can be honed. To cultivate empathy, a humane educator can learn and teach about nonhuman species and their behaviors and body languages; they can encourage careful observation of individual animals and discuss the importance of agency and consent in such an interaction.

One of the most powerful strategies we as humane educators can employ is to model empathy in how we care for all beings, including our fellow humans (Springirth 2021). Practicing active listening is one way to do this. We should engage in authentic dialogue and create space for others to share their experiences and values with us (Spanjol 2020). This may open the door for us to share our own stories, including ones about the nonhuman animals in our lives. Indeed, storytelling can help us find common ground and cultivate empathy, trust, and community.

One can often see the power of storytelling in practice on animal sanctuaries. On The Open Sanctuary Project's website, Springirth describes storytelling as a key strategy for deepening empathy for farmed animals. Sharing individual stories is "a wonderful way to illuminate the lived realities, experiences, and perspectives of [. . .] sanctuary residents," Springirth shares (2021, "Build Perspective-Taking"). Springirth also discusses the importance of word choice when talking to and about other animals. For example, we should avoid referring to them with the pronoun "it," as this usage reduces sentient beings to commodifiable objects. To embrace other animals as subjects with meaningful inner lives and experiences, we should refer to them by their names and with pronouns like "she," "he," or "they" (Springirth 2021).

Many animal sanctuaries have adopted this approach of sharing their residents' stories with the public. For example, on Woodstock Farm Sanctuary's website, we can read about Dani the turkey, who was rescued with her sisters from a corporate turkey farm:

> Like the 46 million turkeys who are killed every year for Thanksgiving, Dani's toes were cut off at the joint and she was de-beaked—extremely cruel, but normal practices in the industry, all done without any pain relief or anesthetic. When Dani first arrived to Woodstock Sanctuary, she was scared. But thanks to the daily love, care, and compassion from our shelter team, Dani learned quickly that she could be her bold, talkative self. Dani can be found enjoying her days with her friends Beatrice and Loren. Once a timid, fearful turkey, she is now the most social of the flock and will walk right up to you and say hello. (Woodstock Farm Sanctuary 2015)

Dani's story and the stories of other animals like her have the power to deepen empathy and inspire critical reflection. Through the cultivation of these skills, humane education promotes compassionate action (Spanjol 2020). Ultimately, we believe that critical thinking, empathy, and compassion are necessary components of coexistence.

Taking Action for Compassionate Coexistence

Empathy and compassion are often used interchangeably, yet empathy has also been described as a prerequisite for compassion (Saari 2018). While empathy enables us to acknowledge suffering, it's compassion that inspires action to decrease this suffering and improve well-being (Pfattheicher, Sassenrath, and Schindler 2016; Young, Khalil, and Wharton 2018). Compassion is a cornerstone of humane education, and both empathy and action are central to its definition. This sets humane education apart from more traditional forms of education.

Conventional education is centered on increasing knowledge, but more knowledge rarely culminates in changed behavior (Philpotts, Dillon, and Rooney 2019). Arbour, Signal, and Taylor (2009) note a gap between positive attitudes toward nonhuman animals and actual behavioral change to help those animals. While humane education also increases knowledge by fostering critical thinking skills, this knowledge must translate to compassionate action in order to reduce suffering. Humane educators aim to strengthen compassion by, among other things, empowering learners to consider how their behavior affects others (Weil 2004). Both formal and informal humane educators can guide people to make behavioral changes that will ultimately allow all animals and nature to not just survive but thrive in our human-dominated world.

Additionally, as humane educators, we should support each other given how difficult it can be to make the changes necessary for compassionate coexistence. As Haupt (2009) puts it: "Coexistence [. . .] will sometimes involve a vague uneasiness. Can we come to live comfortably in this slight discomfort? Can we rejoice in its meaning?" (179). Humane education acknowledges and embraces this inevitable discomfort through its emphasis on critical reflection and community. There can be many barriers to altering diet and other consumption habits, for example. With community support such as the sharing of easy and affordable vegan recipes, these barriers can be much easier to navigate. Support is especially helpful as we strive to overcome the most formidable of barriers: our own beliefs. We can gently guide each other to challenge our own assumptions and welcome new ways of seeing—and thus interacting with—the world (Cranton 2016). By fostering critical reflection and community, humane education supports people through transforming their perspectives and, ultimately, their actions.

Again, the most powerful way we can spark action for compassionate coexistence is to model it ourselves. While anyone can be a humane educator, one must be willing to embody this role in one's daily life, embrace discomfort, and make some complicated choices—and to find meaning and joy in the process (Weil 2009). Necessarily, we must acknowledge that perfection isn't attainable, but that shouldn't stop us in our pursuit of a better world. There are many possibilities for how this pursuit might unfold for each of us, and it is important that we consider factors such as access to resources and cultural traditions. Veganism is one such possibility. Additional actions we can take toward compassionate coexistence include becoming more mindful consumers and reducing our ecological footprints (Weil 2009). As Weil shares, "what matters is that we commit to the path, however we each come to understand it" (2009, xiv).

CONCLUSION

In his 2014 book *Rewilding Our Hearts*, Bekoff states that "if we set any lower standard than compassionate coexistence, we can be sure that everyone will lose eventually" (51). Later, Bekoff describes humane education as a valuable tool for cultivating compassion and reverence, especially for other animals and our shared planet, in school-aged children. Although humane education continues to be geared primarily toward youth, we contend that expanding its purview to include adults would lead to even greater, more accelerated social change. Humane education espouses many of the same principles, skills, and personal qualities as other movements and disciplines advocating for nonhuman animals, such as the total liberation movement and critical animal studies. For example, the interconnectedness of oppressions is a common theme. Meanwhile, the sense of curiosity nurtured within humane education and its principle of doing the most good could be useful additions to the work being done in these adjacent movements and fields. Perhaps because of its initial target audience, humane education is intentionally approachable, allowing it to be to incorporated into the daily lives of both educators and learners.

As mentioned earlier, we can choose to employ the principles of humane education in our personal decision-making and in our encounters with others. Being cognizant of individual and collective trauma, its effects, and common triggers helps us create a healing-centered atmosphere in which education can flourish. Mindfulness also facilitates healing, as well as increased recognition and acceptance of other beings and surrounding environments. Further, mindfulness has been described as the first step of critical reflection—an essential component of learning—as it requires that we challenge our own assumptions (Wergin 2019). It is through humane education's encouragement of critical thinking, action, and reflection that we are perpetually learning and growing. And it is through humane education's promotion of empathy, responsibility, and empowerment that we can inspire people of all ages to take action toward compassionate coexistence with others, human and nonhuman, and the natural world.

CHAPTER TWELVE

Building an Effective Animal Liberation Movement: Beyond Educational Outreach

Kiana Avlon

When I became active in the animal liberation movement in 2018, the most visible form of advocacy to get involved in was educational outreach, whereby animal advocates would hold screens displaying footage of the horrors of the animal agriculture industry and talk with pedestrians who would pause to watch. Part of the preparation for participating in this advocacy work was watching videos of men who had risen to social media influencer status within the movement with their apparent ability to disarm anyone in a debate with memorized talking points. When I engaged in this type of outreach myself, it felt immediately gratifying to be able to encourage a stranger to begin changing their mind on the ethics of eating, wearing, and using animals. This feeling was validated by the group I had joined, which spoke of how we were "planting seeds" and turning the world vegan one person at a time. However, this narrative didn't hold up when I learned the number of animals slaughtered yearly was constantly rising. Furthermore, I felt increasingly uncomfortable with the hero worship of a handful of men who would fundraise within the movement to record debates with meat-eaters for their online branding. I saw peers in adjacent social movements engage in campaigns with specific demands, targets, and sometimes concrete wins, while here

I was, in the animal rights scene, spending my time just talking—with no metrics to measure efficacy.

This chapter will begin by exploring who are elevated to leadership positions within the animal liberation movement. It will then discuss how the movement's hyperfocus on debates favors single-issue influencers who perpetuate a capitalist framework by taking an aggressive and antagonistic stance and promoting plant-based consumerism rather than veganism as an ideology that extends beyond food choices. I argue that activists' time in the movement would be better spent building coalitions to work toward a shared goal of total liberation. The chapter concludes with a broad discussion about strategy, highlighting the importance of addressing all five points of intervention and embracing a diversity of tactics and strategies from an intersectional, anti-capitalist lens in order to achieve not just animal liberation but liberation for all. Despite my many criticisms of how the animal liberation movement fixates on educational outreach, I'm not trying to minimize the importance of conversation, public speaking, rhetoric, and persuasion; rather, I'm taking issue with the debate culture that treats "owning" someone in the marketplace of ideas as the ultimate goal and that the animal liberation movement glorifies and pours money into.

REDEFINING LEADERSHIP: RATIONALISM AND DEBATE FIXATIONS

With educational outreach seemingly considered the pinnacle of animal liberation activism, the misconception that we can simply talk our way to a vegan world has brought about a specific idea of who is a leader. Leadership is often associated with fame, and those who rise to fame and secure ample funding are generally conventionally attractive, white, cis-hetero men promoting single-issue, white veganism. For example, Ed Winters from the United Kingdom and Joey Carbstrong and James Aspey from Australia are three individuals who are placed on a pedestal in the mainstream movement. But what unique contributions do they make that are supposedly worthy of so many people's support? Ed Winters, at least, runs a nonprofit, Surge, and an animal sanctuary. So the majority (though by no means the entirety) of my criticism is aimed at Carbstrong and Aspey, who win debates with strangers on the street.

With memorized elevator pitches and statistics, they swiftly respond to any counterargument thrown their way. My aim is not to minimize the importance of communication skills but to argue that the fetishized recording and posting of debates dunking on nonvegans is not an overall effective tactic for the movement. Since men are considered uniquely rational under patriarchy—in contrast with "emotional" women and "instinctual" animals (Figueroa-Helland and Lindgren 2016)—the obsession with educational outreach leads to the majority of attention and financial resources being disproportionately spent on debates such as Winters's, Carbstrong's, and Aspey's rather than on animal sanctuaries or other invaluable efforts. Janet O'Shea (2021) addresses these gendered lines of activism that sideline what is considered feminized labor, like the care sanctuaries provide. There are many examples of organizations that do crucial work in the movement—such as Food Empowerment Project, which advocates food choices that oppose animal abuse, natural-resource depletion, poor working conditions, and food apartheid, or Black Vegans Rock, a platform founded by theorist and indie digital media producer Aph Ko, which is dedicated to spotlighting Black vegans and debunking the myth that veganism is for white people. To rattle off a few more, Rancher Advocacy Program (RAP) helps farmers and ranchers transition out of animal agriculture; Agriculture Fairness Alliance (AFA) created the first hub to centralize vegan voters to push for policy change; and Coalition to Abolish the Fur Trade (CAFT) is a stellar example of an effective pressure campaign against a major industry as demonstrated by the work of its U.S.-based organizers, who have forced all eight companies they've targeted to date to go fur-free (CAFT 2022). These examples represent the numerous types of advocacy that are instrumental in actualizing a vegan world and that are deserving of our time and resources—beyond simply winning debates.

We must challenge the perception that white men are our sole leaders and the ensuing hero-worshipping from much of the mainstream movement that believes they will talk everyone into veganism. pattrice jones from VINE Sanctuary in Vermont urges us to "rethink the starstruck tenor of much of the animal rights movement," writing:

175

> I understand the utility of sometimes asking celebrities to use their platforms to advocate for animals or demonstrate the deliciousness of veganism. But this has somehow morphed into a kind of celebrity culture within the animal rights movement itself, in which "conferences" consist of movement "stars" pontificating to the masses rather than peers conferring with each other. (jones 2014)

This highlights the current culture wherein a few talking heads are unquestioned, thereby taking away from the necessary community conversations and decision-making that foster a diversity of perspectives and approaches. Converging with jones's stance, Brockington's (2014) analysis of celebrity influence in movements leads to the suggestion that "these associations are best avoided" or that we significantly limit when celebrity appearances are considered appropriate and useful (104). Likewise, Jake Conroy (2021a), known as The Cranky Vegan, gives valuable commentary on the danger of treating influencers as beyond reproach to the point where civil discourse is stifled and criticism is "met with hostility," noting that he believes James Aspey and Joey Carbstrong have "all reached that point." It's not surprising that these individuals rose to stardom when we consider how conventional forms of leadership place importance on individual charisma, assertiveness, aggressiveness, and public speaking. Since these are characteristics that men are encouraged to embody, "the dominant model of leadership in our society is a masculinized one," making leadership heavily influenced by patriarchy (Dixon 2014, 177).

Hegemonic ideas of leadership and who can be a leader are showcased in online media. As Zeynep Tüfekçi (2017) describes it, "although online media are indeed more open and participatory, over time a few people consistently emerge as informal but persistent spokespersons—with large followings on social media" (xxiii). Clashes in the online space between these "de facto spokespersons" and others in the movement can be frustrating when the movement has "few means to resolve their issue or make decisions" (Tüfekçi 2017, xxiii–xxiv). Though social media allows everyone to access its platforms, certain personalities will rise to the top and have the largest sway in the movement, which can lead to tension, insularity, and marginalization of truly revolutionary, intersectional, anti-capitalist perspectives on veganism.

To relate the dynamics of social media to the context of influencers in the animal liberation movement, I draw upon my earlier mention of Ed Winters, who, in addition to his endless debates, runs an animal sanctuary. This is noteworthy because activism that's feminized, such as caretaking, is also minimized (Dixon 2014)—despite how crucial it is, especially in the case of the animal liberation movement. Vergès's book *A Decolonial Feminism* (2022) is a brilliant illustration of feminized work on a global scale and a powerful call for solidarity with the women who clean and care for the world under a hetero-patriarchal, extractivist, capitalist organization of the economy. Her decolonial feminism witnesses the entanglement of capitalism, imperialism, and patriarchy—all of which marginalize the crucial work of cleaning, which is overwhelmingly done by women of color. Within the animal liberation movement, animal sanctuaries play the vital role of caring for nonhuman individuals who freed themselves through escape or were liberated by activists and given the ability to live out the rest of their lives free of exploitation and systemic violence. Yet this work does not appear to drum up the fanfare or funding that the Patreon of a man recording himself debating in a YouTube video or Instagram post does. A critique of this misguided prioritization within the animal liberation movement is not new, as McGregor (2022) writes:

> In place of the logic of domination, ecofeminists have explored alternative values and approaches that have been repressed by the privileging of white male masculinities. Feminine values such as empathy (Gruen 2013), compassion (Curtin 2014), joy (Slicer 2014), and care (Donovan and Adams 2007) are promoted as important influences for improved more-than-human relations. (314)

Moreover, many ecofeminists have long since identified how feminized labor (e.g., the grueling work of taking care of rescued animals in sanctuaries) is sidelined in favor of more masculine forms of advocacy. This indispensable labor must be brought to the forefront of the movement.

In the case of Ed Winters's sanctuary, the marketing imagery deviates from that of sanctuaries that focus on the animal residents. Winters, given his celebrity status, is often the focal point: one image used to promote the sanctuary features him centered, with the animals shown as small images in the backdrop. While the matter may seem trivial, I argue that this is intentional branding that draws the focus to the celebrity activist rather than to the farmed animals we (and Winters) are supposedly fighting for. So, in a case in which a celebrity activist engages in care labor, he still manages to make himself the center of attention—which indicates our vulnerability to the trap of funneling the movement's resources to a handful of charismatic celebrities rather than to effective grassroots organizing.

Rather than elevating a select few spokespeople as heroes of animal liberation, the movement would benefit from shifting to an inclusive and empowering ideal of leadership whereby a leader is defined as "someone who thinks about the group and helps it function effectively" (Myers-Lipton 2017, 22). In this sense, potentially everyone can be a leader. To provide a concrete example, this shift would mean fighting against James Aspey and his pump-and-dump cryptocurrency scams (The Cranky Vegan 2022a)—schemed by his financial advisor Randy, an incoherent Trump and QAnon supporter (The Cranky Vegan 2021b; Kirkwood 2021)—and reallocating funds to the many struggling animal sanctuaries around the world, to nonprofits and pressure campaigns serving the collective good.

The animal liberation movement must prefigure the world we are actively working toward. There is tension between a goal of total liberation and a movement that glorifies a handful of men debating, thereby overshadowing the vital projects taken on by a diverse community of vegans. As Dixon (2014) puts it: "We struggle with thorny social hierarchies as they play out in our movements and in society more generally. We try to build the world we would like to see through the ways in which we struggle" (4). A struggle that values only one tactic and one identity will never succeed in achieving total liberation (and may not even succeed in achieving its singular goal). Perhaps we'd also benefit from this principle for community organizing (PICO): "No permanent allies, no permanent enemies, only permanent interests" (Institute for Community Organization n.d., 1). Rather than focusing on the identities and images of vegan influencers and celebrities who are beyond reproach, we must return to the end goal of total liberation.

Moreover, the gendered nature of social hierarchies in the movement is illustrated in pattrice jones's (2014) book *The Oxen at the Intersection*—an account of Green Mountain College's steadfast pursuit to kill two oxen held captive and enslaved for labor, Bill and Lou, once they no longer held any use value to humans, despite a global public outcry. jones witnessed people, particularly men, jump into the discourse, making the situation an abstract intellectual exercise in debate, rather than centering the life-or-death stakes playing out in real time. Furthermore, these men didn't bother asking jones and the others at VINE Sanctuary, which had started the campaign to save Bill and Lou in the first place, about their strategy and the role they played. As neighbors of Green Mountain College, those at VINE Sanctuary had familiarity with the context of animal agriculture in the state of Vermont and other place-based knowledge that would undeniably benefit a united effort to liberate Bill and Lou. Reflecting on how the logic of domination and rationalism undermined the focus on Bill and Lou, jones pointedly states that "in preferring reason to emotion and pretending that they are separate, [Bill and Lou's advocates] may have inadvertently endorsed the very mind-over-matter mentality that led the oxen to be in such a precarious position to begin with" (2014, 185). Instead of asking how animal advocates could work together, these men hijacked the situation to further their careers through garnering online attention via "rational" debates.

Building Coalitions and Rejecting the Vegan-versus-Nonvegan Framing

The mainstream animal movement is fixated on the social media accounts and personalities of a handful of vegan influencers, like Winters, Carbstrong, and Aspey, rather than focusing on the collective good, coalition building, and tactical diversification to achieve animal liberation. This current framing of veganism as an individual consumer choice is one that people like Winters perpetuate when they focus on commodities like Beyond Meat products as "solutions" rather than on an analysis of how animal exploitation is embedded in the fabric of the economic order. To better address speciesism, the movement should frame veganism as a social and political problem. Myers-Lipton (2017) discusses how recognizing what might initially seem to be a personal problem as actually a social problem can lead to collective action and thus progress. This is not as simple as denouncing capitalism and yelling something abstract like "smash capitalism," which cannot be turned into a simple plan or action item. A better use of our time and energy is "collectively fashioning more elaborated visions [to develop] strategies that are genuinely revolutionary" (Dixon 2014, 137).

We must begin coalition building by framing our calls to action in a way that resonates with future allies. An effective framing is value-laden and forges connections to values shared with future allies and the general public (Myers-Lipton 2017). It's integral to the success of a movement to tie its values into larger collective values because we need power in numbers to create change. As Montréal-based organizer Tatiana Gomez says, "I don't think we're going to build a movement with about a hundred anarchists in every major city" (Dixon 2014, 117). When our messaging stays within the confines of our like-minded social groups, we do not build momentum in movements. When the radical politics of anarchism is limited to self-marginalizing anarchists, there is no chance of a societal shift (Dixon 2014). And within the self-marginalizing left, leftist animal liberation activists, already a small faction, further segregate themselves as "orphans of the Left" in an all-too-common pursuit of a single-issue approach to veganism that alienates other causes (Kymlicka and Donaldson 2014, 1). Instead of falling into this trap, "we need to engage with ordinary people and popular struggles" to make animal liberation applicable to our communities at large, to people who may not share our love of animals (Dixon 2014, 117). That is not to say that we should abandon studying the intersections of animal liberation and anarchist philosophy, but this should not be our baseline expectation to grant entry into the movement.

We build coalitions by looking at our spectrum of allies—a term created by the Ruckus Society (n.d.)—that is, the gradient from people who are ideologically aligned with us, to those who marginally sympathize with part of our cause, to our active opponents. It is valuable to map out who makes up the groups on this spectrum, to help us deliberate how to move each group closer toward us. Unfortunately, the animal liberation movement has struggled to intentionally move the popular imagination regarding which ideas are considered to be permissible, often getting stuck in purity politics. It's more productive to partner with communities fighting against corporations putting factory farms in their towns on account of the environmental destruction and decreased property values, for instance, than to whine that they aren't vegan and refuse to collaborate. In addition to inviting other social justice activists into the animal liberation movement, animal activists must recognize the interconnected nature of human and animal oppressions and organize alongside these other activists for mutual expansion and integration of our inherently linked causes. Each activist, scholar, and journalist who contributed to Z. Zane McNeill's *Vegan Entanglements* (2022) identifies the enmeshed nature of speciesism and capitalism, which necessitates a collective liberation approach that we can make possible only by working alongside one another and addressing the intersections of oppressive systems, manifested as the animal–industrial complex, the prison–industrial complex, and more, underpinned by the same carceral and white-supremacist logics. As Stubler (2022) puts it, the animal liberation movement "urgently need[s] to stop instrumentalizing other struggles and instead begin to authentically join their fight" to build multi-justice coalitions that are mutually beneficial for marginalized animals and human communities alike (116).

Instead of looking at how we can harness shared interests, the animal liberation movement perpetuates a divisive framing that focuses on the duality of vegans versus nonvegans and that deters coalition building. One need not look further than celebrity activist Joey Carbstrong's YouTube videos with titles like "SLAUGHTERHOUSE WORKER VS VEGAN," "FARMER VS VEGAN," "VEGAN VS MEATEATER," in a playlist aggressively titled "JOEY VERSUS THE PUBLIC" (Carbstrong 2022, emphasis original). Recognizing that part of the strategy is producing clickbait titles to drive engagement, I still do not believe this framing is in the movement's long-term best interest as it pits Carbstrong, the vegan, against the public when he should be building rapport and recruiting new vegan activists. In particular, pitting slaughterhouse workers against vegans is a grave misstep: as Stubler (2022) points out, animal advocates commonly vilify slaughterhouse workers, many of whom are undocumented immigrant workers or poor people of color and are marginalized. Pinning the blame on disenfranchised workers obscures the real perpetrators of violence—the capital owners and corporations profiteering from animal agriculture. This blame game often ends in the imprisonment and/or deportation of the lowest-level workers—people in dire straights—rather than the punishment of their bosses, those guilty of crimes against humans and animals alike. To move the needle, animal liberation activists must band together with champions of worker and immigrant rights and address these intersecting problems from an anti-capitalist, anti-racist lens; we must cease attacking incredibly vulnerable workers who were forced into one of the most dangerous occupations, from which they're likely to suffer from Perpetration-Induced Traumatic Stress Disorder (PITS) and severe injuries (Dillard 2008).

Moreover, we need to sit at the table with vegans, nonvegans, and veg-curious folks to create alliances instead of perpetuating this harsh divide. Viewing others as not-yet-vegans could aid in this shift in praxis. Also potentially helpful is this principle for community organizing (PICO): "People cannot be held responsible for what they do not understand" (Institute for Community Organization n.d., 1). Rather than shutting down nonvegans or "owning" them in debates, we must see speciesism for what it is—a largely invisible and unquestioned oppressive system that many were indoctrinated into during childhood. This gets us away from vegan exceptionalism, defined by Shelton (2023) as "the harmful idea that vegans are different from and morally superior to other people," which undermines collective liberation by failing to acknowledge how the systems and structures perpetuating speciesism also oppress marginalized humans, thereby throwing people to the wayside rather than organizing together (123). It takes copious amounts of unlearning to dream of a non-speciesist world and acknowledge the need for educational outreach, yet it is far from the only work to be done.

The apparent unwillingness to work with a spectrum of allies who may not be 100 percent ideologically aligned may in part be perpetuated by a celebrity culture in the movement wherein top-tier activism is seen as flashy YouTube video titles rather than forged partnerships across movements. Jennai Bundock's presentation "The Hidden Cost of Patriarchy" (2014) asks why we're surprised to be surrounded by domineering men and why our organizers' meetings can feel so frustrating when our recruitment materials target the lowest common denominator through, for example, sexualized images of women's bodies, as in the case of PETA. For her graduate research, Bundock studied veganism as a social movement and people's journeys to becoming vegan. She found that many men came to the movement because of organizations like PETA, which uses street demonstrations sexualizing women to recruit animal advocates. As she argues, "we aren't actively recruiting the people we want to see sitting next to us in our movement," as demonstrated by the rampant sexual harassment and violence in the animal activism space. Most important, Bundock encourages us to make a conscious effort to recruit our friends "that are with it, and [. . .] understand some other struggle" by going to, for example, "the anti-nuke movement and feminist organizing circles"—and to require worthwhile conversations about why animal liberation should be taken seriously (Bundock 2014). This is a particularly salient point about the current state of the animal liberation movement because until we can forge these relationships with adjacent social justice movements, we will not build coalitions—especially not with framings like "vegan versus farmer" or "vegan versus the public" that circumvent the systemic drivers of speciesism and only blame individuals.

RETHINKING THE ENTIRE STRATEGY

The previous sections have discussed the shortcomings of focusing only on and glorifying educational outreach, as well as the need to reallocate resources through redefining leadership and building coalitions. This section will focus on the importance of strategy in the animal liberation movement. Educational outreach has been a staple in the movement since its inception, yet the number of nonhuman animals killed per year continues to rise, the government still heavily subsidizes animal agriculture, and a global pandemic has not been enough to push the general public to rethink humankind's relationship with other species, even though "3 in every 4 new or emerging infectious diseases in people come from animals" (CDC 2021, n.p.). Insanity is often described as doing the same thing over and over and expecting different results; if so, educational outreach increasingly feels like insanity. For this reason, the animal liberation movement must look at a strategic diversification of tactics to fight for collective liberation.

Harkening back to Dixon's (2014) notion that "we try to build the world we would like to see through the ways in which we struggle" (4), we should note that the animal liberation movement is largely about bodily autonomy and consent, yet many big names in the mainstream movement violate these principles in secretly recording passers-by at outreach events and posting their conversations online for thousands or millions of people to view. While the outreachers may be "winning" the debates with their memorized talking points and an arsenal of statistics, I'd argue it is not a good look to use this skill as a weapon against pedestrians who were not expecting to have their core, if invisible, beliefs challenged on their way to grab a coffee or run errands, let alone have the conversation (likely the first) in which this fundamental part of them is challenged be posted online. Therefore, it's imperative that we, as animal activists, reassess how we approach educational outreach based on actual studies of human psychology.

We should take a step back to see how educational outreach fits into a larger strategy in order to leverage it as one important piece of the broader puzzle. With each educational outreach event, we could work toward a win by tying it to a specific ask, whether that's signing on to a campaign, writing a letter to legislators, or something else. In his *Are We Winning?* series, Jake Conroy encourages a shift toward pressure campaigns that achieve concrete wins to inspire activists to continue their grassroots work in the long haul, thereby building our collective resiliency and strength (The Cranky Vegan 2021c; 2022b).

ADDRESSING THE FIVE POINTS OF INTERVENTION

Story-based strategy "is a participatory approach that links movement building with an analysis of narrative power and places *storytelling at the center of social change*" (Center for Story-Based Strategy n.d.). The Center for Story-Based Strategy outlines five major points of intervention to help orient change-making efforts. The shortcomings of hyperfocusing on one type of advocacy aside, educational outreach addresses only one point of intervention, the point of assumption (The Cranky Vegan 2020), in challenging "underlying beliefs" and "control mythologies" (Center for Story-Based Strategy n.d.). While this is indeed an important part of changing culture, I believe it's incredibly unlikely that we can create a vegan world without also focusing on the other four points of intervention. To help animal liberation activists apply this framework to their work, Conroy lists a few examples with each point:

- Point of production: Factories, breeders
- Point of destruction: Slaughterhouses, fur/dairy/meat farms, and laboratories
- Point of consumption: Restaurants, grocery stores
- Point of decision: Board room, office building, and neighborhood (where contracts are signed)
- Point of assumption: Beliefs, politics, and values

In the video, he also creates an incredibly helpful visual of the five points of intervention, using an anti-dairy campaign as an example, that can be a guide for animal activists to map out a strategic campaign (The Cranky Vegan 2020). For further examples of the five points of intervention in social movement organizing, Andrew Boyd's *Beautiful Trouble: A Toolbox for Revolution* (2016) (see also Reinsborough and Canning 2016 in Boyd) has a chapter dedicated to case studies that can inspire animal liberation activism.

The success of educational outreach can't be quantified. No matter how effective our talking points may be at persuading folks to consider going vegan, the rate at which new people are born and raised as nonvegans far exceeds the rate of our *hopeful* conversions (I emphasize "hopeful" because we don't track who becomes vegan after these one-off conversations). A counterargument is that the same conversations, when recorded and posted on YouTube and social media, will reach thousands or millions of people. A view on YouTube is counted when a person watches at least thirty seconds of a video (Google/YouTube Help 2022) and a view on Facebook lasts at least three seconds (Meta n.d.). So, going by the number of views alone, we do not know how many have completed the video, nor do we know how this translates to interest in or actual veganism. With this format, we do not have the data to ascertain if these debating activists are mostly preaching to the choir—vegan viewers seeking the catharsis of vicariously winning debates—or actually reaching and changing the hearts and minds of veg-curious and not-yet-vegan folks.

INTERCONNECTIONS OF CAPITALISM AND SPECIESISM

Given the shortcomings of the movement's overreliance on educational outreach, it's obligatory that we rethink our overarching strategies, which is no small feat. Creating a strategy requires us to wrestle with the questions of why the problem exists and why it hasn't been solved, as well as to theorize about what we can do to solve it. As Ganz (2015) writes:

> And because those who resist change (and who don't have the problem) often have access to greater amounts of resources, those who seek change (and do have the problem) have to be more resourceful. And we have to use our resourcefulness to create the capacity—the power—to get the problem solved. It's not so much about getting "more" resources as it is about using one's resources. Strategy is creative, linking resources to outcomes through intentional choice of tactics. (4)

Indeed, there may be an incentive for famous vegan influencers to lean into educational outreach and fixate on plugging Beyond Burgers and selling the idea that we can shop our way to a vegan world. This approach to advocacy does not challenge the status quo as it buys into the capitalist fallacy of "voting with one's dollar"; thus, vegan influencers keep their donors' pockets lined and their Patreons placated with familiar propaganda. The rich and privileged remain unchallenged when our movement is watered down to consumer purchases that corporations profit from. We'd be more likely to succeed if we reallocated our limited resources toward attacking the supply rather than the demand chain. There is no incentive for a business to limit its own clientele when it can make more money by diversifying its products, selling both animal- and plant-based foods. Richard White (2018), for example, offers a thoughtful analysis of how the mainstream adoption of the vegan diet has detached veganism from its radical leftist roots and transformed it into a profitable market. Therefore, we must be strategic in our approach so that we are not stuck in a cycle of talking individuals into changing their grocery lists—we will never reach a tipping point this way. The explicit tie between capitalism and speciesism, briefly touched on elsewhere in this chapter, has been analyzed abundantly by scholars: Bob Torres (2007), in his book *Making a Killing: The Political Economy of Animal Rights*, investigates how the converging issues of labor, property, and commodification sustain animal exploitation and thus why the animal liberation movement needs to be anti-capitalist. David Nibert (2017) details in the two-volume set *Animal Oppression and Capitalism* how capitalism leads to unimaginable amounts of harm to animals, humans, and the environment. And White (2017) posits that capitalism has enveloped much of the animal liberation movement, replacing radical vegan sentiments with optional, consumer or lifestyle choices.

Ultimately, to escape these capitalist trappings, we can force corporations to capitulate to our demands through strategic campaigning with explicit targets, the success of which has been continually proven by organizations like CAFT. Instead of wishful thinking that "planting seeds" through educational outreach will turn everyone vegan, we need concrete campaign goals that "build on our ethical commitments and ground us in popular struggles" (Dixon 2014, 137). We can set such goals using the SMART criteria (**s**pecific, **m**easurable, **a**ctivating, **r**ealistic, and **t**ime-specific) to hold ourselves accountable.

IDENTIFYING THE AUDIENCE, THE ASK, AND THE TARGET

Another major component of strategizing is identifying the audience. To do this, we need to be able to say *whom* we are organizing, to *what* outcome, *how*, and by *when*—taking the campaign beyond the educational component (Ganz 2015, 10). We need to decide, say, if a particular effort is targeting meat-avoiders or meat-eaters, as a Faunalytics study suggests that certain approaches are more effective for particular groups based on their eating habits. The same study also finds that graphic content is polarizing: many people are moved to sadness, disgust, or anger by the shocking reality it exposes, while just as many become disengaged (Polanco, Parry, and Anderson 2022). Likewise, University of Buffalo professor Sunyee Woon's study on the "guilt of the meat-eating consumer" finds that "when most people feel guilty about eating meat, they don't eat less of it" but "simply justify their choice by picking a meat dish that's prepared in a healthier way." Based on the overall result, Yoon suggests that effective messaging aimed at reducing meat consumption should both induce guilt by elevating animals' human-like characteristics and debunk misinformation about meat's nutritional value (Biddle 2021). Thus, the animal liberation movement would benefit from presenting information in a multitude of ways to anticipate different psychological responses across the population.

After identifying its audience, a campaign needs to have one to three demands directed at the person with the authority to meet the demand(s) (Myers-Lipton 2017). It can take much necessary groundwork to devise effective campaigns, yet the results are far more tangible than the "seeds" planted through educational outreach that cannot be measured. It's important to note that not all asks are equally conducive to data collection. For example, the ask in educational outreach is often that individuals try a vegan diet for however many days, but there's a lack of data on the impact of such vegan challenges (Polanco, Parry, and Anderson 2022). Ergo, it would be worthwhile to design asks that can lead to concrete wins, like a company no longer selling a particular product.

Closing Thoughts:
Finding a Home for Education Outreach in Pressure Campaigns

Educational outreach, including online videos of in-person conversations, could still be integrated into campaigns so that we aren't just spreading awareness but also asking people to engage with the movement. As Jake Conroy puts it:

> We can continue to do educational outreach. Educational outreach
> is a super important part of broader corporate campaigns—of pres
> sure campaigns. Can you imagine if the million people that are
> watching each of your videos not only considered veganism—[but]
> also wrote an email or signed a petition or went to a demonstra
> tion or participated in a specific campaign to target an individual
> corporation? [. . .] Let's start tearing these systems down at the roots,
> right? At the slaughterhouses, at the corporations that are fund
> ing these places, the places that are subsidizing them—the places
> that are making this an acceptable thing in society. Instead of just
> simply asking the individual, "Hey, maybe you can change your
> diet?" Because this is not working. (The Cranky Vegan 2018, 6, 40)

By combining educational outreach and pressure campaigning, we could build power by mobilizing large groups of people to coerce a particular target into meeting our demands. As the Ruckus Society (n.d.) lays out, the educational component, taking the form of, say, workshops, is often the beginning of a campaign. However, the campaign does not end here: afterward comes organization building, whereby we work on nurturing coalitions and alliances, negotiating with the target, devising low-level confrontational tactics if necessary, and so on (Ruckus Society n.d.). Taking a hard look at strategy allows us to move beyond debating the validity of tactics toward "considering how those tactics fit into overall plans to achieve something" (Dixon 2014, 113).

To begin building more campaigns and strengthening the powerful work many grassroots organizations are already engaged in, we need to diversify our activism. An incredible resource is Andrew Boyd's book *Beautiful Trouble: A Toolbox for Revolution* (2016), a collection of stories, tactics, theories, principles, and methodologies for creative, effective organizing that can support the movement's efforts. To grow both personally and collectively, we "go in dumb, come out smart" (Institute for Community Organization n.d., 1), finding what works and what doesn't and sharing our experiences with fellow organizers—to expand our collective skillsets beyond memorized elevator pitches for educational outreach.

The animal liberation movement has been stagnating from pouring too many resources into educational outreach, mistakenly viewed as the pinnacle of tactics. Besides the fact that it is never wise to bank on one tactic to solve everything, the "debate me" style of educational outreach meant to generate maximum online clicks, especially, has been counterproductive since it is shaped by dominant ideas of leadership that are exclusive to certain identities and does not leave enough resources to support other types of leaders, coalition building, or strategic pressure campaigns with tangible goals. And worshipping straight, white men who argue with unsuspecting strangers is even less helpful. To achieve animal liberation, we need to challenge structures and systems, using a diversity of tactics and working within a larger strategy that is unapologetically anti-capitalist and intertwines our movement with human rights movements. Until we collectively reflect on our failings and reorganize our movement, the number of nonhuman animals killed per year will continue to rise. Planting seeds is not enough. It's time to get organized, launch campaigns, and coexist with our fellow organizers in intersecting movements.

CHAPTER THIRTEEN

Teaching and Learning Critical Animal Studies: Treading and Shredding the Line

Sarah May Lindsay

INTRODUCTION

I am neither a scholar nor an activist. I am an imposter.

I was a graduate student, teaching other graduate students about a field I felt aligned with yet excluded from. At course end, I was hopeful, proud, and enormously empty. But this was just a class, all these feelings would pass, and the students would move on and forget. And this might be okay if it was just any course, but it was not. It was an introduction to critical animal studies (CAS), and at the time, it was the only sociological orientation I knew of that "felt right."

Critical animal studies is interdisciplinary; indeed, it must be to tackle the complexity and "everywhereness" of its focus: speciesism and anthropocentrism (Matsuoka and Sorenson 2018; Sorenson and Matsuoka 2022), and the so-called truncated narrative (Kheel 1993) upheld in dominant discourse about the magnitude and impact of oppressive power structures, which are built upon intersectional "isms." These "isms" are socially constructed categories often used to maintain or create oppressive conditions and tied to discrimination based on supposed differences. They are compounding and intersecting, creating unique experiences of injustice and power imbalances (see, for example, Crenshaw 1990).

This critical auto-ethnography focuses on the experience of intro-ducing CAS to students in an animal studies graduate program. Three themes emerge in my analysis: imposter syndrome, activist-scholar-ship, and welfarism versus liberationism. These themes are in some ways deductive, as teaching about CAS includes discussing the various stances held in human societies about nonhuman-animal care, relation-ships, uses or purposes, and liberation. Although I write from a domi-nant, Western societal perspective, it is remarkable (and horrible) that one would be hard-pressed to find a human society on Earth that does not use nonhuman animals in some way, let alone to locate an inclu-sive, equitable, multispecies society. I am also familiar with imposter syndrome as well as activist-scholarship; the latter describes the orien-tation of my dissertation. Inductively, I identify a set of assumptions I unconsciously had about myself; the course; the school, department, and program; and my students. These beliefs are examined thematically and self-*reflexively* in the following sections.

Approach and Grounding

I felt an odd and almost unmanageable excitement about interacting with folks and discussing other animals intentionally. For me, the COVID-19 pandemic solidified where my comfort and strength in academia lie, and even though I have had all sorts of support and teaching positions, I was perpetually angst- and anxiety-ridden, absolutely hating what I was doing. I preferred to grade and evaluate (yes, really), and learn and research. Having to "show up" and be an "authority" made me tremble physically, sweat, and vomit, and I relied on tranquilizers and random explosions of rage to combat what I knew: I hated to teach others; I wanted to work independently. Every lesson was a countdown until it was done. Every week was one fewer that I had to endure. And this remains true, but there are two enormous improvements that have removed a significant portion of the discomfort: online classes and not having to travel.

This is not to say that the course in question (which was held online and mostly asynchronous) was not anxiety-producing: I still disliked having to record lectures, and the "live" group chats reliably produced stomach and nerve responses. But I can say that I did not hate teaching the course. And the experience and interactions moved me to tears, evoked a sense of pride, and renewed my flame, so I could continue. So, what to do with the contradictory feelings that the experience left me with? There was an odd sense of finding my space but then realizing I did not have a space at all—I had nowhere to continue this work; I felt that it was rejected or not supported in my PhD project. (This was somewhat of a misconception: I had failed to champion it, tease it apart, and fully deploy it in my dissertation analysis, but there was no pushback on its eventual use in my research.) This was but one course, and there was no guarantee that I would ever teach it again. However, the "not just a course" theme arose not through a bureaucratic brawl about the content and relevance as Flynn (2003) and undoubtedly countless others experienced in early (and maybe even current) attempts to include other animals in sociology, but out of my inexperience teaching CAS and the unexpected effects that teaching what I was passionate about would have.

Thus, this chapter is self-reflexive. "The term 'reflexive' is used to denote actions that direct attention back to the self and foster a circular relationship between subject and object" (Probst 2015, 37). The task is to critically observe and evaluate the self, or (to attempt) to objectively work with the self as the subject (Probst 2015). In other words, in this chapter, I review my thoughts and actions and examine and specu-late on their reasons and effects. The "data" are my feelings, actions, and thoughts. Specifically, here, how I emotionally, intellectually, and cognitively experienced the course and my interactions with students is the focus. As Probst (2015) notes, this is an epistemological point, not a methodological one. Methodologically, this study is qualitative, relying on self-reflection.

Critical auto-ethnography (CAE) is an "interdisciplinary approach to research [that] centers the self as a site of inquiry" (Marx, Pennington, and Chang 2017, 2). The "critical" component, as in all critical sociologi-cal approaches, seeks to uncover, understand, and challenge or change power imbalances and oppression. The course at hand is based specifi-cally on work that illuminates and critiques speciesist and anthropocen-tric power structures and systems; it is "on animals" and "for animals." Further, self-reflexivity is used here to identify and interrogate or begin to work with (1) my thoughts and beliefs about myself, (2) if and how my actions impact myself as well as others, and (3) my belief in the exceptional and "only" or "right" way for/to animal liberation (whatever that means).

It is hard to avoid self-reflection when you habitually review the minutiae of your actions ad nauseam. For example, as I think, say, or type each word, I evaluate it, aiming to not misspeak, to share only informed points of view, to not be "wrong." I review my actions at length for days afterward and at random times seemingly until forever, with fleeting mental "check marks" for things well done but recurring "stomach flips" of anger and embarrassment about what I did or did not do—a constant orchestra of screwups, with a backup choir of critics (i.e., whoever I was speaking to and people who may "hear about it"; sometimes, my late mom even pops in with a few scathing remarks). Why do I do this? Is it useful? Is it to search for little glimmers of reassurance or recognition? Perhaps it would be if I dwelled on successes, but this is not the case.

However, self-reflexivity is made easier by this "neurosis." "Critical auto-ethnography" is perhaps just another way of saying "informed searching and confrontation." The technique is performed by the subject on the subject, with a parallel understanding that the process will be uncomfortable, perhaps painful, as one attempts to evaluate the self: one's actions, thoughts, and "worldview." In this process (and because of it), one learns about the self—oneself. Critical theorists are trained to see the system and the individual, as well as the system in the individual and the individual in the system, and to use methods such as ethnography to immerse themselves in/with their subjects. However, adding the "auto" (self) to "critical ethnography" presents a slew of additional challenges as well as rewards. I had to answer to more than external evaluators. In this case, I use CAE to examine how I designed and conducted my first course in CAS, based on assumptions about the topic, the learners, and my role. I had to cast my change-oriented, critical gaze on my knowledge, my work, and my self-world. This was perhaps made messier by the disparaging way I view and speak to myself. At the same time, there is no better reason to take this approach, since one can control and work with only oneself: the saying "change starts with you" could not be more relevant and instructive (and powerful) in critical auto-ethnographical work.

ASSUMPTIONS

I identify four types of assumptions I held about this course in critical animal studies. They were present vaguely for the most part, although assumptions about the course structure arose out of the inescapable necessity to develop the syllabus (there was none provided to me, and the finished document was accepted without question). I also made assumptions about challenges the course might present for students (individually or collectively) in general, and about the students. These assumptions were not recognized at course conception and were unconsciously tested throughout the course. They were only recognized through self-reflexivity, which was central to the analysis.

Assumptions about the students:
• I knew who the audience was.
• Students would be, at the very least, "animal lovers."
• Student demographics would vary, but there would likely be more women/femmes and younger, recently graduated students.
• There might be differences in prior knowledge, familiarity with teaching traditions/styles, and expectations due to the course's not being in my location and training/education system.

Assumptions about the course structure:
• Students would appreciate:
    • The fairly minimal workload and assignment distribution;
    • The chance to interact with peers;
    • The chance to discuss and connect their own lives to the course material and;
    • The creative and fairly unrestricted zine format of the final assignment.
• Engagement would be good, but similar to that in an upper-year undergraduate course.
• Documentaries would be more effective than articles/chapters in evoking reactions and reflections from the students.
• The most effective way of running weekly meetings and judging participation would be interactive discussion boards.

195

- The frequency of discussion posts and interactions would likely be minimal/fair to good.

Assumptions about challenges the course might present for students (individually or collectively):

- There might be emotional and passionate discussions.
- There might be some students unable to engage with (some of) the material.
- It might be difficult to encourage and sustain discussion and engagement each week.

Other assumptions:

- It would be challenging for me to (re)engage with the material at length.
- There might be some dissatisfaction with a graduate student teaching other graduate students.
- I might be "called out" as unqualified, biased, ineffective, or "too emotional" by the students.

THEMATIC SELF-REFLECTION

Some of the above assumptions seem benign, more like observations. Others clearly affect the students. All reflect how I interpret my strengths, abilities, and place as a vegan, an academic, and as a teacher. They also indicate a level of ignorance or bias (my own). Of course, this is unavoidable: one cannot be unbiased, as we all see and interact with our environment from a particular, unique point of view. This exercise in self-reflexivity is meant to expose my bias and question why I perceive and behave as I do. I take the perspective that perceptions and beliefs are fluid, cumulative, and changeable; this ontology is hopeful, applied to nonhuman-animal liberation (I write more about this later). Next, I analyze the act of teaching CAS via the themes of activist-scholarship, welfarism versus liberationism, and imposter syndrome.

ACTIVIST-SCHOLARSHIP

"Activist-scholarship" (Meyer 2005) refers to work that combines academic study with political activism, that leverages teaching, research, and related activities in support of social movements or community-based initiatives (Reynolds et al. 2018). It involves using one's academic skills and knowledge to challenge and critique systems of power and oppression, while also working toward social justice and transformation. A dichotomy is often supposed between those working in academia and those in the field or "on the ground" (Reynolds et al. 2018). Activist-scholarship produces knowledge while striving for positive social change.

As a vegan activist-sociologist working in the area of social inequity, specifically with injustices related to/impacting nonhuman animals, I have found myself confronted with the reality of inhabiting both academia and a social movement numerous times in my career. My research over-all, and this chapter, can thus be described as activist-scholarship.

Through a critical lens, a few of the preceding assumptions denote an activist-scholarship orientation. The assumption that "documentaries would be more effective than articles/chapters in evoking reactions and reflections from the students" is so oriented in two ways. First, students would get to see and be made to confront practices they may or may not have been aware of but undoubtedly participate in, at the very least as consumers. The film *Earthlings*, for example, portrays the use, abuse, enslavement, and murder of nonhuman animals for five key purposes: for food, entertainment, scientific experimentation, petkeeping, and clothing (Monson 2005). The simple (clearly demonstrating the subject) and graphic (real) nature of *Earthlings* makes the film a "go-to" for educators in fields like CAS: it explains and exposes the ways humans objectify, maim, and manipulate other beings, and it is difficult to watch. For these reasons, I chose it as the first of several documentaries in the course. Through a self-reflexive lens, parts of *Earthlings* have never left me. Two scenes, in particular, haunt me: a "stray" dog being thrown into the back of a garbage truck and crushed, and a fox being "skinned" alive. The film evoked a guttural response and sense of urgency in me—a feeling of horror, of rage and sadness. When I recall these scenes, I can almost feel them happening to me: my heart races, and I start to panic and quickly try to "turn off" the memory. I hoped that the film would have the same profound impact on my students. I wanted them to feel it too. I wanted them to care.

Second, documentaries would add visual and aural elements to the course. I wanted the group to understand why animal liberation is essential. Interestingly, during course design, I chose relevant documentaries hoping to explain and "make real" the course content. I speculated that perhaps students needed "to believe" by seeing and hearing nonhuman-animal abuse themselves, so that they would more clearly understand the subject. I assumed that students might not be aware, that they might be ignorant (why else would they participate in these horrific systems?). I did not know much about theories of learning—how we remember and apply knowledge (Ross, Maureen, and Schultz 2001)—at the time; this exposes the fact that at no point in my education had I received "teacher training," had I been presented with frameworks for learning or "learning styles." Since the course, I have investigated learning strategies and found a body of work that identifies sense-based elements of knowledge acquisition. The VARK model, with the first two letters in the acronym standing for Visual and Aural, suggests that different sensory modalities are used in learning—that is, some learn best by watching and/or listening to someone demonstrate or describe something (see, for example, Drago and Wagner 2004; Moazeni and Pourmohammadi 2013; VARK Learn Limited 2023). Without knowing it, I made the course more accessible to different types of learners by complementing the readings, lecture notes, and discussions with audio-visual material throughout. It seemed obvious to me that documentaries should be central to the course. Through a critical lens, I see that it was obvious not because I considered the varied learning styles of my students but because I wanted them to be offended, enraged, worried, mortified, and motivated. Were they? My attempt to use exposure as persuasion can be considered an activist tactic (however loosely designed).

Although I cannot draw directly from students' responses here for ethical (confidentiality) reasons, *Earthlings* did indeed move and mortify several students: a few mentioned that they had consciously avoided the film for years; some others spoke of how the assignment was so pain-ful that they could only watch portions of the film or that they had to spread viewing over several days. I was pleased with these expressions of discomfort through exposure (does this mean I do not actually care about individual students?). I was not surprised (but disappointed) that a few students took the "out" I provided, as with all the other docu-mentaries in the course: that they could "skip" the film if they took the time to read and respond to other students' summaries and reactions. Why did I give this option? In review, this was not out of respect for the students' "feelings" or "sensitivity," as I believe they should see and know the realities documented in the film. Ignorance is not an excuse. The nonhuman animals in the film, as well as those who came before and after it, must be seen and their stories known; the ongoing anthropo-centric notions that they are "ours" to do with as we wish, that they are "here for us," and that it is "normal" to use, abuse, enslave, torture, rape, and murder them are constructed fallacies based on power and domina-tion. I was disappointed with students who did not watch the assigned documentaries. Upon reflection, I see that this option emerged out of my concern about what I was "allowed" to do in the eyes of the depart-ment/program/school; I was worried that students might complain, that I could "get in trouble" for assigning such "disturbing" material. There was no such feedback before, during, or after the course, so this concern seems unfounded.

Another documentary, *Seaspiracy* (Tabrizi 2021), had a different effect, introducing students to the intersectionality of the subject. I included this film as an alternative to *The Cove* (Psihoyos 2009), another impor-tant account of "fishing" or, more accurately, the catching and killing of animals who live in water. Access was a determining factor, which, in retrospect, reveals a tactical concern for activist-scholars as well as documentary makers: if I could not find the documentary free online or through the institution's library, and if I did not have digital copy to share with the class, it would be unadvisable to assign the film for accessibility reasons. This point also highlights the expectation held by students and instructors alike that students should not have to pay (more) to obtain course material. Indeed, in my experience, in Canadian academic contexts, articles and even some e-textbooks are expected to be free to distribute, supported by access and distribution laws. I felt it unfair to ask students to pay for, say, a Netflix account or a digital copy in order to access audio-visual materials. This seems straightforward in hindsight, but I paid little attention to access rules and regulations in the school's region, which are different from those in my region and my experience, and could have run into a problem. Upon reflection, I am concerned that activist-scholars may encounter socioeconomic and/or regulatory roadblocks to distributing or facilitating access to pay-per-view or licensed materials. We should also question the barrier that is access to the internet, and a computer or another device to connect to it with, in order to pay for and obtain knowledge in the first place. My class was online, so this point may be moot. But that learners all have internet access is another assumption, is it not?

What was unexpected was that some students remarked most strongly on the inclusion of *Seaspiracy*, not *Earthlings*. These folks pointed out the controversy around the film—that some statistics and claims had since been said to be untrue or taken out of context; that classism and racism were apparent, with regional, cultural, and economic "needs" ("fishing" being "essential" for some people in some areas) negatively targeted; and that the film had a naivety stemming from an "extreme" Western "animal welfare" view (see, for example, Allen 2021; McVeigh 2021). It is remarkable how in tune some were with the subject, much more than I. Why was this? In retrospect, my view that fishing is unacceptable at all times clearly dismisses claims like "it's my job" or "we have no choice."

This reflection is troubling, especially since I believe in the concept of intersectionality, that oppression (caused by divisive categories built by/for control and power) compounds and is experienced uniquely by each individual and connected to their identity or sense of self (see, for example, Crenshaw 1990). Why did I not consider this element? I can conclude that I did, but I really did not care; I remain steadfast that the making and taking of "marine life" is unnecessary, environmentally and systemically destructive, and morally wrong. Is this a shortcoming or a dogmatic stance? Does this mean that I value nonhuman animals more than humans (this is, of course, a common criticism of nonhuman-animal rights activists)? What if the answer is yes? I did not directly express such a view, and this also reflects my discomfort with criticism and confrontation. I am uncomfortable openly "demonstrating"—or engaging in discussions in which I may have to defend—my liberationist view and alliance with "other animals." I do not want to argue. I want to point to and expose injustices, but I do not want to convince or lobby. Or is that what I am doing right now? These reflections highlight the messy line of activist-scholarship, which is more of a dance with emotions, politics, "customs" or "traditions," and the anthropocentricity of our systems and institutions.

I am certain of the urgency and essentiality of nonhuman-animal liberation, and I lean into the activist tactics of leading by example with a vegan lifestyle and exposing evils and injustices on social media, in my conversations, research, and teaching—this is outreach. What I have learned about this social position is that it is made easier by my whiteness, my place of residence and education (Canada), my first language (English), and my empathic tendencies. My actions are intentional, meant to embrace and demonstrate the ease of plant-based and environmentally conscious consumer choices and ways of living as important steps on a long-term journey to self-sufficiency and sustainability. My actions are also for and with other beings and energies in the environment, with "my" home—an urban space abutting a six-lane road and a bus stop—being shared with community (homeless) and "rescued" cats, skunks, possums, raccoons, squirrels, mice, birds, insects, and a few groundhogs; with bat houses, pollinator pathways, "mole zones," and under- and over-story trees and shrubs. All in an effort to "re-wild" and release, to connect and nurture, to respect, to live and let live.

Also, in the sanctuary I am creating and connecting with, I wrestle with two contradictions, points of tension in my orientation of kindness and of ahimsa (the principle of "do no harm") and my critical study: cats and plants. The CAS course introduces two "animal rights camps": welfare and liberation. Such "camps" or "factions" (Wrenn 2012) are more of a continuum. All of them are concerned with nonhuman-animal well-being, the difference being one of scope and degree: for example, welfarists primarily seek to improve living conditions for animals here and now, entangled in human systems; liberationists strive to break these systems and stop nonhuman-animal captivity, abuse, enslavement, torture, and murder; some liberationists, or abolitionists, advocate humankind's complete disentanglement from and non-interference in other beings' lives.

THE WELFARE–LIBERATION CONTINUUM, CATS, AND PLANTS

The CAS course brought together folks from across the welfare–liberation continuum and elsewhere. I was not quite right in my assumption that "students would be, at the very least, 'animal lovers,'" but they did share an interest in other species. I myself entered the course being near the most "extreme" abolitionist point on the continuum but was troubled by plants and cats, and by a seeping discomfort with this position as the class went on. I described to my students how cats just "show up" in my life and accept me and my space. How I have sought to "rescue" homeless cats trapped in shelters and worked with and for foster organizations. How I regret spaying Cleo, a community cat whom I found yowling atop a three-story house, in heat, as dozens of (male?) cats watched from the ground, all around her. How she was forced to stay inside in my cramped little attic apartment with other cats and a chihuahua and recover from a surgery that I had arranged, violating her reproductive rights. How she "went out" one day months later and never returned. We talked about Cleo and the supposed "pet overpopulation crisis" just as *Roe v. Wade* was challenged in the United States; we saw gender/sex, power, and species intersect.

I described my interest and education in environments. I talked about how shelter, place, and space impact us and others on emotional, physical, and intellectual levels; how energy, our environment, and individual *Umwelts* ("self-worlds") (von Uexküll 1964) are inextricable, unique, and primary. How our life chances are dramatically affected by where we are and what we do when we are there. This last point clearly encompasses the nonhuman animals sharing our environments and affected by our choices—and thus our positions on the welfare–liberation continuum.

Yet, what is not spoken about enough in any "animal" camp? Plants. Are they not beings too? And the insects and other animals affected not only by agribusiness but also by "my" vegetable garden/ing? They are collateral damage. What of the fact that "growing food" and horticulture are striking examples of anthropocentric activity, as "our wee gardens," homesteads, community gardens, small-scale "produce" farms, and monstrous monocrop fields all disrupt and destroy the ecosystem, all force and cease life, manipulate and mould, and take, take, take. And then there is the right that every plant should have—to life. Maybe the way to do the least harm is not to be vegan but to be a raw fruitarian, one who only consumes what falls from a plant and then defecates in the same spot for seed scarification and soil nutrition; and the cycle contin- ues. Even then, I am choosing to nourish myself by taking from other beings who could live off the fruit, and I may be eating small organisms on the fruit . . . how far need I go? Plants—where are they in our libera- tion movement? Why should this movement end at animals?

I Am (Not) an Imposter

My assumptions that "there might be some dissatisfaction with a grad- uate student teaching other graduate students" and that "I might be 'called out' as unqualified, biased, ineffective, or 'too emotional' by the students" seem unfounded. Upon reflection, I did not read any feedback that expressed such sentiments or else find much evidence to support them. But I am not a fruitarian, and I do not go to demonstrations (though I love that they are there, and I love those who stand with and for the oppressed). I currently float in the postdoctoral ether; I am not a professor in a critical animal studies program; I have but a flicker of hope for funding for research related to nonhuman-animal homeless- ness; and I have numerous drafts and "survival" jobs. I share the images and "facts" of the eternal Treblinka—the genocide and domination of everyone and everything by "us"—on social media channels, images that also serve as a constant reminder that nonhuman-animal libera- tion and peace are, for the most part, still pipe dreams. And that we are hurtling toward complete collapse.

Teaching the CAS course helped me to "keep up the fight" by blow- ing up my sail a fair bit. I smiled and cried—a lot. It also affirmed the necessity and legitimacy of teaching as activism, or knowledge as power. It was one strike against the phenomenon known as imposter syndrome, whereby one feels unqualified and insufficient, whereby one waits to be called out and denied acceptance and legitimacy—a condition often found in "high achievers" who do not feel great at all about their capabilities and achievements (see, for example, Clance and Imes 1978; Sakulku and Alexander 2011; Young and Vermilyea 2020).

I was so very cautiously energized by the proclamations of "reconsidering" made by several students: with regard to their diet, their roles, even the actions of those they love. If all we have is a self, it is what that self does that we control. More than "just making real" the plight of nonhuman animals in an anthropocentric world, which could just as easily (and sometimes did) provoke "so what?" responses, I witnessed an accelerating breaking down of assumptions, an emotional entanglement with the topics and course material, and even apparent revisions in points of view. I rejoiced in (seemingly) similar gangly steps and ponderances amongst my students about their ontologies, actions, traditions, understandings, and intentions.

CONCLUSION

So, a very dark and light end note: I am disappointed that I could not just keep teaching CAS, and hopeful that my small effort may have helped nonhuman animals immediately and/or in the longer term by targeting the source of the problem (broadly, humans; specifically, nonvegan humans). I gave my students the information (now go do!). I was and remain overwhelmed and angry that there is so much work to do. I lug around the weight of change, feeling tired, sensitive, alone, and vulnerable—only able to "protect" my small square, right here—but also remembering the interconnectivity of it all, how one thing affects and is entangled with the others, how knowledge can be powerful and once you know, you cannot unknow. Or, more deeply, respecting entropy and energy, respecting the fact that we are all energy, and energy cannot be created or destroyed.

Why do I "need" to be . . . something? What is that something? Right? Good? Just? Different? Radical? When will I know I am that? In the end, my wrestling is all with myself. Teaching this CAS course was painful in its force: I "had to" address and explain acts and beliefs that send rage and anguish straight from my toes to my scalp. The great leveling is the inescapability of my humanness. I am neither a scholar nor an activist. I am just human. To live by the principle of ahimsa is impossible; to live, I choose to take and use the lives and bodies of other beings. "Being vegan" is not enough; complete abolition would be the cessation of all human interference with other beings and environments—which is, in its purest form, human extinction. Upon critical self-reflection, I am left confronted with the observation that if all humans were to die today, the Earth would flourish (the obvious best scenario) but that as things are, the Earth is angry, and no matter how "radical" our reforms and remediations are, it is likely too late for us and innumerable other beings. And it is our fault. How do you live with being the greatest problem the Earth has ever known? Maybe, I teach . . . and learn. That is activism, that is peacekeeping, that is . . . worth it. I have to do *something* with this rage and sadness or it will continue to consume me. Maybe that is enough.

CHAPTER FOURTEEN

Nonhuman Animals: Laboratory or Liberation? A Critical Analysis of the Defense of Vivisection

Lynda M. Korimboccus

"Liberty means you receive rights because of what you are, with-
out being compared to anyone."
—Wise 2002, 232
"Pain is pain regardless of species."
—Ryder 2002, 9

The use of nonhuman animals in biomedical research is a contentious
issue, with both proponents and opponents entrenched in their respective views. Cartesian ideas of nonhuman animals as automatons are
now dismissed as pre-Darwinian and out of touch (Ryder 2002)—with
some exceptions (see Carruthers 1989). In any case, the deontology of
this issue is not analyzed here. This chapter seeks to explore the more
up-to-date defense of vivisection—that is, the use of live nonhuman
animals in medical research. Whilst the industry may acknowledge
sentience in many of its "subjects," it also appeals to the presupposed
notion that humans are morally superior and thus worth the sacrifice
of other, less worthy species. Many millions of often incredibly painful procedures are conducted worldwide each year by universities and

pharmaceutical-company laboratories, allegedly to further the goal of improving human health. Yet cures for many human ailments remain out of reach whilst the industry keeps growing and gaining profit (Ismail 2011).

This acknowledgement of "speciesism" appears to serve a dual purpose for those involved in biomedical research involving animals: first, to accept that harm, actual or potential, is inflicted on so-called laboratory animals during testing, thus reducing guilt in the lay supporter of medical research involving animals; second, to enable themselves to justify the treatment of nonhuman animals in their charge. In the case of the former, it could be argued that "honesty" appeals to wider social needs to excuse the continuance of such experimentation since it is an increasingly unpopular practice (Anderegg et al. 2006). In a nation of self-professed animal lovers such as the United Kingdom (UK), most people are likely relieved not to have to be directly involved in what is oft regarded as a "necessary evil."

Proponents of vivisection such as Carol Cohen (1986) and Susan Lederer (1992) invoke this very "necessary evil" argument—and add to the mix a suggestion that those in opposition are merely reacting emotionally or subjectively to a process that requires objective detachment. It is such claims of objectivity that this piece will aim to debunk, and with it all justification for the use of nonhuman animals in human biomedical research. Despite increasing opposition, and the great technological advances in the development of methods dubbed "alternatives," animal models remain the preferred choice in the pursuit of treatments and cures for many human ailments—not to mention that these models have never been scrutinized or scientifically validated (Fano 1997).

Our case commences with a (very) brief history of nonhuman-animal use in medicine. As early as 302 BC, animals were used by physicians to further their understanding of general physiology (Chow et al. 2008, 1). This practice would, over time, traverse disciplines from comparative anatomy into physiology and, in the late nineteenth century, microbiology. Research involving live nonhuman animals increased over the following century (Chow et al. 2008, 9) and into the twenty-first; today, it remains a widely accepted method of investigating human ill health.

A recent survey estimates that over 100 million nonhuman animals are used for research each year (Humane Society International n.d.).

The controversy surrounds the ethics and morals of such use rather than the pursuit of medical progress. Ethical objections to animal experimentation are most strongly pushed back by those who acknowledge the moral relativism of their own position—most notably Carl Cohen (1986). Cohen assumes there to be only two objections, both of which he believes to be unsound: the first is that vivisection involves violations of the rights of the animals involved; the second is that vivisection causes sentient animals to suffer. Cohen identifies and then counters each of these in turn. His defense of research using animals is openly speciesist throughout. The term "speciesism" was first coined in the 1970s by Richard Ryder to refer to the unjust and irrational act of inflicting "unconsented-to pain" on nonhuman animals simply because they are not human (Ryder 2002, 1).

To summarize Cohen's speciesist counterarguments, his first is straightforward: There are no rights violations since nonhuman animals cannot have rights. Rights are necessarily human. Human beings have a unique nature, including an ability to comprehend complex concepts and to be morally autonomous beings. Nonhuman animals are not the right *kind* of beings to warrant such consideration: "we do not violate their rights, because they have none to violate" (Cohen 1986, 95). In a way, he accuses animal rights advocates of making a category mistake by purporting that life alone constitutes rights—rights are not afforded to everything else that lives, so why should nonhuman animals receive special treatment?

Cohen pragmatically continues, arguing that with rights come responsibilities and so the absence of rights for nonhuman animals does not give humans carte blanche to treat them in any way they please. He takes life with his dog as an example, explaining that though she has no right to walks and shelter, it is his responsibility to ensure her basic necessities are met. A typical response at this point would be to point out that there are some humans for whom such comprehension is difficult, if not impossible, but how Cohen approaches this common Singer-esque objection questioning whether incapacitated—or "marginal"—human beings have rights is interesting. He views such objections as flawed since human capacities are still human capacities, whether certain individuals can even be aware of, let alone exercise them (1986, 95).

Cohen's discussion of what he claims is the second anti-vivisection stance places him even more firmly in the realm of speciesism (particularly as Ryder would define it), which he happily accepts and in fact advocates. He deals with this objection—that there should be no distinction between human and nonhuman animals in the prevention of suffering since humans are not that special or unique—by highlighting, again, that only humans are morally autonomous, and so speciesism in this case is entirely appropriate. The trade-off problem referred to by Ryder is relevant here: "It is always wrong to cause pain to A [. . .] to increase the pleasure of B. [. . .] However, when we consider causing pain to A [. . .] to reduce the pain of B [. . .] a very grey and difficult area [opens]" (Ryder 2002, 4).

The first error of the anti-vivisectionist, according to Cohen, is to afford all species equal weighting in such a calculation. Sentience (or "painience" in the case of Regan and Ryder) is often referenced to oppose testing involving nonhuman animals, culminating in a claim that the ends do not justify the means. Animal experimentation must be stopped because the speciesist preference of humans rather than dogs or rats is akin to the racism and sexism of bygone eras (Cohen 1986, 7). This, Cohen claims, is not only an unsound objection but an offensive one, though Cohen is unclear as to who would take offense here.

Whilst he agrees racism has no rationale as there is "no morally relevant distinction" between races, he draws the line at species. Cohen argues that his speciesism is essential—indeed, morally obligatory (Cohen 1986, 97)—else one is left with a bizarre choice of consequence of either both humans *and* nonhuman animals or *neither* humans *nor* nonhuman animals having rights. He explains thus: even if all mammals must be weighed similarly in any cost-benefit analysis of vivisection, the good resulting from it must also be included alongside the harm caused. And the benefits are so "beyond quantification" (98), Cohen claims, that *not* to test on animals is as morally deplorable, as it would be questionable not to consider likely future medical breakthroughs. It would be cruel to humans not to. Any ban on animal experimentation would result in human clinical trials of drugs running without prior animal data; no drug testing; or reduced drug testing (99), none of which is a desired outcome for those committed to medical advancement. Animals are used before humans "to limit risk/maximize safety" (Cohen 1986, 99), and so it is likely that testing would increase rather than decrease as new products make their way to market. This supports Wise's fears that "too many rights for too many nonhuman animals will lead to no nonhuman animals attaining rights" (Wise 2002, 235). Wise opposes abolition, opting instead to advocate a "realizable minimum" use of animals in experimentation (Wise 2002, 235). Ryder, too, aims to reduce only pain, not necessarily the number of animals used (Ryder 2002, 8). Others point to the compromise reached between the two opposing camps in countries like the Netherlands (Rudacille 2000, 276–82) as an illustration of how all sides can work together to at least reduce the scale of vivisection.

Cohen's final flourish (which he accepts is ad hominem in nature) is that those opposed to vivisection cannot reasonably be so whilst still consuming animal products. He argues that a death in the laboratory is less stressful than one in the slaughterhouse, but that both involve discomfort and killing (Cohen 1986, 99). For consistency's sake, any anti-vivisection campaigner must avoid not just eating meat but also wearing fur and leather and supporting other industries that regularly use animals by buying, for instance, certain household products. He highlights the virtually "universal" social approval of animal use in all other areas of life except experimentation and rightly notes differences in the scale of use—for example, many more animals are slaughtered in one day in factory farming than are used as subjects in a laboratory in a year. Cohen raises a significantly valid point here, acknowledging the ethical vegan view as "the only fully coherent position" (Cohen 1986, 99) while concluding that the rights-based and consequences-based arguments against vivisection are both fallacious.

Several writers have sought to dismantle Cohen's justification for vivisection more generally and the paper referred to herein specifically—including Nathan Nobis (2004), who addresses Cohen's categorization of humans as a particular "kind," and Hugh LaFollette and Niall Shanks

(1996), who address his discussion of speciesism. I will present these counterclaims here, though it is a yet-unaddressed objection to speciesism, based on Alix Fano's scientific evidence (1997), that would receive the checkered flag—an objection with regard to animal experimentation's scientific validity (or rather, lack thereof). Fano's empirical data would serve as evidence that all of Cohen's arguments (and those of others like him) miss the point entirely, on occasion committing the logical fallacy of affirming the consequent and throughout creating a false dilemma within an invalid and therefore unsound pro-vivisection agenda.

Nobis's introduction hits straight below Cohen's belt by pointing out that it is inconsistent to support the idea of utility whilst at the same time wishing to minimize suffering (2004, 43). To rub a little salt in any wound he succeeds in creating, he continues by noting that Cohen's definition of rights is not too far from that of animal rights advocate Tom Regan.

The vast majority of Nobis's 2004 work centers around Cohen's treatment of his category idea of "kind" as somehow normative, though in reality, the "kind" of which Cohen speaks simply refers to "humankind," else his argument fails when considering that moral rights are attributed to "marginal" humans, as it is not any more normal for them to have conscious morality than for them to have the ability to make pasta. Nobis initially gives Cohen the benefit of the doubt, however, and wonders if he really means *natural* rather than *normal*, though this would elicit the same response, since by "natural" Cohen essentially means *human* nature.

Nobis then wonders if perhaps Cohen means *potential* rather than normal or natural. In the case of normally developing infants, they may well end up able to make pasta. What about fetuses, then? Indeed, what about human menstrual blood? Nobis rightly takes the argument to its logical conclusion: if moral rights are to be attributed to all potential beings, then these must also count (44). This may be an absurd-consequences move on the surface, but upon closer inspection, it is logical if Cohen's point is to be upheld. Moreover, Nobis draws a distinction between capable humans and "marginal" humans, explaining that some in the latter group will likely never be able to make pasta. In this case, some may argue that if rights are to be afforded to someone medically incapable of observing the duties that accompany rights, then Cohen must concede that nonhuman animals also fit this category (cited in Nobis 2004, 49).

Ultimately, Nobis's final dissection of Cohen's paper shows that what Cohen really means is that humans are special "because they are human" (2004, 50), which is what Ryder claims is an illogical and unintelligent position (2002, 7). If we can give "marginal" humans rights because they share the property of being "human," that property could just as easily read "sentient," thus giving nonhuman animals access to said rights (Nobis 2004, 51). Nobis argues further that the same property-based argument could be reversed to put humans in the same "kind" category as any "thing on earth" (2004, 51), and most such things are not moral agents. If Cohen objects, turning to biological similarity as a metric, then there are yet other nonhuman beings who may fit the new category (great apes, for example). Cohen's argument could likewise be countered by the substitution of another shared property—being human is a neither necessary nor sufficient condition in order to grant moral consideration and, subsequently, rights. Therefore, Nobis shows that "Cohen's 'getting-rights-by-association-in-a-kind' strategy," which is employed by other pro-vivisectionists to the same effect, and his "Getting a Property by Association Principle" (2004, 53), with its illogical consequences, both illustrate the absurdity of his argument.

Nobis concedes that perhaps Cohen means humans *understand the concept* of rights and it is this comprehension that affords them those rights. Quite cleverly, Nobis simply applies this to nonhuman animals to illustrate that the ability to conceptualize is also irrelevant—a dog has no concept of being a dog, but it does not prevent them from being one (55). Nobis surmises (adding more salt) that Cohen's is essentially an animal rights position since he claims animals shouldn't be needlessly harmed—and he is willing to admit (without much fanfare) that they are in order to produce commodities for humans' consumption (56).

Nobis commences his conclusion by addressing claims that vivisection has never been proven necessary for medical progress or designated the best research method. He notes that it cannot be justified even on utilitarian grounds, since there have been no calculations weighing the actual harm to animals against merely possible benefits to humans (2004, 56). Ryder shares this view, pointing out the difficulties in using nonhuman animals to predict human biological responses and adding that any "alleged benefits [. . .] still lie in the future" (2002, 5). Indeed, empirical analysis shows nonhuman-animal models to be very poor predictors for humans: "Animal studies can neither confirm nor refute hypotheses about human physiology or pathology; human clinical investigation is the only way such hypotheses can be tested. [. . .] There are countless other, far superior ways to derive new hypotheses" (cited in Anderegg et al. 2006, 1).

Add to all this the human harms of vivisection—psychological harm in the laboratory from face-to-face interactions with animal "subjects" (Haraway 2008), as well as physiological harm from cross-species contamination, failed clinical trials, or pharmaceutical side effects. With at least 90 percent of drugs passed safe in animal tests failing human trials (Shanks, Greek, and Greek 2009, 7), one wonders how many human cures have been relegated to the cutting-room floor *because* the relevant or required animal data could not be produced. Add still further the extensive funds awarded to animal research that could be redirected to non-animal research methods, medical care for the poor, or wider humanitarian aid, and the argument for vivisection is a poor one at best (Nobis 2004, 59). It seems that drugs have been developed despite, not due to, such experimentation, with its derisory success rate of no more than 10 percent.

Cohen's "kind" is simply a stand-in for an unjustifiable but accepted prejudice based on species—much like one based on race or sex. What "kind" are we, then, if it's not rooted in biology or any other Cohenistic categorization? We are conscious, sentient beings, the same as so many of our nonhuman counterparts, as Nobis concludes (2004, 59). His views echo much of LaFollette and Shanks's 1996 review of speciesism (particularly Cohen's version thereof), which makes it clear that "moral properties and biological properties are categories from different domains" (45) and that "bare speciesism" is essentially discriminatory. In contrast, a focus on the morality of a species would perhaps fit more neatly with "indirect speciesism" (ibid.), though it remains speciesist. LaFollette and Shanks are most effective in highlighting the real dilemma faced by biomedical researchers, whichever view they adopt. To claim that vivisection has utility for humans requires interspecies similarity, but to claim the irrelevance of rights in regard to nonhuman animals requires interspecies difference. This is a "logical trap" (cited in LaFollette and Shanks 1996, 50–51).

Cohen's key claim that speciesism is justifiable based on the greater human good is one he readily accepts and seems unashamed of. At this point, one of the central premises of Cohen's argument must be addressed—that nonhuman-animal experimentation is justified as it provides valid and valuable data for the development of new treatments for human ailments (1986). Should this be true, then the scientific argument for vivisection is valid and sound. However, despite Cohen's dispute with his opponents over the soundness of their arguments, he himself commits a faux pas by failing to recognize the lack of science behind the scientific argument. He is far from alone here, nor is his the only justification provided for the continuance of vivisection, as Fano illustrates in her 1997 work.

Fano details six explicit justifications for the use of nonhuman animals in human biomedical research:

1. There is no need to test on humans or wait for disease to occur naturally.
2. Human cancer and other diseases model well in rodents, especially those genetically modified to be sufficient models.
3. The whole body can be studied in both life and death via biopsy and autopsy since nonhuman animals are accepted models.
4. There are mathematical/statistical ways to deal with interspecies differences and thus make the nonhuman-animal results more relevant to humans.
5. Nonhuman-animal research assists in producing safety standards in terms of toxicology for a variety of products people come into contact with.
6. There exists more data on animals than on humans.

Fano 1997, 47–48

Fano argues that all of these justifications are fallacies, mostly invalidated by either intra- or interspecies differences. Although these differences (and thus limitations of animal models) are acknowledged by the scientific community (Chow et al. 2008, 9), many believe the similarities to be "[sufficient] [. . .] to provide an index of hazard" (cited in Fano 1997, 45). This, along with researchers' ability to thoroughly investigate animal "subjects," means that for pro-vivisectionists, nonhuman animals are "the best, most scientifically valid surrogates for people in biomedical research and testing" (cited in Fano 1997, 46).

Fano details significant interspecies differences between humans and other animals in not only basic biology but also fundamental bodily processes, such as breathing, vomiting, absorption, digestion, and excretion (Fano 1997, 50–57). Indeed, the genetically engineered "lab rat" is not a suitable model even for their own species, let alone for humans (66). Yet another example that reminds us of how prevalent these interspecies differences are: cigarette smoke and arsenic do not affect nonhuman animals much (if at all) and so were once deemed safe for human consumption (cited in Fano 1997). Fano also points to many examples of false positives and negatives in animal research: "the method of allowing 100 cats to represent one million humans [. . .] often produces false negatives, or allows real dangers to be missed [. . .]" (1997, 59). Incidence of cancer at a rate of, say, 5 in 1,000 (0.5 percent) based on a study of 600 animals is statistically insignificant and thus would produce a false-negative result.

Moreover, different research methods can produce different results, even within the same species (Fano 1997, 60). Surprisingly, the lack of ecological validity in animal research is seldom highlighted. The laboratory is an artificial, sterile, fully controlled, "unhealthy and abnormal" environment (ibid.), and the subsequent stress in nonhuman-animal subjects creates changes in their biological systems that surely produce misleading data (Knight 2011). This would clearly contradict Cohen's view that a laboratory death is a preferable one—and one could add that a laboratory life is most certainly a traumatic one. Human error must also be taken into account, especially at the research-cycle stage of data analysis. Even the United Kingdom's powerful Medical Research

Council has admitted that almost three quarters of its reports contain errors in statistical analysis (cited in Fano 1997, 68), notwithstanding purposeful fabrications due to scientific misconduct.

The key argument Fano presents, the same one that is employed against any and all alleged justifications for vivisection, concerns validation. Alternatives to nonhuman-animal research such as in vitro tests require intensive validation (Fano 1997, 69) and scrupulous tests of relevance and reliability. Yet, such alternatives continue to be accused of invalidity, although the very process of and principles for validation are still a matter of debate (cited in Fano 1997, 69). Whatever the validation procedure for the so-called alternatives, however, the most significant fact here is that nonhuman-animal tests *have never been formally validated*, despite claims to the contrary (Chow et al. 2008).

A huge body of non-animal research exists and is widely accepted as scientific: for example, in vitro fertilization and embryonic science (Fano 1997, 73) have been made possible without the use of animals—and more to the point, methods to predict side effects of drugs without relying on animal tests, such as side-effect reporting. That some proponents of vivisection accept some non-animal research but not others represents a double standard. As Fano concludes, if animal testing underwent rigorous validation, the injustice would soon become clear.

An accusation leveled against the anti-vivisection movement dismisses supposedly emotional responses to animal experimentation as unfounded. Many activists believe it is wrong on many levels to subject nonhuman animals to unnatural lives and deaths in the name of "science" that cannot justifiably be termed science at all. Lederer's (1992) work on the language of the laboratory finds that some researchers prefer the term "animal experimentation" to "vivisection" since the latter is associated with descriptions of torture and similarly graphic accounts of experiments using live animals (78–79). She claims that in response to the anti-vivisection culture, researchers have resorted to "creative" reporting (79), further affecting the validity of their research.

As Fano (1997) concludes, humans are the only sufficient model for humans (79), given the sheer volume of evidence supporting human drug trials and the distinct absence of evidence supporting animal experiments. The utilitarian argument holds up only when it is a valid one, which we have now established is not. As LaFollette and Shanks (1996) also conclude: "The straightforward deontological defense of experimentation is implausible. [. . .] [A] utilitarian defense of research is flawed. It is no longer certain how the researchers can morally justify their practice" (61).

What, then, is behind the continuance of such morally objectionable and scientifically invalid practices? Some posit that they are little more than tools employed within the wider "medical–industrial complex" to protect its powerful protagonists (Ismail 2011), while some agree that animal-research policy is hegemonically driven and "skewed" (Lyons 2013, 332). The Medical Research Modernization Committee outlines six possible explanations:

1. Animal research provides legal protection against claims for damage.
2. It is easily publishable, assisting in the building of academic reputation.
3. It is self-perpetuating and helps with grant applications.
4. It is financially lucrative.
5. Laboratory testing is (mistakenly) viewed as more scientific, despite confounding variables linked to stress in the animal "subjects" in such an environment.
6. Use of "appropriate" language (e.g., "sacrifice," "distress") avoids issues of morality and perpetuates speciesism by implying the utilitarian notion of "the ends justify the means."

(Anderegg et al. 2006, 19–21)

The claim of utility to humans as justification for the costs of nonhuman-animal use in research surely necessitates as much scrutiny as is demanded of non-animal alternatives. Pro-vivisectionists have never undertaken such a stringent review, and so the pragmatic or utilitarian-esque arguments for animal experimentation (such as Cohen's) fail at the first hurdle. These views should be immediately dismissed as at best biased and at worst dangerous, and "alternatives" to nonhuman-animal research should be rebranded as the primary route to answers for a healthier future for humankind. What is ironic (for the proponents of vivisection) is that science ultimately prevails. Once current "alternatives" become mainstream and the either/or framing of the debate is exposed for what it is—a false dilemma—we may have a hope of curing the ailments that currently plague so many of our "kind." In so doing, we may finally be able to liberate the animals in laboratories, held there without warrant.

CHAPTER FIFTEEN

UFOs and Animal Exploitation: The Rhetoric of Ridicule

Seven Mattes

INTRODUCTION

A person who has had the exceptional experience of witnessing an unexplainable paranormal event, such as a UFO sighting, will likely be all too familiar with the sense of uncertainty and isolation such a witnessing causes, and the ridicule that arises if they speak openly about their experience. These events can be life-changing, challenging our notions of how the world works, what meaning we give to life or religion, or who we are as a species. Three reactions are common. First, confusion as this encounter challenges major institutions and cultural norms: "Why does no one else talk about this?" "What do I do with this information?" Second, isolation: "Who do I talk to and how will they react?" And third, a shift as the experience challenges worldviews, religious beliefs, and more: "I cannot go back to who I was prior to this knowledge/witnessing." Taken together, the aftermath of such an experience is psychologically and socially complicated.

Talking openly about the experience in this case can lead to unwanted labels and unflattering assumptions, due partially to how doing so challenges the status quo. At worst, it can lead to the loss of one's job, or institutionalization. Not surprisingly, then, many choose to stay quiet, despite the profound impact these events often have on their lives (Denzler 2001; Pasulka 2019). Those who do open up about their experiences find themselves navigating a complex arena and having to decide what to associate or not associate themselves with, for example:

science, not religion; UFO "witness," not "abductee"; "unidentified," not "little green men." Conspiracy theories abound. Where the witness is aligned, which is not always their choice, determines how seriously they will be taken—or how much they will be ridiculed.

The ridicule that accompanies the research into or experience of UFO and alien phenomena is effective. To discredit a whole group of people, you make them ridiculous, their experiences and words ludicrous, and their character suspect. As such, it is not far-fetched to argue that those working for animal liberation share parallel experiences with those who have witnessed UFO phenomena—though objectively distinct, these are, at the very least, both highly ridiculed communities. The similarities do not end there, nor do the lessons the two groups can learn from each other. Both animal liberationists and UFO witnesses challenge the cultural norms that position humans as the most significant and dominant beings in the universe (Wendt and Duvall 2008). Indeed, human exceptionalism is called into question by the overwhelming scientific evidence of nonhuman animals' intelligence and cognitive and emotional capacity, as well as extraterrestrial entities' capacity for intergalactic travel. Both communities rally for scientific legitimacy, struggle to be taken seriously by peers, and are waved away as fanatics with a collection of anecdotes (Wendt and Duvall 2008; Despret 2012). Members of each group share strategies for navigating various fields, socially or professionally, sometimes code-switching and holding back unless in the company of others who understand their cognitive shift.

Waldau (2013) describes the path to transforming our relationship with other animals as a series of doors to be opened—enabling us to gain myriad understandings that may have been previously clouded by dominant anthropocentric narratives. Similarly, as one journeys into the UFO believers' realm, there are many doors along the way, and thus many opportunities to turn back or stay put. That said, one of the most common phrases uttered by both those who have witnessed the reality of animal oppression and those who have witnessed UFO activity references the inability to return to a time when they did not know. This journey is a transformational process (McDonald 2000).

Notably, the purpose of this chapter is not to argue for or against the truthfulness of UFO reports—adhering to the central thesis herein, all claims of UFO witnessing will be taken seriously and the witnesses trusted. The goal here is to understand the impact of ridicule on those who open unclosable doors—doors that others may not even be aware exist. As for those who have inadvertently witnessed UFOs, they may have fallen through the door rather than chosen to open it, but the consequences are similar. Be it a choice or an accident, the next step is up to them. Following these parallels between "ridiculous" groups, the chapter addresses the liberation gained and the lessons learned as they rise above and challenge conformity, making waves in contemporary American culture.

LITERATURE REVIEW

To be ridiculous is to invite derision or mockery. It is to espouse a behavior, argument, or action that is absurd in the context in which it is performed. What or who is ridiculous is determined by the observer. Ridicule is a means of controlling or regulating behavior, and/or a means of reinforcing social norms and maintaining social order. As such, ridiculing laughter directed at a subject can humiliate the subject into conformity. A way to avoid being ridiculed is to take note and pledge compliance with social norms. Just as social norms must be learned, so too must ridicule (Grewell 2013, 15).

Ridicule is commonly used among children as they are enculturated into their social context. This can present in a humorous form, in the form of bullying, or as anything in between. Bryant et al. (1983; 1981) found that older children's behavior was altered when they watched video recordings of a puppet being ridiculed for certain actions. They felt the impact of the derisive laughter on the puppet, understanding and interpreting it as something they wished to avoid. Similarly, in an article aptly named "Jeer Pressure," Janes and Olsen (2000) found that merely seeing another person be ridiculed led to behavioral alterations. Thus, ridicule is also effective indirectly—awareness of the potential of being laughed at or having one's dignity challenged can be enough to shift behavior. Given the power inherent in ridicule, it is no wonder that Foucault considers it one of the functions of the "disciplines," which are aimed at maintaining control over and order among humans in a given social context (Foucault 1995).

Ridicule is also used to discredit arguments. A common fallacy is appeal to ridicule, whereby one frames the opponent's argument as ridiculous or otherwise not worthy of serious inquiry by misrepresenting the opponent's argument or merely responding to it as though it lacks validity or as though it must be a joke. This fallacy might be used to discredit an argument, to avoid engaging with the points presented, or to call into question the general character of the human presenting the argument. And it works. The threat of ridicule is the threat of not merely being laughed at but also losing credibility, which is linked to social standing and social integration. Ridicule has the power to undermine one's intelligence, capabilities, and sanity, depending on the way and context in which it is being wielded.

Finally, ridicule's function is dependent on power relations. On the other hand, ridicule can be used to punch up—call into question the trustworthiness of those in positions of authority, such as politicians during an election cycle. On the other hand, when used to punch down, ridicule is a function of authority itself, reiterating institutional and cultural norms and reaffirming the status quo (Grewell 2013).

RIDICULE AND ANIMAL LIBERATIONISTS

The similarities between the experience of UFO witnesses and that of animal liberationists are many, both within and outside of academia. Animal liberationists arrive at their position in a variety of ways. Some may have been handed a PETA brochure in undergrad and chosen to open it rather than chuck it into the garbage. Others may have tagged along with a friend to a viewing of the groundbreaking documentary *Earthlings*. Yet others may have merely had a moment of awareness, stoked by context or conversation: eating a BBQ sandwich at the zoo in front of the farm animals they had just fed, or listening to a coworker rant about the impacts of industrial animal agriculture on climate change. Whatever it may be, this occasion opens a door that cannot be closed again easily. McDonald (2000) and Hirschler (2011) refer to this as a "catalytic experience," of which there may be many before lifestyle change occurs.

Though they don't always happen as singular events or in a linear progression, the next steps might look like the following: First, there is confusion, as one says to oneself, "Why is no one else talking about this? My family and friends, my co-workers and mentors, and the majority of the world use animal products and participate in animal oppression— I must be missing something." A shift happens, as once the door is opened, it can lead one down a path of awareness. One starts to develop an intersectional understanding of oppression and harsh critiques of the economic and cultural systems that have produced the current accepted reality. Once one piece of the web is ripped down, the others loosen: religious beliefs, worldviews, even understanding of the self can be as fragile as a mirror. Ultimately, one experiences isolation, as the awareness that one has participated in an unjust, deeply problematic system is a lot to take in. Further, the awareness that everyone else is participating and will continue to participate in this system is difficult to understand, and one's social circle may shift in accordance (Hirschler 2011; Bresnahan, Zhaung, and Zhu 2016).

Throughout this process, talking openly about one's experiences can lead to harsh labels, criticisms, and numerous exhausting appeals to ridicule. Animal liberationists are often familiar with "punch-down" ridicule. Challenging strong, long-established cultural institutions that dictate how humans should live with and relate to other species opens them up to mockery.

A multitude of studies on an adjoining phenomenon termed "vegan stigma" illustrate the social and personal impacts of living openly as an animal liberationist (Twine 2014; Greenbaum 2012; Markowski and Roxburgh 2019; Hirschler 2011; Bresnahan, Zhuang, and Zhu 2016). Vegans experience stigma not only because they go against social and cultural norms but also because this choice induces cognitive dissonance in omnivores (Rothgerber 2014; Adams 2001). This discomfort can prompt angry, defensive, and other negative responses, including ridicule. Markowski and Roxburgh (2019) found that the "infamous vegan stigma" can prevent some from practicing veganism; as for vegans, the inevitable friction can put a strain on their relationships: "This tension may result in lost friendships, reduced contact, and/or exclusion from social activities, suggesting that the social costs of veganism can be quite high" (3). This finding is corroborated by McDonald (2000) and Twine

(2014), who documented how vegans undergo incredulous interrogations by friends and family as well as hear condescending words from outsiders, implying that their lifestyle is merely temporary. Similarly, Hirschler (2011) found that vegans can suffer from prejudice and social rejection, while Greenbaum (2012) noted their fear of being perceived as activists due to their choices. Further, men who are vegan have an increased risk of experiencing stigma due to the association of meat consumption with masculinity (Adams 1990; Greenbaum 2018).

However, positive consequences of "vegan stigma" include the ongoing exploration of human–animal relationships and the formation of liberating and accepting communities. In Hirschler's (2011) study, many participants who initially went vegetarian later transitioned to veganism: the learning process doesn't end after the "catalytic experience"; once one door is open, one is much more likely to open the next. As McDonald (2000) explains: "Becoming oriented and open facilitated learning about animal abuse, how to live a vegetarian or vegan lifestyle, or both. Participants became self-directed, goal-directed learners. [. . .] [A]s they learned, participants became more convinced of the moral rightness of their direction" (11). Along this trajectory of compassionate understanding, it is not uncommon that one finds or forms a community of like-minded humans. While veganism results in social distance between vegans and omnivores, it acts as blissful glue among vegans. Vegans find spaces to connect, and they thrive in these accepting environments, strengthening and validating their beliefs and their sense of community. As Twine asserts: "Within the safe bubble of the vegan community its practitioners are noticeably joyous, especially about food. This can be seen at forms of vegan sociality such as potlucks, vegan fairs or CAS conferences" (15).

Case Study: Carol J. Adams's "Beyond Meat Debate"

In February 2022, Carol J. Adams participated in the "Beyond Meat Debate" at the Oxford Union to speak on her concept of the absent referent. In her speech, she noted that the presentation of, conceptions about, and language describing where the meat on one's plate comes from are separated from the reality of the once-living animal it came from. She also listed the basic externalities of meat consumption and the intersections between carnism, misogyny, white supremacy, and colonialism. Smirks, laughter, and other open displays of disrespect filled the room throughout the talk (and you can perhaps imagine the YouTube comment section). Adams ended with, "And I heard all your laughter, I know some of these ideas are new to you or you think they're fringe or whatever . . ." to reframe the audience's reaction for what it was—defensive discomfort.

Adams's work *Living among Meat Eaters* (2001) illustrates that she is well acquainted with the ridicule that one receives when walking through the world as an animal rights advocate. Adams argues, for example, that the best approach to all interactions with meat-eaters is to perceive them as "blocked vegetarians." Their responses are due to their own discomfort and uncertainty around their diet—the presence of a vegetarian/vegan becomes the mere catalyst for their reflection and often-angry projection. The defensive response often takes the form of ridicule, from ignorant jabs about vegans having poor health to collective labeling, exemplified by the pejorative nickname "soy boys" that is meant to emasculate men who eat tofu instead of meat. Much diet-related ridicule focuses on reasserting human domination by pointing out, for example, that humans are meant to be at the top of the food chain and thus vegans are naturally lower and lesser. Comics portraying vegans as having evolved from poorly skilled hunters or otherwise lacking in what omnivores have mastered are so common that they are clichéd.

The use of ridicule extends beyond diet choices. When animal liberationists openly challenge anthropocentrism, human exceptionalism, speciesism, or other, related established norms, the general public commonly responds first with laughter. The perception of such a position as is so prevalent that the infamous animal rights organization PETA capitalizes on it, playing the ridiculous to the extreme in its public campaigns.

RIDICULE AND UFO WITNESSES

Ridicule toward UFO witnesses and alien abductees is so common that it has become a comedy trope (e.g., the drunken redneck raving about being probed by little green men). What UFO witnesses experience, which can be said to be similar to McDonald's "catalytic experience," alien-abduction researcher John E. Mack refers to as an "epistemological shock" (cited in Pasulka 2019, 9). Subsequently, those who are open about the shift that occurs following this shock endure rampant negative reactions and strained social relationships and may find validation and liberation only with others with similar experiences.

While there are parallels between the entry points into the animal liberation movement and the UFO-witness community, the social repercussions of the latter can be more extreme. "A common (though mistaken, classist, and elitist) view is that people who believe in UFOs are poor, uneducated, white, usually American. Poll data suggests otherwise" (Dean 1997, 67). These social repercussions are also not experienced equally—those who merely see a UFO fall into a different social category of ridicule than those who are abductees. UFOs themselves are already a stretch—nonhuman, extraterrestrial contact, or "close encounters of the fourth kind," can expose one to much more ridicule (Denzler 2001). Indeed, negative stereotypes are placed on those who experience such contact almost immediately after the event:

> Official explanations for UFO sightings focused on witnesses' unreliability, on either their moral failings as dishonest or drunk, or their failures of judgment, as caused by lapses in sanity or perception. UFO researchers responded by working to establish the witnesses' credibility. Using scientific and juridical languages, they sought to provide reasons to trust the words of even someone who claims to have seen a flying saucer. This had the effect of shaping the UFO discourse around questions of trust and credibility as much as around empirical evidence. (Dean 1997, 51)

That the discourse surrounding the reality of this phenomenon is focused on the credibility of the human reporting it places the human in a vulnerable position, socially and otherwise. It is no surprise that many choose to stay quiet, or that jobs and reputations have been lost after coming forward. For example, meteorologist Jack Bushong was encouraged to move out of the state after he witnessed UFOs on radar in West Michigan in 1994 (Sippell 2022). Bushong had merely done his job, used the tools he was trained to use, and reported what occurred on his screen. But the credibility of the weather service became threatened due to the unknown nature of what he had experienced and the public media accounts that were now linked to his name.

Those who experience and research UFO phenomena tend to be in this position of being punched down—though they do not go out without a fight. A common assertion by scholars who cover the controversial topic of UFO witnessing and related experiences is that they are widespread, socially and politically significant phenomena that deserve more attention than they get (see Pasulka 2019). The UFO community itself (which is an amorphous collection of witnesses, abductees, and more) has spent decades seeking scientific attention and legitimacy. Such scientific backup would not only offer UFO witnesses an escape from the confusion and isolation but also help reframe inquiry into these topics as based on not irrational belief but scientific questioning. In contrast, the cold shoulder offered by the scientific community has fueled trajectories of conspiracy theories and anti-science sentiments. Pasulka (2019), a religious studies scholar who completed an ethnographic study of extraterrestrial beliefs, notes that there is an "invisible college" of scientists and academics who research UFO and alien phenomena but do not want their research interests in these areas to be publicly known and thus publicly scrutinized. According to Wendt and Duvall (2018), dismissal of UFO phenomena as a legitimate research topic is not only sociological but political in nature, "more like Galileo's ideas were political for the Catholic Church than like the once ridiculed theory of continental drift," and "considerable work goes into ignoring UFOs, constituting them as objects only of ridicule and scorn" (610).

As Denzler (2001), who also researches UFO communities from the perspective of religious studies, states: "Such is the strength of science as arbiter of Reality and thus conferrer of legitimacy that we struggle to find some point of accommodation [. . .] for our beliefs within a scientific framework. [. . .] Others in the UFO community have wondered if perhaps the limits of science's ability to explain reality have been surpassed in UFO encounters" (xvii). Dean (1997) refers to this struggle for the truth of reality as an example of the postmodern "fugitivity of truth": "The alien seduces us into a critical reassessment of our criteria for truth: How do we determine what real is? Why do we believe?" (45).

Arising out of and leading to distrust in science and the government that is historically rooted in major political events such as the Cold War (Denzler 2001), and balancing atop an increasing abundance of anecdotal evidence, the interest in UFO and alien-abduction experiences produces numerous questions to be explored. So why is such a pertinent, ongoing topic ignored? As alien-abduction researcher John E. Mack famously states, "In academia, this topic could ruin your career" (Crowder and Monroe 2021). Scientists are not immune to the fear of being ridiculed. In a review of Denzler's defining book *The Lure of the Edge*, Westrum (2002) declares: "The real reason for scientists' lack of interest in UFOs is social: The wrong set of people takes UFOs seriously. The consequence of this prejudice is that whatever work scientists do on the subject must be covert or they will suffer professional sanctions" (726). Jacobs (1992), an early researcher of alien abductees, speaks of the loneliness of this work: "When I broached the subject to my colleagues at the university, I was met, with few exceptions, with instant ridicule. Jokes about my sanity followed as they tried to humor me. [. . .] A few pointed out that my career could be effectively halted by this research" (27).

Wendt and Duvall (2008), seeking to understand what they call the "epistemology of [UFO] ignorance," or the production of (un)knowledge about UFOs, assert that the UFO taboo is a result of the threat it poses to anthropocentric sovereignty, which is challenged metaphysically by the possibility that UFOs might contain extraterrestrial beings:

> As such, genuine UFO ignorance cannot be acknowledged without calling modern sovereignty itself into question. This puts the problem of normalizing the UFO back onto governmentality, where it can be "known" only without trying to find out what it is—through a taboo. The UFO, in short, is a previously unacknowledged site of contestation in an ongoing historical project to constitute sovereignty in anthropocentric terms. [. . .] We are not saying the authorities are hiding The Truth about UFOs, much less that it is ET. We are saying they cannot ask the question. (612)

This inability to "ask the question" about UFOs is a hindrance to not only scientists but also the large number of witnesses of UFO phenomena who would benefit from the knowledge and respect to be gained.

Case Study: Phoenix Lights

Thousands witnessed the unidentified aerial phenomenon now known as the "Phoenix Lights" on March 13, 1997. Consisting of a multitude of bright lights hovering in formation above Phoenix, Arizona, the Phoenix Lights defied—and continue to defy—scientific explanation. Fife Symington, governor of Arizona at the time, publicly stated that he witnessed the event and that it was "otherworldly," validating his constituents' experiences. The Phoenix Lights were special in that—for once—people were not alone in their witnessing. Governor Symington was with over ten thousand others, including countless people who could hardly be labeled as lacking in credibility. They were perplexed; some were scared of invasion, and some were delighted to share in a paranormal moment. Many anxiously awaited answers to this life-shifting event (see Kitei 2010) as media coverage of it went global. The demand for an explanation was high, and Governor Symington publicly promised a press conference.

Months later, Symington held his infamous press conference regarding the concerning phenomenon. Rather than providing an explanation to eager viewers, he brought out a man in a rubber alien suit, and all present proceeded to laugh—ridiculing those who sought to understand an experience that threatened their norm and reality. Wielding his authority as governor, Symington, in just minutes, threw his constituents into the category of the ridiculous. Not only were their concerns and fears over the extraordinary event left unaddressed, but the path to inquiry was now shrouded in mockery. Over a decade later, the Phoenix Lights continue to haunt the area. In a documentary about the event, Pasulka explains, "We're still talking about it because of the aftereffects the people who experienced it are still having" (Crowder and Monroe 2021).

Case Study: John E. Mack

John E. Mack, a professor of psychiatry at Harvard and a Pulitzer Prize winner, is a well-known, if controversial, figure for his work with alien abductees. When he began researching alien abductees—interviewing them and documenting their astoundingly similar stories over a ten-year period—Mack, already a prominent scholar at the time, was brought up for official review, a divisive action never before taken against a tenure-track professor at Harvard. The committee ultimately "reaffirmed Dr. Mack's academic freedom to study what he wishes and to state his opinions without impediment" (John E. Mack Institute 2022). Jacobs, an associate professor of history at Temple University who studies UFOs and alien abduction, commented on the investigation in 1995: "Questioning the credibility of faculty studying unconventional subjects is not unprecedented. [. . .] If I continue with what I'm doing I will never be promoted to full professor—ever, no matter how many books I write or how many publications I make" (Israel 1995).

Mack originally aimed not to confirm or deny the experiences of his participants, but rather to understand the profound connection that witnesses felt between themselves and extraterrestrials, as well as the impact it had on their lives. His deep and rigorous inquiry into a potential nonhuman intelligence was trailblazing—paving the road for those previously fearful of coming forward about their experiences with nonhuman, extraterrestrial entities. The lived experiences of alien abductees directly challenge common understandings of human exceptionalism:

> UFO abductions and related phenomena suggest first that humans are not the preeminent intelligent beings in a universe more or less empty of conscious life. But abductees' experiences also indicate that we are participating in a cosmos that contains intelligent beings that are far more advanced than we are in certain respects and have the power to render us helpless for purposes we are only just beginning to fathom. (Mack 2007, 408)

Interestingly, Mack's findings have huge implications for how we can reimagine our relationship with our environment and with other species. Both terrestrial and extraterrestrial nonhuman beings are issuing an intense, immersive warning to us—that environmental collapse awaits if we do not change course. Notably, scholars and others have also tried to communicate—by way of listening to, understanding, and communicating with nonhuman others, though this is oft ridiculed—such a message, that change is necessary (see Poirier 2020; Gaard 2017).

Mack's legacy continues to be controversial; questions abound regarding his methods (e.g., hypnotic regression) and the validity he granted to a community that is typically shuffled into the category of the ridiculous, if not mentally ill. Although he is held in high regard by his peers in psychiatry, his reputation is often said to be in spite of this work rather than because of it (Boyce 2012).

CHALLENGING RIDICULE

Acceptance of UFO witnesses has risen in recent years, perhaps partially due to the "slow release" of official videos and information from the US military that reveal the documented reality of UAPs (Unidentified Aerial Phenomena). A groundbreaking *New York Times* article in 2007 made waves by making public the existence of "the Pentagon's mysterious UFO program" and the $22 million that funded it, as well as discussing the video of a "Tic Tac–shaped" UFO. The use of "black money"—the classified allocation of funds—to finance official governmental programs to research UFO phenomena (e.g., the Department of Defense's AATIP program, Project Blue Book) keeps the public in the dark (Cooper, Blumenthal, and Kean 2017). The secrecy of these programs leads to legitimate questions, one of which is: Is the secrecy due to a fear of ridicule or a fear that the outcome of such research could lead to a large-scale "epistemological shock"? While the answer is unknown, we do know that a public announcement of the program's existence did much to validate and empower those who have experienced UFO phenomena.

The "Tic Tac" video, which captures an oblong craft recorded by a Navy fighter jet from the USS *Nimitz* in 2004, remains a significant step toward official, institutional acknowledgement of UAPs. This piece of evidence from a reliable source opened the door for witnesses to come forward. Notably, the pilot of the USS *Nimitz* originally experienced ridicule and isolation. Now that the video is substantiated and publicly known, she is able to break out of these social constraints. In a media article following the video's release, she states that she "wants to reduce the stigma attached to reporting UFO sightings and hopes more people can speak up without fear of ridicule." She adds: "Folks might be concerned about their careers or their church or something like that. They don't want to be the kooky UFO person, so I guess I'm trying to normalize it by talking about it" (George 2021). Similarly, Kevin Day and Gary Voorhees, radar operators of the USS *Princeton* who saw similar "Tic Tac" UFOs, were required to remain publicly silent and were ridiculed and mocked by fellow military officers. Day has reported that the experience manifested into nightmares, while Voorhees has said that the *New York Times* article was substantial. As he recalls: "I kind of went numb, like, people are actually going to believe us now" (Crowder and Monroe 2021).

The official release of the "Tic Tac" video was especially significant because it directly addressed the stereotype that UFO witnesses lack intelligence or respectability. The witnesses to this incident were the most highly trained observers to exist: Navy pilots and radar operators. As Pasulka notes: "They're not mentally deficient, they are tested for psychological aberrations, these people are trusted with the most powerful weapons in our arsenal. They're seeing it with their eyes!" (Crowder and Monroe 2021). In 2021, an official report was issued by the Office of the Director of National Intelligence, acknowledging that UAPs exist, that they might be a threat to national security, and that their causes are unknown (Office of the Director of National Intelligence 2021).

UFO phenomena and alien abductions continue to be popular topics for documentaries, TV shows, books, and online forums. The public's interest and demand for answers (scientific, religious, and otherwise) remain strong—as does the potential of censure of those who address the issue in an open, serious inquiry. With the ongoing acknowledgement of these happenings by those in power, the discourse and the framing therein may well shift.

And what of animal liberationists and those who academically address animal rights issues? Awareness and understanding of such issues continue to increase, along with the prevalence of vegan lifestyles and animal-friendly consumer choices (Minassian 2022). With awareness and acceptance, the space for open discourse grows wider. "The animal turn" in academia, which marks a shift in how animals are studied, is now over two decades old; at academic institutions, animal studies programs (those of the critical variety and beyond) continue to grow. Nonetheless, scholars and activists must choose their battles, navigate context-specific terminology, strategize to reach broader audiences without triggering defensive responses, and find spaces where they can work and publish together in a fully open fashion. They convene in conferences and speak literal volumes about the reality of a world few will ever choose to see. They watch as scholars in other fields openly critique and discuss oppressions and inequalities in public forums— a privilege of studying and working with "isms" that are no longer accepted as cultural norms, as "just the way the world is."

LEARNING FROM THE PARALLELS

Ridicule obliterates power. It isolates and silences. It can turn a credible human in the public's eye into one who is unreliable and potentially unstable. Ridicule forces conformity and a shameful return to the very systems the "catalytic experience" challenges. And it works. The ridiculed communities of animal liberationists and UFO witnesses follow similar trajectories, despite their differences. Thus, they can learn from each other.

First and foremost, it is important to acknowledge and understand how ridicule functions in order to devise strategies for controlling harm and even fighting back. Ridicule and stigma are functional in a society as they reassert norms. Challenging human exceptionalism or anthropocentric sovereignty represents a significant break from said norms— leading to significant backlash. Furthermore, ridicule works indirectly. When Governor Symington held a press conference that publicly invalidated the interests and fears of his constituents through ridicule, it impacted all who watched—even those who read about—the event. Had the thousands of witnesses come together in solidarity to push back on such a cowardly and despicable political response, perhaps the press conference would have opened a road to further investigation rather than constructing a roadblock.

Strength is found in such numbers. Silence begets silence, in both of the communities concerned. The personal is political, as the slogan goes—speaking up can form community and power. Meanwhile, it is also important to acknowledge and understand why some can afford to be more open than others about their UFO experiences, or their animal liberationist philosophy, due to their positionality. Exercise of respect and understanding and appropriate use of one's own power and privilege (when available) are both necessary paths to inclusion.

Recognizing lines of power and privilege can also aid either community in obtaining legitimacy and respectability and avoiding censure. It can be helpful to identify and make use of powerful entities, though such strategies may require reiterating problematic assertions of authority. UFO accounts, for example, often note that the witness is a police officer or a politician and therefore can be trusted—indirectly reaffirming their power and discrediting others. Animal liberationists may identify traditional means of validation as well, such as clinging only to normative science or distancing themselves from terms and trajectories that may paint them as "too radical"—indirectly disparaging the very communities and philosophies they aim to support and endorse. Because Adams and Mack did not hold back—Adams from her openly ridiculed speech at the Oxford "Beyond Meat Debate" and Mack from his open inquiry into alien abductions—they have since inspired, validated, and connected multitudes. Notably, however, both were established scholars when they took on their respective work.

In trying to understand how both groups walked or fell through the doors that led them to these "catalytic experiences" and "epistemological shocks," we can perhaps learn how to best hold the doors open for others. What encouraged them to move forward to the next door? Perhaps it is the strength and validation they gained from community (especially contrasted with the initial ostracization following their epiphany), the seeking and sharing of knowledges previously ignored, or the reframing of extraordinary experiences as empowering and enlightening rather than isolating and burdening. Ridicule is effective and will continue, but we can work together to have the last laugh.

Afterword

Iván Vazquez

Every Friday night, my first stop after I leave the office is, as it has been for the past twenty years or so, the grocery store. It doesn't take long for me to make it to the meat section. I usually hurry past it. I recall that when I was a child, the sight of dead animals being sold caused me enough discomfort that I felt the need to look away. I grew up in Puerto Rico; pork products were the main ingredient in our most popular dishes, and no celebration was complete unless the body of a slain pig was roasting at the center of it. It was common to see brightly colored Whole Roasted Pig for Sale signs hovering over large displays, with the pigs' chilled bodies awaiting purchase. I don't know whether I found the adult pigs' bodies more disturbing, or the piglets'. In the moments when I forced myself to look, I would quietly stare at their faces, not knowing how I should feel. No one else appeared to find it disturbing, so why should I? The only issue shoppers seemed concerned with was the price per pound and whether it was a good bargain or not. At some point—I'm not sure when—cognitive dissonance kicked in for me, and my initial discomfort over the sight of a deceased nonhuman on display faded away. Then I felt nothing.

My first trip to the grocery store after reading through these chapters was very different. I wasn't able to hurry past the meat section as I had in the years since I gave up consuming animal products. Now, I find myself paralyzed by self-reflection—and by fear. Every chapter affected me in a slightly different way. I'll touch on the ones that had the greatest impact on me.

As I read Chapter Two ("The Reproduction of Violence in Resistance to Brahminical Vegetarianism"), I learned about the limitations and complexities surrounding cow protection in India—all new information to me. Previously, I didn't know all the ways in which cows in India are not spared from human greed. The (mis)perception that protection based on religion in at least one corner of the world meant that cows were spared certain types of suffering gave me peace in some ways. Losing that illusion was difficult but necessary. These are the moments of truth that fuel my activism and my personal resolve to maintain a lifestyle that seeks to minimize suffering, though it does not come without hardships. I initially chuckled over the comparison made in Chapter Fifteen ("UFOs and Animal Exploitation: The Rhetoric of Ridicule") between those who are ridiculed for their experiences with UFO sightings and those of us who see nonhuman animals in the same light as we see ourselves and work to have their rights recognized and protected. As I continued to read, I smiled for a different reason, I felt understood. It was brilliant and unexpected! The chapter hit the nail on the head, not just in making that comparison but also in addressing the effects of ridicule in our activist community.

I was vegetarian for nine years before I transitioned to a vegan lifestyle six years ago. What held me back was ignorance. I didn't know the horrors of the dairy industry, and thus I didn't see the need for change until I was given new information by local activists. I eventually joined these activists in their efforts. Educational outreach, as outlined in Chapter Twelve ("Building an Effective Animal Liberation Movement: Beyond Educational Outreach"), is by far my favorite form of activism. It gives me a sense of purpose. It gives me the opportunity to make connections that allow me to nurture and support people whose moral compass opened them up to the need for animal liberation. This form of activism is very dear to me, which is why I appreciate the bravery with which this chapter tackles the very real issues within activist communities, in particular the dangers of hero worship and the need to redefine leadership. My impression has been that this sentiment is shared by many activists, though we don't vocalize it so as to avoid alienation.

Why am I afraid? The book as a whole highlights the physical and spiritual interconnectedness of non/humans and our shared struggles with oppression. We're all soldiers on the same battlefield. "All of us humans are pieced together from our non/human ancestors who paved the way. Non/human liberation struggles are all entangled with each other and there is no real—meaning moral—difference between one and the next." Somewhere along the way, as I reflected on those words, it occurred to me that with all the minority boxes I happen to check off, next to nonhumans, people like myself have the least rights. That thought expanded the ways in which I see myself in my nonhuman brethren and strengthened my connection to them.

I am a pre-op transgender man of color. I've watched so many of my rights—and to some degree, my dignity—slowly being stripped away. The rhetoric around transgender persons and the LGBTQIA+ community in general has been completely dehumanizing, which seems to be the intent. With the increasing efforts to eradicate the transgender population, repeated attacks on the reproductive rights of people assigned female at birth, and never-ending injustices against people of color that go unpunished, I am left to fearfully wonder where the line will finally be drawn. Religious leaders are being cheered on over statements that echo Jason Garber's (a Baptist Church pastor) call for the parents of transgender children to be "convicted in trial, shot in the back of the head and strung up so the public can see the consequences of their wickedness." Politicians who refer to us as "demons and mutants" are applauded by their constituents. Is the endgame of those in power to place everyone who isn't a white cisgender male in the same category as nonhumans in order to justify violence against them? Even if it isn't the plan, is it the inevitable outcome if their efforts succeed? It doesn't seem unreasonable to fear that someday the publicly displayed remains of people like myself might be as easily dismissed as those of nonhuman animals currently are.

I'll admit I was surprised, and intimidated, when one of the editors reached out and asked me to contribute to this project. I am not a scholar. I don't have a formal education. The number of words I had to google to read through some of the chapters in this book surprised me. I've been an activist for some time, but mine is certainly not the loudest voice in the movement. I agreed to participate because I understand oppression from so many different angles, and I hoped there would be value in that. I understand it from the perspective of a woman, a person of color, the parent of a disabled child, a queer/trans person of color, a homeless teen mom . . . . Under those circumstances, there were instances when contributing to the oppression of animals was necessary for survival. I've both intentionally and unintentionally abused what little power I had at times. We tell ourselves it's human nature, but it doesn't need to be, and hopefully the exploration of the topics written about here will open a few more minds to that possibility.

My initial motivation for eliminating animal products from my diet was strictly animal welfare and liberation. Over time, things took a more spiritual turn for me, and I began to understand the cause from a different perspective. Because everything is interconnected, the choice to harm another living being equates to self-harm, as does the choice to overlook this harm. The concept of the Interbeing discussed in Chapter Five ("Interbeing: A Spiritual Insight on the Suffering of Nonhuman Animals") resonated with me in a very meaningful way. Thích Nhất Hạnh's use of a sheet of paper to explain the entanglement of all living things is poetic and illuminating. Non/human coexistence relies on the acceptance that whatever serves others' best interests equally serves ours.

References

Ackelsberg, Martha. 2005. *Free Women of Spain: Anarchism and the Struggle for the Emancipation of Women.* Oakland: AK Press.

Adams, Carol J. 1990. *The Sexual Politics of Meat: A Feminist-Vegetarian Critical Theory.* New York: Continuum.

Adams, Carol J. 1994. *Neither Man nor Beast: Feminism and the Defense of Animals.* New York: Continuum.

Adams, Carol J. 2001. *Living among Meat Eaters: The Vegetarian's Survival Handbook.* New York: Three Rivers Press.

Adams, Carol J., and Lori Gruen, eds. 2022. *Ecofeminism: Feminist Intersections with Other Animals and the Earth*, 2nd ed. New York: Bloomsbury Academic.

Adcock, Cassie S. 2010. "Sacred Cows and Secular History: Cow Protection Debates in Colonial North India." *Comparative Studies of South Asia, Africa, and the Middle East* 30, no. 2: 297–311.

Adcock, Cassie S. 2018. "Cow Protection and Minority Rights in India: Reassessing Religious Freedom." *Asian Affairs (London)* 49, no. 2: 340–54.

Adewale, Omowale, and A. Breeze Harper. 2021. *Brotha Vegan: Black Men Speak on Food Identity, Health, and Society.* New York: Lantern Publishing & Media.

Agriculture Fairness Alliance. 2022. "Vegan Voter Hub." Accessed November 30, 2022. https://agriculturefairnessalliance.org/vegan-voter-hub/.

Akram, Muhammad, Asim Nasar, Muhammad Rizwan Safdar, and Falak Sher. "Restorative Justice Approach to Cow Vigilante Violence in India." *Journal of Ethnic and Cultural Studies* 8, no. 1 (2021): 190–205. doi:10.29333/ejecs/537.

al-Dīn, Mūʾil Yūsuf ʾIzz. 2000. *The Environmental Dimensions of Islam.* Cambridge, UK: The Lutterworth Press.

Ali, Kecia. 2015. "Muslims and Meat-Eating." *Journal of Religious Ethics* 43, no. 2: 268–88.

Allen, Liz. 2021. "Seaspiracy: A Call to Action or a Vehicle of Misinformation?" *Forbes*, April 10, 2021. https://www.forbes.com/sites/allenelizabeth/2021/04/10/seaspiracy-a-call-to-action-or-a-vehicle-of-misinformation/?sh=77ee9dfc23ac.

Alonso, Marta E., José R. González-Montaña, and Juan M. Lomillos. 2020. "Consumers' Concerns and Perceptions of Farm Animal Welfare." *Animals* 10, no. 3: 385–97.

al-Qādir Shaykhalī, Abd. 2006. *Huqūq al-hayawān wa-riāyatuhu fi-l-islām*. Irbid: Dār al-Kitāb al-Thaqāfī.

al-Qarāla, Ahmad Yāsīn. 2009. "Huqūq al-hayawān wa-damānātuhā fī-l-fiqh al-islāmī Al-Majalla al-urduniyya fī-l-dirāsāt al-islāmiyya." *Jordan Journal of Islamic Studies* 5: 23–45.

Anderegg, Christopher, Kathy Archibald, Jarrod Bailey, Murry J. Cohen, Stephen R. Kaufman, and John J. Pippin. 2006. *A Critical Look at Animal Experimentation*. Cleveland, OH: Medical Research Modernization Committee.

Anderson, William C. 2021. *The Nation on No Map: Black Anarchism and Abolition*. Oakland: AK Press.

Anjorin, Elizabeth, Glenn Floyd, John Chesterman, Rene Talbot, and Uwe Pankow. 2019. "Report on the Deprivation of Liberty of Persons with Disabilities." United Nations Human Rights. https://www.ohchr.org/en/issues/disability/srdisabilities/pages/libertyandsecurity.aspx.

Arbour, Rosie, Tania Signal, and Nik Taylor. 2009. "Teaching Kindness: The Promise of Humane Education." *Society & Animals* 17, no. 2: 136–48. doi:10.1163/156853009X418073.

Archibald, Kathy, Katya Tsaioun, J. Gerry Kenna, and Pandora Pound. 2018. "Better Science for Safer Medicines: The Human Imperative." *Journal of the Royal Society of Medicine* 111, no. 12: 433–38.

Arruzza, Cinzia, Tithi Bhattacharya, and Nancy Fraser. 2019. *Feminism for the 99%: A Manifesto*. London and New York: Verso.

Ashraf, Ajaz. 2017. "Why Hindu Farmers and Cattle Traders in Rajasthan Are Angry with Gau Rakshaks." Scroll.in, May 6, 2017. https://scroll.in/article/836477/why-hindu-farmers-and-cattle-traders-in-rajasthan-are-angry-with-gau-rakshaks.

Awry, Wren, ed. 2023. *Nourishing Resistance: Stories of Food, Protest, and Mutual Aid*. Oakland: PM Press.

Bagby-Williams, Atticus, and Nsambu Za Suekama. 2022. *Black Anarchism and the Black Radical Tradition*. Cantley, Quebec: Daraja Press.

Bailey, Cathryn. 2007. "We Are What We Eat: Feminist Vegetarianism and the Reproduction of Racial Identity." *Hypatia* 22, no. 2: 39–59.

Bardon, Yves, Nicolas Boyan, and Chloe Morin. 2018. "Human Rights in 2018." *Ipsos.* https://www.ipsos.com/en-us/news-polls/global-advisor-human-rights-2018.

Bechocha, Julian. 2023. "Two Dead in Suspected Turkish Drone Strikes on Sulaimani." *Rudaw*, April 16, 2023. https://www.rudaw.net/english/kurdistan/16042023.

Bee Health Collective. 2020. "Honey." https://beehealthcollective.org/honey-dashboard.

Bekoff, Marc. 2014. *Rewilding Our Hearts: Building Pathways of Compassion and Coexistence*. Novato, CA: New World Library.

Bem, Daryl J. 1970. *Beliefs, Attitudes, and Human Affairs*. Pacific Grove, CA: Brooks/Cole.

Bendik-Keymer, Jeremy. 2020. *Involving Anthroponomy in the Anthropocene: On Decoloniality*. Oxfordshire, UK: Routledge.

Berger, John. 2009. *Why Look at Animals?* London: Penguin Books.

Best, Steven, Anthony J. Nocella II, Richard Kahn, Carol Gigliotti, and Lisa Kemmerer. 2007. "Introducing Critical Animal Studies." *Animal Liberation Philosophy and Policy Journal* 5, no. 1: 4–5.

Bey, Marquis. 2019. *Them Goon Rules: Fugitive Essays on Radical Black Feminism*. Tucson: University of Arizona Press.

Bey, Marquis. 2020a. *Anarcho-Blackness: Notes towards a Black Anarchism*. Oakland: AK Press.

Bey, Marquis. 2020b. *The Problem of the Negro as a Problem for Gender*. Minneapolis MN: University of Minnesota Press.

Bey, Marquis. 2022. *Black Trans Feminism*. Durham, NC: Duke University Press.

Biddle, Matthew. 2021. "When Meat-Eaters Feel Guilty, They Choose Healthier Meat Dishes—Instead of Veggies." Accessed November 30, 2022. https://www.buffalo.edu/grad/news.host.html/content/shared/university/news/ub-reporter-articles/stories/2021/05/meat-eating-choices.detail.html.

Billet, Alexander. 2021. "Giving Up the Ghost: On the Legacy of Mark Fisher." *Los Angeles Review of Books*. https://lareviewofbooks.org/article/giving-up-the-ghost-on-the-legacy-of-mark-fisher/.

Black Rose Anarchist Federation. 2016. *Black Anarchism: A Reader*. Black Rose Anarchist Federation. http://blackrosefed.org/black-anarchism-a-reader/.

Blanco, Andrea. 2023. "Titanic Sub Implosion: OceanGate CEO's Chilling Words about Titan Revealed as Company Shudders after Disaster." *The Independent*, July 8, 2023. https://www.independent.co.uk/news/world/americas/titanic-tourist-sub-missing-oceangate-implosion-b2371067.html.

Bois, Thomas. 1966. *The Kurds*. Beirut: Khayats.

Bottici, Chiara. 2021. *Anarchafeminism*. London: Bloomsbury.

Bousquet, G. H. 1958. "Des Animaux et de Leur Traitement Selon Le Judaïsme, Le Christianisme et l'Islam." *Studia Islamica* 9: 31–48.

Bowman, Sarah. 2019. "113 Tons of Dead Fish: Indiana's Worst Environmental Disaster, 20 Years Later." *Indianapolis Star*. https://www.dispatch.com/in-depth/news/environment/2019/12/19/guide-corp-s-toxic-discharge-killed-millions-fish-white-river/4385458002/.

Boyce, Niall. 2012. "The Psychiatrist Who Wanted to Believe." *The Lancet* 380, no. 9848: 1140–41.

Boyd, Andrew, ed. 2016. *Beautiful Trouble: A Toolbox for Revolution*. New York: OR Books.

Bresnahan, Mary, Jie Zhuang, and Xun Zhu. 2016. "Why Is the Vegan Line in the Dining Hall Always the Shortest? Understanding Vegan Stigma." *Stigma and Health* 1, no. 1: 3–15.

Brookfield, Stephen D. 2011. *Teaching for Critical Thinking: Tools and Techniques to Help Students Question Their Assumptions*. San Francisco: Jossey-Bass.

Brookfield, Stephen D. 2013. *Powerful Techniques for Teaching Adults*. San Francisco: Jossey-Bass.

Brookfield, Stephen D., and Mary E. Hess. 2021. *Becoming a White Antiracist: A Practical Guide for Educators, Leaders, and Activists*. Sterling, VA: Stylus Publishing.

Brueck, Julia Feliz. 2019. *Veganism of Color: Decentering Whiteness in Human and Nonhuman Liberation*. Sanctuary Publishers.

van Bruinessen, Martin. 1992. *Agha, Shaikh and State: The Social and Political Structures of Kurdistan*. London; Atlantic Highlands, NJ: Zed Books.

Bryant, Jennings, Dan Brown, and Sheri L. Parks. 1981. "Ridicule as an Educational Corrective." *Journal of Educational Psychology* 73, no. 5: 722–27.

Bryant, Jennings, Dan Brown, Sheri L. Parks, and Dolf Zillmann. 1983. "Children's Imitation of a Ridiculed Model." *Human Communication Research* 10, no. 2: 243–55.

Bundock, Jennai. 2022. "The Hidden Cost of Patriarchy." Filmed July 2014. Video, 1:04:01. https://vimeo.com/100087331.

CAFT. 2022. "Victories." Accessed November 30, 2022. https://caftusa.org/victories/.

Callicott, J. Baird. 1980. "Animal Liberation: A Triangular Affair." *Environmental Ethics* 2: 311–37.

Camp, Jon. 2014. "One Million Leaflets!" Vegan Outreach. Accessed April 5, 2023. https://veganoutreach.org/one-million-leaflets/.

Campbell, Ian J. 2018. "Animal Welfare and Environmental Ethics: It's Complicated." *Ethics and the Environment* 23, no. 1: 49–69.

Carbstrong, Joey. 2016. "Slaughterhouse Worker vs Vegan I." Filmed November 19, 2016. Video, 16:26. https://www.youtube.com/watch?v=fPXW2dSM1g&list=PL9H0QfopRsccyAOFBAqB38gdPPbrWVNvb&index=24.

Carbstrong, Joey. 2017. "Vegan vs Farmer [A Moral Dilemma]." Filmed August 18, 2018. Video, 17:29. https://www.youtube.com/watch?v=PHl2efS8ZXQ&list=PL9H0QfopRsccyAOFBAqB38gdPPbrWVNvb&index=62.

Carruthers, Peter. 1989. "Brute Experience." *The Journal of Philosophy* 86, no. 5: 258–69.

Castricano, Jodey, and Rasmus Simonsen, eds. 2016. *Critical Perspectives on Veganism*. London: Palgrave Macmillan.

"Cat Breeds: The Hidden Problem of Inherited Diseases." *Veterinary Ireland Journal*. Last modified March 2019. http://www.veterinaryirelandjournal.com/small-animal/74-cat-breeds-the-hidden-problem-of-inherited-diseases.

Celermajer, Danielle, and Darren Chang. Forthcoming. "A Grateful Acknowledgement: Gender Theory and Multispecies Justice." In *The Routledge Companion to Gender and Animals*, edited by Chloë Taylor. London: Routledge.

Celermajer, Danielle, David Schlosberg, Lauren Rickards, Makere Stewart-Harawira, Mathias Thaler, Petra Tschakert, Blanche Verlie, and Christine Winter. 2021. "Multispecies Justice: Theories, Challenges, and a Research Agenda for Environmental Politics." *Environmental Politics* 30, no. 1–2: 119–40.

Center for Story-based Strategy. n.d. "Story-Based Strategy." Accessed November 28, 2022. https://www.storybasedstrategy.org/what-is-storybased-strategy.

Centers for Disease Control and Prevention. 2021. "Zoonotic Diseases." Accessed November 30, 2022. https://www.cdc.gov/one-health/about/about-zoonotic-diseases.html.

Chao, Sophie, Karin Bolender, and Eben Kirksey. 2022. *The Promise of Multispecies Justice.* Durham, NC: Duke University Press.

Cherry, Elizabeth. 2016. "'The Pig That Therefore I Am': Visual Art and Animal Activism." *Humanity and Society* 40, no. 1: 64–85.

Chigateri, Shraddha. 2008. "'Glory to the Cow': Cultural Difference and Social Justice in the Food Hierarchy in India." *South Asia* 31, no. 1: 10–35.

Chigateri, Shraddha. 2010. "Negotiating the 'Sacred' Cow: Cow Slaughter and the Regulation of Difference in India." In *Democracy, Religious Pluralism and the Liberal Dilemma of Accommodation*, edited by Monica Mookherjee, 137–59. Dordrecht: Springer Netherlands.

Chilis on Wheels. n.d. "What Is Chilis on Wheels?" Accessed April 23, 2023. https://www.chilisonwheels.org/about/.

Chiorando, Maria. 2020. "Exclusive: Earthling ED to Open Animal Sanctuary." *Plant-Based News.* Accessed November 28, 2022. https://plantbasednews.org/culture/ethics/earthling-ed-open-surge-sanctuary/.

Chow, Pierce K. H., Robert T. H. Ng, and Bryan E. Ogden. 2008. *Using Animal Models in Biomedical Research: A Primer for the Investigator.* Singapore: World Scientific.

Clance, Pauline Rose, and Suzane Ament Imes. 1978. "The Imposter Phenomenon in High Achieving Women: Dynamics and Therapeutic Intervention." *Psychotherapy: Theory, Research and Practice* 15, no. 3: 241–47.

Clark, John, and Camille Martin, eds. and trans. 2013. *Anarchy, Geography, Modernity: Selected Writings of Elisée Reclus.* Oakland: PM Press.

Clutton-Brock, Juliet. 1999. *A Natural History of Domesticated Mammals.* Cambridge, UK: Cambridge University Press.

Cohen, Carl. 1986. "The Case for the Use of Animals in Biomedical Research." *The New England Journal of Medicine* 315: 94–100.

Colling, Sarat, Sean Parson, and Alessandro Arrigoni. 2014. "Until All Are Free: Total Liberation through Revolutionary Decolonization, Groundless Solidarity, and a Relationship Framework." In *Defining Critical Animal Studies: An Intersectional Social Justice Approach for Liberation*, edited by Anthony Nocella, John Sorenson, Kim Socha, and Atsuko Matsuoka, 51–73. New York: Peter Lang.

Collins, Patricia Hill. 2022. *Black Feminist Thought: Knowledge, Consciousness, and the Politics of Empowerment*, 3rd ed. Oxfordshire, UK: Routledge.

Combahee River Collective. 1977. "The Combahee River Collective Statement." Accessed on February 28, 2023. https://www.blackpast.org/african-american-history/combahee-river-collective-statement-1977/.

Cooney, Nick. 2011. *Change of Heart: What Psychology Can Teach Us about Spreading Social Change*. Brooklyn: Lantern Books.

Cooper, Helene, Ralph Blumenthal, and Leslie Kean. 2017. "Glowing Auras and Black Money, The Pentagon's Mysterious UFO Program." *New York Times*, December 16, 2017. https://www.nytimes.com/2017/12/16/us/politics/pentagon-program-ufo-harry-reid.html.

Cornish, Amelia, Bethany Wilson, David Raubenheimer, and Paul McGreevy. 2018. "Demographics Regarding Belief in Non-Human Animal Sentience and Emotional Empathy with Animals: A Pilot Study among Attendees of an Animal Welfare Symposium." *Animals* 8, no. 10: 174. doi:10.3390/ani8100174.

The Cranky Vegan. 2018. "Are We Winning // A Challenge to James Aspey." Filmed July 3, 2018. Video, 8:31. https://www.youtube.com/watch?v=pApTaNTZqJc&list=PLDi86oKRn2xs2khTFEO6WhTsV0A872gq8&index=12.

The Cranky Vegan. 2021a. "3MT: I Agree with James Aspey, Joey Carbstrong & Anonymous for the Voiceless." Filmed January 28, 2021. Video, 9:20. https://www.youtube.com/watch?v=WnpTXJ2irgQ.

The Cranky Vegan. 2021b. "3MT: James Aspey – Con Man or Conned?" Filmed February 11, 2021. Video, 13:36. https://www.youtube.com/watch?v=-6i6XnD6lyY.

The Cranky Vegan. 2021c. "Disrupt These Points // S03 E05 // Are We Winning." Filmed May 21, 2020. Video, 10:01. https://www.youtube.com/watch?v=5J0MgYzp_aE&list=PLDi86oKRn2xuu8vr0WiN_jNdDD56BAPo&index=7.

The Cranky Vegan. 2022. "3MT: James Aspey Is BACK!" Filmed November 10, 2022. Video, 10:33. https://www.youtube.com/watch?v=mOD0cF3G9fg.

Cranton, Patricia. 2016. *Understanding and Promoting Transformative Learning: A Guide to Theory and Practice*, 3rd ed. Sterling, VA: Stylus Publishing.

Crenshaw, Kimberlé. 1990. "Mapping the Margins: Intersectionality, Identity Politics, and Violence against Women of Color." *Stanford Law Review* 43: 1241–300.

Christman, Phil. 2020. "Turning Nothings into Somethings: 'Postcapitalist Desire'." *Commonweal*, December 3, 2020. https://www.commonwealmagazine.org/turning-nothings-somethings.

CrimethInc. 2019. "Against the Logic of the Guillotine." https://crimethinc.com/2019/04/08/against-the-logic-of-the-guillotine-why-the-paris-commune-burned-the-guillotine-and-we-should-too.

Crowder, Paul, and Mark Monroe, dirs. 2021. *UFO.* Showtime Documentary Films and Bad Robot. Film.

Cornell University College of Veterinary Medicine. 2017. "Obesity." Cornell Feline Health Center. https://www.vet.cornell.edu/departments-centers-and-institutes/cornell-feline-health-center/health-information/feline-health-topics/obesity.

Cudworth, Erika. 2005. *Developing Ecofeminist Theory.* Hampshire, UK: Palgrave MacMillan.

Curtin, Deane. 1996. "Toward an Ecological Ethic of Care." In *Beyond Animal Rights: A Feminist Caring Ethic for the Treatment of Animals,* edited by Josephine Donovan and Carol J. Adams, 60–76. New York: Continuum.

"Dani." 2015. Woodstock Farm Sanctuary. Last modified October 8, 2015. https://woodstocksanctuary.org/meet-the-rescued-animals/danis-story.

Dean, Jodi. 1997. "The Truth Is Out There: Aliens and the Fugitivity of Postmodern Truth." *Camera Obscura* 14, no. 1–2: 42–74.

Deemer, Danielle R., and Linda M. Lobao. 2011. "Public Concern with Farm-Animal Welfare: Religion, Politics, and Human Disadvantage in the Food Sector." *Rural Sociology* 76, no. 2: 67–196.

Defenders of Wildlife. 2022. "Sonoran Pronghorn." https://defenders.org/wildlife/sonoran-pronghorn.

Denzler, Brenda. 2001. *The Lure of the Edge: Scientific Passions, Religious Beliefs, and the Pursuit of UFOs.* Berkeley: University of California Press.

Department of Homeland Security. 2021. "Border Wall System." https://web.archive.org/web/20210121203240/https://www.cbp.gov/border-security/along-us-borders/border-wall-system.

Despret, Vincent. 2012. *What Would Animals Say if We Asked the Right Questions?* Minneapolis: University of Minnesota Press.

Dhont, Kristof, and Gordon Hodson, eds. 2020. *Why We Love and Exploit Animals: Bridging Insights from Academia and Advocacy.* Oxfordshire, UK: Routledge.

Dhont, Kristof, Gordon Hodson, A. Leite, and A. Salmen. 2020. "The Psychology of Speciesism." In *Why We Love and Exploit Animals: Bridging Insights from Academia and Advocacy,* edited by Kristof Dhont and Gordon Hodson, 29–49. Oxfordshire, UK: Routledge.

Dietz, Thomas. 2015. "Environmental Value." In *Handbook of Value: Perspectives from Economics, Neuroscience, Philosophy, Psychology, and Sociology,* edited by Tobias Brosch and David Sander, 329–49. Oxford: Oxford University Press.

Dietz, Thomas, Summer Allen, and Aaron M. McCright. 2017. "Integrating Concern for Animals into Personal Values. *Anthrozoös* 30, no. 1: 109–22.

Dillard, Jennifer. 2008. "A Slaughterhouse Nightmare: Psychological Harm Suffered by Slaughterhouse Employees and the Possibility of Redress through Legal Reform." *Georgetown Journal on Poverty Law and Policy* 15, no. 2: 1–18.

Dixon, Chris. 2014. *Another Politics: Talking across Today's Transformative Movements.* Oakland: University of California Press.

Dominick, Brian A. 1997. *Animal Liberation and Social Revolution: A Vegan Perspective on Anarchism or an Anarchist Perspective on Veganism.* Critical Mess Media.

Donovan, Josephine. 2009. "Tolstoy's Animals." *Society & Animals* 17, no. 1: 38–52.

Doshi, Vidhi. 2017. "To Protest Modi, These Indians Are Cooking Beef in Public." *Washington Post,* June 6, 2017. https://www.washingtonpost.com/world/asia_pacific/protests-against-the-governments-anti-beef-laws-spread-in-india/2017/06/05/8aa05dfc-489e-11e7-bcde-624ad94170ab_story.html.

Drago, William A., and Richard J. Wagner. 2004. "Vark Preferred Learning Styles and Online Education." *Management Research News* 27, no. 7: 1–13.

Driscoll, Carlos A., Marilyn Menotti-Raymond, Alfred L. Roca, Karsten Hupe, Warren E. Johnson, Eli Geffen, Eric H. Harley, Miguel Delibes, Dominique Pontier, Andrew C. Kitchener, Nobuyuki Yamaguchi, Stephen J. O'Brien, and David W. Macdonald. 2007. "The Near Eastern Origin of Cat Domestication." *Science* 317, no. 5837: 519–23.

Dunn, Kirsty. 2019. "Kaimangatanga: Maori Perspectives on Veganism and Plant-Based Kai." *Animal Studies Journal* 8, no. 1: 42–65.

Ehsan, Mir. 2015. "Independent MLA behind 'Beef Party' Asks Government to Serve Beef in J&K House." *The Indian Express,* October 28, 2015. https://indianexpress.com/article/india/india-news-india/independent-mla-behind-beef-party-asks-government-to-serve-beef-in-jk-house/.

Ervin, Lorenzo Kom'boa. 2022. *Anarchism and the Black Revolution.* London: Pluto Press. First published 1979.

Evans, Brodie, and Hope Johnson. 2021. "Contesting and Reinforcing the Future of 'Meat' through Problematization: Analyzing the Discourses in Regulatory Debates around Animal Cell-Cultured Meat." *Geoforum* 127: 81–91.

Evans, Katy M., and Vicki J. Adams. 2010. "Proportion of Litters of Purebred Dogs Born by Caesarean Section." *The Journal of Small Animal Practice* 51, no. 2: 113–18.

Falvey Memorial Library. 2022. "The Nativist Movement." Villanova University Falvey Memorial Library. https://exhibits.library.villanova.edu/index.php/chaos-in-the-streets-the-philadelphia-riots-of-1844/nativism.

Fano, Alix. 1997. *Lethal Laws: Animal Testing, Human Health and Environmental Policy.* London: Zed Books Ltd.

Farouk, Mustafa M., Joe M. Regenstein, Maryann R. Pirie, R. Najm, Alaa ED Bekhit, and Scott O. Knowles. 2015. "Spiritual Aspects of Meat and Nutritional Security: Perspectives and Responsibilities of the Abrahamic Faiths." *Food Research International* 76: 882–95.

Feather, Norman T. 1995. "Values, Valences, and Choice: The Influences of Values on the Perceived Attractiveness and Choice of Alternatives." *Journal of Personality and Social Psychology* 68, no. 6: 1135–51.

Feliz, Julia, and Z. McNeill, eds. 2020. *Queer and Trans Voices: Achieving Liberation through Consistent Anti-Oppression*. Sanctuary Publishers.

Femia, Joseph V. 1987. *Gramsci's Political Thought Hegemony, Consciousness and the Revolutionary Process*. Oxford: Clarendon.

Fernand, Malcolm. 2022. *Decolonial Ecology: Thinking from the Caribbean World*. Cambridge, UK: Polity Press.

Fernández, Laura. 2020. "The Emotional Politics of Images: Moral Shock, Explicit Violence and Strategic Visual Communication in the Animal Liberation Movement." *Critical Animal Studies* 17, no. 4: 53–80.

Figueroa Helland, Leonardo E., and Tim Lindgren. 2016. "What Goes around Comes Around: From the Coloniality of Power to the Crisis of Civilization." *Journal of World-Systems Research* 22, no. 2: 430–62.

Fisher, Mark. 2010. *Capitalist Realism: Is There No Alternative?* Hampshire, UK: Zero Books.

Fisher, Mark. 2013. "Exiting the Vampire Castle." *Open Democracy*, November 24, 2013. https://www.opendemocracy.net/en/opendemocracyuk/exiting-vampire-castle/.

Fisher, Mark. 2014. *Ghosts of My Life: Writings on Depression, Hauntology and Lost Futures*. Hampshire, UK: Zero Books.

Fisher, Mark. 2017. *The Weird and the Eerie*. London: Repeater.

Fisher, Mark. 2018. *K-Punk: The Collected and Unpublished Writings of Mark Fisher from 2004–2016*. Edited by D. Ambrose. London: Repeater.

Fisher, Mark. 2020. *Postcapitalist Desire*. Edited by M. Colquhoun. London: Repeater.

Fletcher, Robert. 2017. "Environmentality Unbound: Multiple Governmentalities in Environmental Politics." *Geoforum* 85: 311–15. doi:10.1016/j.geoforum.2017.06.009.

Flynn, Clifton P. 2003. "A Course Is a Course, of Course, of Course (Unless It's an Animals and Society Course): Challenging Boundaries in Academia." *International Journal of Sociology and Social Policy* 23, no. 3: 94–108.

Foltz, Richard. 2001. "Is Vegetarianism Un-Islamic?" *Studies in Contemporary Islam* 3, no 1: 39–54.

Food Empowerment Project. n.d. "Missions and Values." Accessed April 23, 2023. https://foodispower.org/mission-and-values/.

Foucault, Michel. 1995. *Discipline and Punish: The Birth of the Prison*. Translated by Alan Sheridan. New York: Vintage.

Fraiman, Susan. 2022. "Pussy Panic versus Liking Animals: Tracking Gender in Animal Studies." In *Ecofeminism: Feminist Intersections with Other Animals and the Earth*, 2nd ed., edited by Carol J. Adams and Lori Gruen, 283–312. New York: Bloomsbury Academic.

Friedman, Uri. 2017. "What Is a Nativist?" *The Atlantic*, April 11, 2017. https://www.theatlantic.com/international/archive/2017/04/what-is-nativist-trump/521355/.

Gaard, Greta C. 1993. *Ecofeminism: Women, Animals, Nature*. Philadelphia: Temple University Press.

Gaard, Greta C. 2017. *Critical Ecofeminism*. Lanham: Lexington Books.

Ganz, Marshall. 2015. "Strategizing." Lecture notes from Leadership, Organizing and Action: Leading Change workshop.

George, Amber E., and J. L. Schatz, eds. 2016. *Screening the Nonhuman: Representations of Animal Others in the Media*. Lanham: Lexington.

George, Pavithra. 2021. "'Normalizing' UFOs – Retired U.S. Navy Pilot Recalls Tic Tac Encounter." *Reuters*, June 25, 2001. https://www.reuters.com/lifestyle/science/normalizing-ufos-retired-us-navy-pilot-recalls-tic-tac-encounter-2021-06-25/.

Giles, Richard Eugene. 2022. "Under the Skin: Assessing the Ideological Underpinnings and Material Reality of Cultured Meat." Doctoral thesis, University of Waterloo.

Gillespie, Kathryn, and Rosemary-Claire Collard, eds. 2015. *Critical Animal Geographies: Politics, Intersections and Hierarchies in a Multispecies World*. Oxfordshire, UK: Routledge.

Ginwright, Shawn. 2020. "The Future of Healing: Shifting from Trauma Informed Care to Healing Centered Engagement." *Medium*, December 9, 2020. https://ginwright.medium.com/the-future-of-healing-shifting-from-trauma-informed-care-to-healing-centered-engagement-634f557ce69c.

Goodfellow, Aiyana. 2021. *Radical Companionship: Rejecting Pethood and Embracing Our Multispecies World*. Active Distribution.

Google/YouTube Help. 2022. "How Engagement Metrics Are Counted." Accessed November 28, 2022. https://support.google.com/youtube/answer/2991785?hl=en.

Gormezano, Linda J., and Robert F. Rockwell. 2013. "What to Eat Now? Shifts in Polar Bear Diet during the Ice-Free Season in Western Hudson Bay." *Ecology and Evolution* 3, no. 10: 3509–23.

Gorski, Paul, Stacy Lopresti-Goodman, and Dallas Rising. 2019. "'Nobody's Paying Me to Cry': The Causes of Activist Burnout in United States Animal Rights Activists." *Social Movement Studies* 18, no. 3: 364–80.

Granovetter, Sara. 2021. "Activist as Symptom: Healing Trauma within a Ruptured Collective." *Society & Animals* 29, no. 7: 659–78.

Greenbaum, Jessica. 2012. "Managing Impressions: 'Face-saving' Strategies of Vegetarians and Vegans." *Humanity & Society* 36, no. 4: 309–25.

Greenbaum, Jessica, and Brandon Dexter. 2018. "Vegan Men and Hybrid Masculinity." *Journal of Gender Studies* 27, no. 6: 637–48.

Greig, Kieran. 2017. "Leafletting Intervention Report." Animal Charity Evaluators. Accessed April 2, 2023. https://animalcharityevaluators.org/research/reports/leafleting/#report.

Grewell, Greg. 2013. "Rhetoric of Ridicule." Doctoral thesis, University of Arizona.

Gruen, Lori. 2004. "Empathy and Vegetarian Commitments." In *Food for Thought: The Debate over Eating Meat*, edited by Steve. F. Sapontzis, 284–92. Buffalo: Prometheus.

Gruen, Lori. 2015. *Entangled Empathy: An Alternative Ethic for Our Relationships with Animals*. New York: Lantern Publishing & Media.

Gundimeda, Sambaiah. 2009. "Democratiazation of the Public Sphere: The Beef Stall Case in Hyderabad's Sukoon Festival." *Broadsheet on Contemporary Politics* 29, no. 2 (September): 127–49.

Gundimeda, Sambaiah, and V. S. Ashwin. 2018. "Cow Protection in India: From Secularising to Legitimating Debates." *South Asia Research* 38, no. 2: 156–76.

Hall, K. Melchor Quick. 2021. "Darkness All around Me: Black Waters, Land, Animals, and Sky." In *Mapping Gendered Ecologies: Engaging with and beyond Ecowomanism and Ecofeminism*, edited by K. Melchor Quick Hall and Gwyn Kirk, 17–32. Lanham: Lexington Books.

Hall, K. Melchor Quick, and Gwyn Kirk, eds. (2021). *Mapping Gendered Ecologies: Engaging with and beyond Ecowomanism and Ecofeminism*. Lanham: Lexington Books.

Halsey, Mark, and Rob White. 1998. "Crime, Ecophilosophy and Environmental Harm." *Theoretical Criminology* 2, no. 3: 345–71.

Handwerk, Brian. 2018. "How Accurate Is Alpha's Theory of Dog Domestication?" *Smithsonian Magazine*, August 15, 2018. https://www.smithsonianmag.com/science-nature/how-wolves-really-became-dogs-180970014/.

Haraway, Donna. 2008. *When Species Meet*. Minneapolis: University of Minnesota Press.

Harper, Breeze A. 2010. *Sistah Vegan: Black Female Vegans Speak on Food, Identity, Health, and Society*. New York: Lantern Books.

Harris, Malcolm. 2022. "Just Beans: What Was Ethical Consumption under Capitalism?" *The Drift*, November 1, 2022. https://www.thedriftmag.com/just-beans/.

Haupt, Lyanda Lynn. 2009. *Crow Planet: Essential Wisdom from the Urban Wilderness*. New York: Back Bay Books.

Heberlein, Thomas A. 2012. *Navigating Environmental Attitudes*. New York: Oxford University Press.

Herzog, Harold A., and Lauren L. Golden. 2009. "Moral Emotions and Social Activism: The Case of Animal Rights." *Journal of Social Issues* 65, no. 3: 485–98.

Hirschler, Christopher. 2011. "'What Pushed Me over the Edge Was a Deer Hunter': Being Vegan in North America." *Society & Animals* 19, no. 2: 156–74.

Hodge, Paul, Andrew McGregor, Simon Springer, Ophélie Véron, and Richard J. White, eds. 2022. *Vegan Geographies: Spaces beyond Violence, Ethics beyond Speciesism.* Brooklyn: Lantern Publishing & Media.

Holst, Mirja Annalena A. 2021. "'To Be Is to Inter-Be': Thích Nhất Hạnh on Independent Arising." *Journal of World Philosophies* 6, no. 2 (Winter): 17–30. https://scholarworks.iu.edu/iupjournals/index.php/jwp.

hooks, bell. 1984. *Feminist Theory: From Margin to Center.* Boston: South End Press.

hooks, bell. 2009. *Belonging: A Culture of Place.* New York: Routledge.

Hsiung, Wayne. 2022. "How Harvard Justifies Animal Torture with the Doctrine of 'Necessary Evil.'" https://simpleheart.substack.com/p/how-harvard-justifies-animal-torture.

HSUS. n.d. "Outdoor Cats FAQ." The Humane Society of the United States. Accessed August 3, 2023. https://www.humanesociety.org/resources/outdoor-cats-faq.

HSUS. 2021. "Puppy Mills: Facts and Figures." The Humane Society of the United States. https://www.humanesociety.org/sites/default/files/docs/puppy-mills-facts-and-figures.pdf.

The Humane League. 2023. "Research Reports." Accessed April 1, 2023. https://thehumaneleague.org/research-reports.

Humane Society International. n.d. "About Animal Testing." https://www.hsi.org/news-resources/about/.

Hurwitz, Heather McKee. 2021. *Are We the 99%? The Occupy Movement, Feminism, and Intersectionality.* Philadelphia: Temple University Press.

Hussain, Grace. 2021. "How Many Animals Are Killed for Food Every Day?" *Sentient Media.* December 17, 2021.

Irvine, Leslie. 2002. "Animal Problems/People Skills: Emotional and Interactional Strategies in Humane Education." *Society & Animals* 10, no. 1: 63–91. doi:10.1163/156853002760030888.

Isfahani-Hammond, Alexandra. 2023. "Memes about Animal Resistance Are Everywhere – Here's Why You Shouldn't Laugh off Rebellious Orcas and Sea Otters Too Quickly." *The Conversation*, August 18, 2023. https://theconversation.com/memes-about-animal-resistance-are-everywhere-heres-why-you-shouldnt-laugh-off-rebellious-orcas-and-sea-otters-too-quickly-210622.

Ismail, Asif. 2011. "Bad for Your Health: The U.S. Medical Industrial Complex Goes Global." In *The Global Industrial Complex: Systems of Domination*, edited by Steven Best, Richard Kahn, Anthony J. Nocella, and Peter McLaren. Plymouth: Lexington.

Israel, Lana. 1995. "Mack's Research Is Under Scrutiny." *Harvard Crimson,* April 17, 1995. https://www.thecrimson.com/article/1995/4/17/macks-research-is-under-scrutiny-pdean/.

Jacobs, David. 1992. *Secret Life: Firsthand Documented Accounts of UFO Abductions.* New York: Simon & Schuster.

Jaffrelot, Christophe. 2008. "Hindu Nationalism and the (Not So Easy) Art of Being Outraged: The Ram Setu Controversy." *South Asia Multidisciplinary Academic Journal* 2. doi:10.4000/samaj.1372.

Jameson, Frederic. 1991. *Postmodernism, or the Cultural Logic of Late Capitalism.* Durham, NC: Duke University Press.

Jameson, Frederic. 2003. "Future City." *New Left Review* 21 (May/June). https://newleftreview.org/issues/ii21/articles/fredric-jameson-future-city.

Janes, Leslie M., and James M. Olson. 2000. "Jeer Pressure: The Behavioral Effects of Observing Ridicule of Others." *Personality and Social Psychology Bulletin* 26, no. 4: 474–85.

Jasper, James M., and Jane D. Poulsen. 1995. "Recruiting Strangers and Friends: Moral Shocks and Social Networks in Animal Rights and Anti-Nuclear Protests." *Social Problems* 42, no. 4: 493–512.

Jeppesen, Sandra. 2019. "Toward an Anarchist-Feminist Analytics of Power." In *The Anarchist Imagination,* edited by Carl Levy and Saul Newman, 110–31. Oxfordshire, UK: Routledge.

Jha, Satish. 2016. "Dalit Asmita Yatra: Crowds Brave Rain, New Leaders Take Centrestage." *Indian Express,* August 11, 2016. https://indianexpress.com/article/india/india-news-india/dalit-asmita-yatra-crowds-brave-rain-new-leaders-take-centrestage-2969601/.

jones, pattrice. 2007. *Aftershock: Confronting Trauma in a Violent World: A Guide for Activists and Their Allies.* New York: Lantern Books.

jones, pattrice. 2014. *The Oxen at the Intersection.* New York: Lantern Books.

jones, pattrice. 2021. "Eros and the Mechanisms of Eco-Defense." In *Ecofeminism: Feminist Intersections with Other Animals and the Earth,* 2nd ed., 123–38. New York: Bloomsbury Academic.

Kabat-Zinn, Jon. 2013. *Full Catastrophe Living: Using the Wisdom of Your Body and Mind to Face Stress, Pain, and Illness,* revised and updated ed. New York: Bantam Books.

Kahneman, Daniel. 2011. *Thinking Fast and Slow.* New York: Farrar, Straus, and Giroux.

Kalvapalle, Rahul. 2017. "Many Americans Think Chocolate Milk Comes from Brown Cows: Study." *Global News,* June 16, 2017. https://globalnews.ca/news/3535819/chocolate-milk-brown-cows-survey/.

The Kennel Club. n.d. "About Breed Standards." Accessed on January 3, 2020. https://www.thekennelclub.org.uk/activities/dog-showing/breed-standards/about-breed-standards/.

Kheel, Marti. 1993. "From Heroic to Holistic Ethics: The Ecofeminist Challenge." In *Ecofeminism: Women, Animals, Nature*, edited by Greta Gaard, 243–71. Philadelphia: Temple University Press.

Kheel, Marti. 2004. "Vegetarianism and Ecofeminism: Toppling Patriarchy with a Fork." In *Food for Thought: The Debate over Eating Meat*, edited by Steve F. Sapontzis, 327–41. Amherst, NY: Prometheus Books.

Kight, Pat. 2012. "Asian Carp Fact Sheet." Oregon Sea Grant. https://seagrant.oregonstate.edu/sites/seagrant.oregonstate.edu/files/invasive-species/toolkit/asian-carp-factsheet.html.

Kim, Claire Jean. 2015. *Dangerous Crossings: Race, Species, and Nature in a Multicultural Age*. Cambridge, UK: Cambridge University Press.

King, Tiffany Lethabo. 2019. *The Black Shoals: Offshore Formations of Black and Native Studies*. Durham, NC: Duke University Press.

Kinna, Ruth. 2018. "Anarchism and Feminism." In *Brill Companion to Anarchism and Philosophy*, edited by Nathan Yun, 253–80. Leiden, Netherlands: Brill.

Kirk, Gwyn, and K. Melchor Quick Hall. 2021. "Maps, Gardens, and Quilts." In *Mapping Gendered Ecologies: Engaging with and beyond Ecowomanism and Ecofeminism*, edited by K. Melchor Quick Hall and Gwyn Kirk, 1–16. Lanham: Lexington Books.

Kirkwood, Brandon. 2021. "Cancelled: James Aspey Cons His Followers." Accessed November 28, 2022. https://vegannews.press/2021/02/11/cancelled-james-aspey-cons-his-followers/.

Kitei, Lynne. 2010. *The Phoenix Lights: A Skeptics Discovery That We Are Not Alone*. Newburyport, MA: Hampton Roads Publishing.

Knight, Andrew. 2011. *The Costs and Benefits of Animal Experiments*. Hampshire, UK: Palgrave Macmillan.

Ko, Aph, and Syl Ko. 2017. *Aphro-ism: Essays on Pop Culture, Feminism, and Black Veganism from Two Sisters*. New York: Lantern Books.

Kopnina, Helen, Haydn Washington, Bron Taylor, and John J. Piccolo. 2018. "Anthropocentrism: More than Just a Misunderstood Problem." *Journal of Agricultural and Environmental Ethics* 31, no. 1: 109–27. doi:10.1007/s10806-018-9711-1.

Korte, Gregory, and Alan Gomez. 2018. "Trump Ramps up Rhetoric on Undocumented Immigrants: 'These Aren't People. These Are Animals.'" *USA Today*, May 16, 2018. https://www.usatoday.com/story/news/politics/2018/05/16/trump-immigrants-animals-mexico-democrats-sanctuary-cities/617252002/.

Koshy, Susan, Lisa Marie Cacho, Jodi A. Byrd, and Brian Jordan Jefferson, eds. 2023. *Colonial Racial Capitalism*. Durham, NC: Duke University Press.

Krausman, Paul R., Lisa K. Harris, Ryan R. Wilson, James W. Cain III, and Kiana K. G. Koenen. 2007. "Bombing and Sonoran Pronghorn: A Clear and Present Danger?" *The Journal of Wildlife Management* 71, no. 8: 2820–23.

Kropotkin, Peter. 1902. *Mutual Aid: A Factor of Evolution*. New York: McClure Phillips & Co.

Kymlicka, Will, and Susan Donaldson. 2014. "Animal Rights, Multiculturalism, and the Left." *Journal of Social Philosophy* 45, no. 1: 116–35.

LaFollette, Hugh, and Niall Shanks. 1996. "The Origin of Speciesism." *Philosophy* 71, no. 275: 41–61.

Land Conservation Assistance Network. 2017. "Sonoran Pronghorn Captive Breeding Program." Cooperative Conservation America. http://www.cooperativeconservation.org/viewproject.aspx?id=407.

Lederer, Susan E. 1992. "Political Animals: The Shaping of Biomedical Research Literature in Twentieth-Century America." *Isis* 83, no. 1: 61–79.

Lee, David. 2013. *Rise of Animals: Triumph of the Vertebrates*. DVD. London: BBC.

Lestel, Dominique. 2016. *Eat This Book: A Carnivore's Manifesto*. New York: Columbia University Press.

Levitt, Peggy, and Sally Merry. 2009. "Vernacularization on the Ground: Local Uses of Global Women's Rights in Peru, China, India and the United States." *Global Networks (Oxford)* 9, no. 4: 441–61.

Lupinacci, John, and Alison Happel-Parkins. 2016. "(Un)Learning Anthropocentrism: An Ecojustice Framework for Teaching to Resist Human-Supremacy in Schools." In *The Educational Significance of Human and Non-Human Animal Interactions: Blurring the Species Line*, edited by Suzanne Rice and A. G. Rud, 13–30. New York: Palgrave Macmillan US.

Lynch, Michael J., and Paul B. Stretesky. 2014. *Exploring Green Criminology: Toward a Green Criminological Revolution*. Surrey, UK: Ashgate Publishing Ltd.

Lyon, Melissa Lynn, Kathy L. Sikes, Patti H. Clayton, and Robert G. Bringle. 2022. "Designing Transformative Service-Learning: Mindfulness and Healing-Centered Engagement." In *Handbook of Research on Learner-Centered Approaches to Teaching in an Age of Transformational Change*, edited by Billi L. Bromer and Caroline M. Crawford. Hershey, PA: IGI Global.

Lyons, Dan. 2013. *The Politics of Animal Experimentation*. Hampshire, UK: Palgrave Macmillan.

Machin, David, and Andrea Mayr. 2012. *How to Do Critical Discourse Analysis: A Multimodal Introduction*. Los Angeles: Sage.

Mack, John. 2007. *Abduction: Human Encounters with Aliens*. New York: Scribner.

Mack, John. 2022. "Exploring the Frontiers of Human Experience." John E. Mack Institute. http://johnemackinstitute.org/.

Marceau, Justin. 2019. *Beyond Cages: Animal Law and Criminal Punishment.* Cambridge, UK: Cambridge University Press.

Markowski, Kelly Lorraine, and Susan Roxburgh. 2019. "'If I Became a Vegan, My Family and Friends Would Hate Me': Anticipating Vegan Stigma as a Barrier to Plant-Based Diets." *Appetite* 135: 1–9.

Marx, Sherry, Julie L. Pennington, and Heewon Chang. 2017. "Critical Auto-ethnography in Pursuit of Educational Equity: Introduction to the IJME Special Issue." *International Journal of Multicultural Education* 19, no. 1: 1–6.

Mathew, Liz. 2015. "After 'Beef' Blip, Buffalo Meat Back on Kerala House Menu." *Indian Express*, December 25, 2015. https://indianexpress.com/article/cities/delhi/after-beef-blip-buffalo-meat-back-on-kerala-house-menu/.

Matsuoka, Atsuko Karin, and John Sorenson, eds. 2018. *Critical Animal Studies: Towards Trans-Species Social Justice.* New York: Rowman & Littlefield International.

Maynes, Jeffrey. 2015. "Critical Thinking and Cognitive Bias." *Informal Logic* 35, no. 2: 183–203. doi:10.22329/il.v35i2.4187.

Mbah, Sam, and I. E. Igariwey. 1997. *African Anarchism: The History of a Movement.* Tucson: See Sharp Press.

McAfee, Alison. 2020. "The Problem with Honey Bees." *Scientific American.* Last modified November 4, 2020. https://www.scientificamerican.com/article/the-problem-with-honey-bees/.

McDonald, Barbara. 2000. "'Once You Know Something, You Can't Not Know It': An Empirical Look at Becoming Vegan." *Society & Animals* 8, no. 1: 1–23.

McGregor, Andrew 2022. "Vegan Environmentalism." In *Vegan Geographies: Spaces beyond Violence, Ethics beyond Speciesism,* edited by Paul Hodge, Andrew McGregor, Simon Springer, Ophélie Véron, and Richard J. White, 306–33. New York: Lantern Books.

McKittrick, Katherine. 2006. *Demonic Grounds: Black Women and the Cartographies of Struggle.* Minneapolis: University of Minnesota Press.

McPhall, Dana. n.d. "What I've Learned by Applying an Antiracist Framework to My Animal Advocacy." *Sentient Media.* Accessed December 1, 2022. https://sentientmedia.org/what-ive-learned-by-applying-an-antiracist-framework-to-my-animal-advocacy/.

McVeigh, Karen. 2021. "Seaspiracy: Netflix Documentary Accused of Misrepresentation by Participants." *Guardian*, March 31, 2021. https://www.theguardian.com/environment/2021/mar/31/seaspiracy-netflix-documentary-accused-of-misrepresentation-by-participants.

Melzener, Lea, Karin E. Verzijden, A. Jasmin Buijs, Mark J. Post, and Joshua E. Flack. 2021. "Cultured Beef: From Small Biopsy to Substantial Quantity." *Journal of the Science of Food and Agriculture* 101, no. 1: 7–14.

Menor-Campos, David J., Sarah Knight, Carolina Sánchez-Muñoz, and Rocío López-Rodríguez. 2019. "Human-Directed Empathy and Attitudes toward Animal Use: A Survey of Spanish Veterinary Students." *Anthrozoös* 32, no. 4: 471–87. doi:10.1080/08927936.2019.1621518.

Merriam-Webster. n.d. "Invasive." https://www.merriam-webster.com/dictionary/invasive.

Meta. n.d. "Meta for Business." Accessed November 28, 2022. https://www.facebook.com/business/news/Coming-Soon-Video-Metrics.

Meyers, Phil. 2000. "Camelidae: Camels, Llamas, and Relatives." Animal Diversity Web. https://animaldiversity.org/site/accounts/information/Camelidae.html.

Mika, Marie. 2006. "Framing the Issue: Religion, Secular Ethics and the Case of Animal Rights Mobilization." *Social Forces* 85, no 2: 915–41.

Mills, C. Wright. 1959. *The Sociological Imagination.* New York: Oxford University Press.

Minassian, Liana. 2022. "Why the Global Rise in Vegan and Plant-Based Eating Is No Fad (30x Increase in US Vegans + Other Astounding Vegan Stats)." *Food Revolution Network*, February 19, 2022. https://foodrevolution.org/blog/vegan-statistics-global/.

Moazeni, Somaych, and Hamid Pourmohammadi. 2013. "Smart Teaching Quantitative Topics through the VARK Learning Styles Model." In *2013 IEEE Integrated STEM Education Conference (ISEC).* Piscataway, NJ: IEEE.

Monson, Shaun, dir. 2005. *Earthlings.* Documentary. Nation Earth. http://www.nationearth.com.

Morales, Aurora Levins. 2021. "Rematriation: A Climate Justice Migration." In *Mapping Gendered Ecologies: Engaging with and beyond Ecowomanism and Ecofeminism,* edited by K. Melchor Quick Hall and Gwyn Kirk, 87–96. Lanham: Lexington Books.

Mudde, Cas, and Cristóbal Rovira Kaltwasser. 2017. *Populism: A Very Short Introduction.* Oxford University Press.

Mukherjee, Rheea Rodrigues. 2022. "Being Vegan and Anti-Caste: Why We Need to Hear from Marginalised Communities." *The News Minute*, September 19, 2022. https://www.thenewsminute.com/article/being-vegan-and-anti-caste-why-we-need-hear-marginalised-communities-168030.

Munro, Lyle. 2005. "Strategies, Action Repertoires, and DIY Activism in the Animal Rights Movement." *Social Movement Studies* 4, no. 1: 75–94.

Murdza, Katy, and Walter Ewing. 2021. "The Legacy of Racism within the U.S. Border Patrol." American Immigration Council. Last modified February 9, 2021. https://www.americanimmigrationcouncil.org/research/legacy-racism-within-us-border-patrol.

Murray, Hunter. 2012. "Dependent Origination as Natural Governing Law." *Contemporary Readings in Law and Social Justice* 4, no. 2: 116–77.

Muzaffar Chishti, Jessica Bolter Muzaffar Chishti, and Jessica Bolter. 2019. "'Merit-Based' Immigration: Trump Proposal Would Dramatically Revamp Immigrant Selection Criteria, but with Modest Effects on Numbers." Migration Policy Institute. Last modified May 30, 2019. https://www.migrationpolicy.org/article/merit-based-immigration-trump-proposal-immigrant-selection.

Myers-Lipton, Scott. 2017. *Change! A Student Guide to Social Action.* New York: Routledge.

Nair, Sobhana K. 2015. "Kerala House Beef Drama Ends on a Palatable Note." *Mumbai Mirror*, October 27, 2015. https://mumbaimirror.indiatimes.com/news/india/Kerala-House-beef-drama-ends-on-a-palatable-note/articleshow/49560314.cms.

Narayanan, Yamini. 2018a. "Animal Ethics and Hinduism's Milking, Mothering Legends: Analysing Krishna the Butter Thief and the Ocean of Milk." *Sophia* 57, no. 1: 133–49.

Narayanan, Yamini. 2018b. "Cow Protection as 'Casteised Speciesism': Sacralisation, Commercialisation and Politicisation." *South Asia* 41, no. 2: 331–51.

Narayanan, Yamini. 2019. "'Cow Is a Mother, Mothers Can Do Anything for Their Children!' Gaushalas as Landscapes of Anthropatriarchy and Hindu Patriarchy." *Hypatia* 34, no. 2: 195–221.

NatureMapping Foundation. n.d. "Bumblebee." http://naturemappingfoundation.org/natmap/facts/bumblebee.html.

Neima, Hemin, and Khasraw Hassan. 2020. "Trends in Livestock Production and Red Meat Industry in Sulaymaniyah Governorate, Kurdistan Region of Iraq: A Review." *Journal of Animal and Poultry Production* 11, no. 5: 189–92.

Nelson, Anitra, and Ferne Edwards, eds. 2020. *Food for Degrowth: Perspectives and Practices.* Oxfordshire, UK: Routledge.

Newitz, Annalee. 2017. "Cats Are an Extreme Outlier among Domestic Animals." *Ars Technica*. Last modified June 19, 2017. https://arstechnica.com/science/2017/06/cats-are-an-extreme-outlier-among-domestic-animals/.

Newman, Saul. 2016. *Postanarchism.* Cambridge, UK: Polity Press.

Nguyen, Hanh. 2019. *Tongue Tied: Breaking the Language Barrier to Animal Liberation.* Brooklyn: Lantern.

Nhất Hạnh, Thích. 1987. *Interbeing: Fourteen Guidelines for Engaged Buddhism.* Berkeley, CA: Parallax Press.

Nhất Hạnh, Thích. 1991. *Peace Is Every Step: The Path to Mindfulness in Everyday Life.* New York: Bantam Books.

Nhất Hạnh, Thích. 1998. *The Heart of the Buddha's Teaching.* London: Rider.

Nhất Hạnh, Thích. 2010 *L'unico Mondo che Abbiamo. La Pace e L'ecologia Secondo L'etica Buddhista.* Firenze: Terra Nuova Edizioni.

Nhất Hạnh, Thích. 2017. *The Art of Living*. London: Penguin.

Nibert, David. A. 2013. *Animal Oppression and Human Violence: Domesecration, Capitalism, and Global Conflict*. New York: Columbia University Press.

Nibert, David. 2017. *Animal Oppression and Capitalism*. Santa Barbara, CA: Praeger.

Nikolopoulou, Kalliopi. 2000. "*Homo Sacer*: Sovereign Power and Bare Life (Review)." *SubStance* 29, no. 3: 124–31.

Nobis, Nathan. 2004. "Carl Cohen's 'Kind' Arguments for Animal Rights and against Human Rights." *Journal of Applied Philosophy* 21, no. 1: 43–59.

Nocella II, Anthony J., John Sorenson, Kim Socha, and Atsuko Matsuoka, eds. 2014. *Defining Critical Animal Studies: An Intersectional Social Justice Approach for Liberation*. New York: Peter Lang.

Nocella II, Anthony J., Richard J. White, and Erika Cudworth, eds. 2015. *Anarchism and Animal Liberation: Essays on Complementary Elements of Total Liberation*. Jefferson, NC: McFarland.

Noske, Barbara. 1997. "Speciesism, Anthropocentrism, and Non-Western Cultures." *Anthrozoös* 10, no. 4: 183–99.

Office of the Director of National Intelligence. 2021. *Preliminary Assessment: Unidentified Aerial Phenomena*. https://www.dni.gov/files/ODNI/documents/assessments/Prelimary-Assessment-UAP-20210625.pdf.

Olivelle, Patrick, trans. 2008. *Upanisads*. Oxford University Press.

Olson, Sarah Rose. 2019. "Dismantling the Human/Animal Divide in Education: The Case for Critical Humane Education." In *Teaching Liberation: Essays on Social Justice, Animals, Veganism, and Education*, edited by Agnes Trzak, 26–45. New York: Lantern Books.

O'Shea, Janet. 2021. "Sentimentality or Prowess? Animal Advocacy and (Human) Physical Labor." *Journal for Critical Animal Studies* 18, no. 3: 4–26.

Ottuh, Peter, and Onos Godwin Idjakpo. 2021. "Animal Care and Ethics in Contemporary Religious Debates." *Jurnal Sosialisasi: Jurnal Hasil Pemikiran, Penelitian Dan Pengembangan Keilmuan Sosiologi Pendidikan* 8, no. 2: 128–41.

Oxford English Dictionary. n.d. "Husbandry." OED Online. https://www.oed.com/dictionary/husbandry_n?tl=true.

Pacific Institute for Community Organization. n.d. "PICO Organizing Principles." https://clintonwhitehouse4.archives.gov/Initiatives/OneAmerica/Practices/pp_19980930.6405.html.

Painter, Corinne. 2016. "Non-Human Animals within Contemporary Capitalism: A Marxist Account of Non-Human Animal Liberation." *Capital & Class* 40, no. 2: 325–43.

Pande, Suchi. 2016. "How an Assault on Banjaras by Gau Rakshaks Sparked an UNA-Like Movement in Rajasthan." Scroll.in, November 11, 2016. https://scroll.in/article/821047/how-an-assault-on-banjaras-by-gau-rakshaks-sparked-an-una-like-movement-in-rajasthan.

Pandey, Geeta. 2017. "Why Are Indian Women Wearing Cow Masks?" *BBC News*, June 27, 2017. https://www.bbc.com/news/world-asia-india-40404102.

Pascal, Blaise. 1995. *Pensées*. Translated by J. Krailsheimer. New York: Penguin Books.

Pasulka, Diana. 2019. *American Cosmic: UFOs, Religion, Technology*. Oxford: Oxford University Press.

Pedersen, Helena. 2010. *Animals in Schools: Processes and Strategies in Human-Animal Education*. West Lafayette, IN: Purdue University Press.

Pedersen, Helena, and Vasile Stanescu. 2011. "Introduction." In Kim Socha, *Women, Destruction, and the Avant Garde*, x–xi. New York: Rodopi.

Pellow, David Naguib. 2014. *Total Liberation: The Power and Promise of Animal Rights and the Radical Earth Movement*. Minneapolis: University of Minnesota Press.

Pellow, David Naguib. 2018. *What Is Critical Environmental Justice?* Cambridge, UK: Polity Press.

Perspectives Editorial Collective. 2016. *Anarchafeminism: A Special Issue of Perspectives on Anarchist Theory*. Portland: Eberhardt Press.

Pfattheicher, Stefan, Claudia Sassenrath, and Simon Schindler. 2016. "Feelings for the Suffering of Others and the Environment: Compassion Fosters Proenvironmental Tendencies." *Environment and Behavior* 48, no. 7: 929–45. doi:10.1177/0013916515574549.

Philpotts, Izzic, Justin Dillon, and Nicola Rooney. 2019. "Improving the Welfare of Companion Dogs—Is Owner Education the Solution?" *Animals* 9, no. 9: 662. doi:10.3390/ani9090662.

Piazza, Jared, Matthew B. Ruby, Steve Loughnan, Mischel Luong, Juliana Kulik, Hanne M. Watkins, and Mirra Siegerman. 2015. "Rationalizing Meat Consumption. The 4Ns." *Appetite* 91: 114–28.

Pieroni, Andrea, Hawre Zahir, Hawraz Ibrahim M. Amin, and Renata Sõukand. 2019. "Where Tulips and Crocuses Are Popular Food Snacks: Kurdish Traditional Foraging Reveals Traces of Mobile Pastoralism in Southern Iraqi Kurdistan." *Journal of Ethnobiology and Ethnomedicine* 15, no. 1: 59.

Plumwood, Val. 2000. "Integrating Ethical Frameworks for Humans, Animals, and Nature: A Critical Feminist Eco-Socialist Perspective." *Ethics and the Environment* 5, no. 2: 285–322.

Plumwood, Val. 2003. "Animals and Ecology: Towards a Better Integration." Working/technical paper. Australian National University Digital Collection. https://digitalcollections.anu.edu.au/handle/1885/41767.

Plumwood, Val. 2004. "Gender, Eco-Feminism and the Environment." In *Controversies in Environmental Sociology*, edited by Robert White, 43–60. Cambridge, UK: Cambridge University Press.

Polanco, Andrea, J. Parry, and J. Anderson. 2022. "Planting Seeds: The Impact of Diet & Different Animal Advocacy Tactics." *Faunalytics*. https://faunalytics.org/relative-effectiveness/#.

Pollan, Michael. 2006. *The Omnivore's Dilemma: A Natural History of Four Meals*. London: Penguin Books.

Pope Alexander VI. 1493. "The Papal Bull Inter Caetera of May 4, 1493." Introduced and translated by Sebastian Modrow and Melissa Smith. *Doctrine of Discovery Project*. https://doctrineofdiscovery.org/assets/pdfs/Inter_Caetera_Modrow&Smith.pdf.

Porcher, Jocelyne. 2011. "The Relationship between Workers and Animals in the Pork Industry: A Shared Suffering." *Journal of Agricultural and Environmental Ethics* 24, no. 1: 3–17.

Poirier, Nathan. 2020. "Issue Introduction: Learning to Listen." *Journal for Critical Animal Studies* 17, no. 3: 1–2.

Probst, Barbara. 2015. "The Eye Regards Itself: Benefits and Challenges of Reflexivity in Qualitative Social Work Research." *Social Work Research* 39, no. 1: 37–48.

Psihoyos, Louie, dir. 2009. *The Cove*. Lionsgate.

Purdy, Chase. 2020. *Billion Dollar Burger: Inside Big Tech's Race for the Future of Food*. New York: Penguin Books.

Puumala, Eeva. 2013. "Political Life Beyond Accommodation and Return: Rethinking Relations between the Political, the International, and the Body." *Review of International Studies* 39, no. 4: 949–68.

Quinn, Emilia, and Benjamin Westwood, eds. 2018. *Thinking Veganism in Literature and Culture: Toward a Vegan Theory*. Oxford: Palgrave Macmillan.

Rahman, Sira Abdul. 2017. "Religion and Animal Welfare—An Islamic Perspective." *Animals: An Open Access Journal from MDPI* 7, no. 2: 11.

Rancher Advocacy Program. n.d. "Home." Accessed November 30, 2022. https://rancheradvocacy.org/.

Rao, Smitha. 2011. "Saffronisation of the Holy Cow: Unearthing Silent Communalism." *Economic and Political Weekly* 46, no. 15: 80–87.

Reddy, Akanksha V. 2022. "Contesting the Animal-Right: The Liberationist Challenges Imposed by Dalit Vegans and Animal Rights Advocates." *Indian Journal of Society and Politics* 9, no. 1: 75–76. https://www.ijsp.in/admin/mvc/upload/901_15_CONTESTING%20THE%20ANIMAL-RIGHT.pdf.

Reese, Ashanté M. 2019. *Black Food Geographies: Race, Self-Reliance, and Food Access in Washington, DC*. Chapel Hill: UNC Press Books.

Reinsborough, P., and D. Canning. 2016. "Points of Intervention." In *Beautiful Trouble: A Toolbox for Revolution*, edited by Andrew Boyd, 250–53. OR Books.

Rich, Adrianne. 1980. "Compulsory Heterosexuality and Lesbian Existence." *Signs: Journal of Women in Culture and Society* 5, no. 4: 631–60.

Rincon, Paul. 2020. "Earliest Evidence for Humans in the Americas." *BBC News.* https://www.bbc.com/news/science-environment-53486868.

Ritchie, Hannah, Pablo Rosado, and Max Roser. 2019. "Meat and Dairy Production." Our World in Data. https://ourworldindata.org/meat-production.

Robinson, Cedric. 2021. *Black Marxism: The Making of the Black Radical Tradition,* 3rd edition. Chapel Hill: North Carolina University Press.

Robinson, Margaret. 2013. "Veganism and Mi'kmaq Legends." *Canadian Journal of Native Studies* 33, no. 1: 189–96.

Robinson, Margaret. 2017. "Intersectionality in Mi'kmaw and Settler Vegan Values." In *Veganism in an Oppressive World: A Vegans-Of-Color Community Project,* edited by Julia Feliz Brueck, 71–89. Sanctuary Publishers.

Rodrigues, Saryta. 2018. *Food Justice: A Primer.* Sanctuary Publishers.

Rokeach, Milton. 1973. *The Nature of Human Values.* New York: The Free Press.

Ross, Jonathan L., Maureen T. B. Drysdale, and Robert A. Schultz. 2001. "Cognitive Learning Styles and Academic Performance in Two Postsecondary Computer Application Courses." *Journal of Research on Computing in Education* 33, no. 4: 400–12.

Rothgerber, Hank. 2014. "Efforts to Overcome Vegetarian-Induced Dissonance among Meat Eaters." *Appetite* 79: 32–41.

Rott, Nathan. 2020. "The World Lost Two-Thirds of Its Wildlife in 50 Years. We Are to Blame." *NPR,* September 10, 2020. https://www.npr.org/2020/09/10/911500907/the-world-lost-two-thirds-of-its-wildlife-in-50-years-we-are-to-blame.

Ruckus Society. n.d. "The Ruckus Action Strategy Guide." https://ruckus.org/training-manuals/the-action-strategy-guide/Story-based strategy.

Rudacille, Deborah. 2000. *The Scalpel and the Butterfly: The Conflict between Animal Research and Animal Protection.* Berkeley, CA: University of California Press.

Rumford, Regina A. 2018. "Shaping the Future of Humane Education toward Creating Systemic Change." PhD Diss., Saybrook University. http://search.proquest.com/docview/2189860577/abstract/64222EF0EC1A4948PQ/1.

Ryder, Richard D. 2002. "The Ethics of Painism: The Argument against Painful Experiments." *Between the Species* 13, no. 2: 1–9.

Saari, Maria Helena. 2018. "Re-Examining the Human–Nonhuman Animal Relationship through Humane Education." In *Research Handbook on Childhoodnature: Assemblages of Childhood and Nature Research,* edited by Amy Cutter-Mackenzie, Karen Malone, and Elisabeth Barratt Hacking, 1–11. New York: Springer International Publishing. doi:10.1007/978-3-319-51949-4_69-1.

Sakulku, Jaruwan, and James Alexander. 2011. "The Impostor Phenomenon." *International Journal of Behavioral Science* 6, no. 1: 73–92.

Samudzi, Zoé, and William C. Anderson. 2018. *As Black as Resistance: Finding the Conditions for Liberation.* Oakland: AK Press.

Sathyamala, Christina. 2019. "Meat-Eating in India: Whose Food, Whose Politics, and Whose Rights?" *Policy Futures in Education* 17, no. 7: 878–91.

Schlaepfer, Martin A., Dov F. Sax, and Julian D. Olden. 2011. "The Potential Conservation Value of Non-Native Species." *Conservation Biology: The Journal of the Society for Conservation Biology* 25, no. 3: 428–37.

Schwartz, Shalom. 1992. "Universals in the Content and Structure of Values: Theoretical Advances and Empirical Tests in 20 Countries." *Advances in Experimental Social Psychology* 25: 1–65.

Schwartz, Shalom. 2012. "An Overview of the Schwartz Theory of Basic Values. *Online Readings in Psychology and Culture* 2, no. 1: 1–20.

Scully, Matthew. 2003. *Dominion: The Power of Man, the Suffering of Animals, and the Call to Mercy.* New York: St. Martin's Press.

Senior, Donald. 1990. *The Passion of Jesus in the Gospel of Matthew.* Collegeville, MN: Liturgical Press.

Shanks, Niall, Ray Greek, and Jean Greek. 2009. "Philosophy, Ethics, and Humanities in Medicine." *Philosophy, Ethics, and Humanities in Medicine* 4, no. 2: 1–20.

Shapiro, Paul. 2018. *Clean Meat: How Growing Meat without Animals Will Revolutionize Dinner and the World.* New York: Simon and Schuster.

Shelton, Samuel Z. 2022. "Toward Collective Liberation: Vegan Exceptionalism, Eco-Accountability, and the Urgency of a New Animal Solidarity." In *Vegan Entanglements: Dismantling Racial and Carceral Capitalism,* edited by Z. McNeill, 119–38. New York: Lantern Publishing & Media.

Sinclair, Upton. 1906. *The Jungle.* New York: Doubleday.

Sinha, Nitin. 2008. "Mobility, Control and Criminality in Early Colonial India, 1760s–1850s." *The Indian Economic and Social History Review* 45, no. 1: 1–33.

Sippell, Margeaux. 2022. "Unsolved Mysteries Director Seeks Answers to UFO Questions That Have Haunted Jack Bushong for Decades." Moviemaker. https://www.moviemaker.com/unsolved-mysteries-ufo-jack-bushong-haunted/.

Sirwan, Dilan. 2022. "Turkish Bombardment Damages a House in Duhok Village." Rudaw Media Network, April 15, 2022. https://www.rudaw.net/english/kurdistan/150420222.

Sizemore, Grant. 2015. "Cats and Birds." American Bird Conservancy. Last modified May 28, 2015. https://abcbirds.org/program/cats-indoors/cats-and-birds/.

Socha, Kim. 2011. *Women, Destruction, and the Avant-Garde: A Paradigm for Animal Liberation.* Leiden, Netherlands: Brill.

Sorenson, John, and Atsuko Matsuoka. 2022. "Moral Panic over Fake Service Animals." *Social Sciences* 11, no. 10: 439. doi:10.3390/socsci11100439.

Spade, Dean. 2020. *Mutual Aid: Building Solidarity during This Crisis (and the Next).* New York: Verso.

Spanjol, Kimberly. 2020. "Teaching Process over Content: Addressing Underlying Psychological Processes and Biases in Learners When Including Non-Human Animals in Education and Social Justice Discourse." *International Journal of Humane Education* 1, no. 1: 66–104.

Spiegel, Marjorie. 1988. *The Dreaded Comparison: Human and Animal Slavery.* Gabriola Island, BC: New Society Publishers.

Springer, Simon. 2016. *The Anarchist Roots of Geography: Toward Spatial Emancipation.* Minneapolis: University of Minnesota Press.

Springer, Simon. 2021. "Total Liberation Ecology: Integral Anarchism, Anthroparchy, and the Violence of Indifference." In *Undoing Human Supremacy: Anarchist Political Ecology in the Face of Anthroparchy,* edited by Simon Springer, Jennifer Mateer, Martin Locret-Collet, and Maleea Acker, 235–54. Lanham: Rowman & Littlefield.

Springirth, Andie. 2021. "Fostering Empathy towards Farmed Animals." The Open Sanctuary Project. Last modified June 8, 2021. https://opensanctuary.org/fostering-empathy-towards-farmed-animals/.

Srinivasan, Krithika, and Rajesh Kasturirangan. 2016. "Political Ecology, Development, and Human Exceptionalism." *Geoforum* 75: 125–28.

Srinivasan, Krithika, and Smitha Rao. 2015. "'Will Eat Anything That Moves': Meat Cultures in Globalising India." *Economic and Political Weekly* 50, no. 39: 13–15.

Stanescu, James, and Kevin Cummings, eds. 2016. *The Ethics and Rhetoric of Invasion Ecology.* Lanham: Rowman & Littlefield.

Staples, James. 2017. "Beef and Beyond: Exploring the Meat Consumption Practices of Christians in India." *Ethnos* 82, no. 2: 232–51.

Steg, Linda. 2016. "Values, Norms, and Intrinsic Motivation to Act Proenvironmentally." *Annual Review of Environmental Resources* 41: 277–92.

Steg, Linda, Goda Perlaviciute, Ellen van der Werff, and Judith Lurvink. 2014. "The Significance of Hedonic Values for Environmentally Relevant Attitudes, Preferences, and Actions." *Environment and Behavior* 46, no. 2: 163–92.

Steiner, Gary 2013. *Animals and the Limits of Postmodernism.* New York: Columbia University Press.

Stella, Judith L., and Candace C. Croney. 2016. "Environmental Aspects of Domestic Cat Care and Management: Implications for Cat Welfare." *The Scientific World Journal* 2016, no. 1. doi:10.1155/2016/6296315.

Stern, Paul C., Thomas Dietz, and Gregory A. Guagnano. 1998. "Social Structural and Social Psychological Bases of Environmental Concern." *Environment and Behavior* 30, no. 4: 450–71.

Stibbe, Arran. 2017. "Positive Discourse Analysis: Re-Thinking Human Ecological Relationships." In *The Routledge Handbook of Ecolinguistics*, edited by Alwin F. Fill and Hermine Penz, 165–78. London: Routledge.

Stubler, Nico. 2022. "Abolitionary Advocacy: Expanding Empathy toward Total Liberation." In *Vegan Entanglements: Dismantling Racial and Carceral Capitalism*, edited by Z. McNeill, 107–18. Lantern Publishing & Media.

Suarez-Villa, Luis. 2009. *Technocapitalism: A Critical Perspective on Technological Innovation and Corporatism*. Philadelphia: Temple University Press.

Subramani, A. 2015. "Lawyers Consume Beef on HC Campus to Protest Maharashtra Ban." *Times of India*, March 7, 2015. https://timesofindia.indiatimes.com/city/chennai/Lawyers-consume-beef-on-HC-campus-to-protest-Maharashtra-ban/articleshow/46481522.cms.

Suchyta, Mark. 2021. "Environmental Values and Americans' Beliefs about Farm Animal Well-Being." *Agriculture and Human Values* 38, no. 4: 987–1001.

Sunder, Jason. 2019. "Religious Beef: Dalit Literature, Bare Life, and Cow Protection in India." *Interventions* 21, no. 3: 337–53.

Swartz, Elliot, and Claire Bomkamp. n.d. "The Science of Cultivated Meat." Accessed February 24, 2023. https://gfi.org/science/the-science-of-cultivated-meat/.

Swenson, Shea 2022. "The Untapped Potential for Urban Agriculture in Detroit." *Modern Farmer*, April 8, 2022. https://modernfarmer.com/2022/04/urban-farms-in-detroit/.

Tabrizi, Ali, dir. 2021. *Seaspiracy*. Netflix.

Taylor, Nicola, and Tania D. Signal. 2005. "Empathy and Attitudes to Animals." *Anthrozoös* 18, no. 1: 18–27.

Taylor, Paul W. 1981. "The Ethics of Respect for Nature." *Environmental Ethics* 3. https://rintintin.colorado.edu/~vancecd/phil308/Taylor.pdf.

Taylor, Sunaura. 2017. *Beasts of Burden: Animal and Disability Liberation*. New York: The New Press.

Thomas, Cassidy, and Leonardo E. Figueroa Helland. 2021. "Agri(cultural) Resistance: Food Sovereignty and Anarchism in Response to the Sociobiodiversity Crisis." In *Inhabiting the Earth: Anarchist Political Ecology for Landscapes of Emancipation*, edited by Martin Locret-Collet, Simon Springer, Jennifer Mateer, and Maleea Acker, 79–98. Lanham: Rowman & Littlefield.

Thomas, Chris D. 2017. *Inheritors of the Earth: How Nature Is Thriving in an Age of Extinction*. New York: PublicAffairs.

Thompson, Paul. 2015. *From Field to Fork: Food Ethics for Everyone*. New York: Oxford University Press.

Tlili, Sarra. 2012. *Animals in the Qur'an*. Cambridge, UK: Cambridge University Press.

Tlili, Sarra. 2018. "Animal Ethics in Islam: A Review Article." *Religions* 9, no. 9: 269.

Tolstoj, Lev. 2020. *Contro la caccia e il mangiar carne.* Milano: Ledizioni.

Tolstoy, Leo. 1900a. *The First Step: An Essay on the Morals of Diet, to Which Are Added Two Stories.* Manchester: Albert Broadbent.

Tolstoy, Leo. 1900b. *The Slavery of Our Times.* Revolt Library. http://www.revoltlib.com/anarchism/the-slavery-of-our-times-tolstoy-leo-1900/.

Tolstoy, Leo. 1902. *Karma.* The Internet Archive. https://archive.org/details/Karma_LevTolstoy/page/n3/mode/2up.

Tolstoy, Leo. 1908. *Letter to a Hindu.* Revolt Library. http://www.revoltlib.com/anarchism/letter-to-a-hindu-subjection-of-cause-tolstoy-leo-1908/.

Tolstoy, Leo. 1911. *Essays and Letters.* London: Oxford University Press.

Tolstoy, Leo. 2011. *Walk in the Light and Twenty-Three Tales.* Rifton, NY: Plough Publishing House.

Tolstoy, Leo. 2016. *War and Peace.* Translated by Louise Maude and Aylmer Maude. Digireads. First published 1865–1869.

Tolstoy, Leo. 2021. *Esarhaddon, King of Assyria.* The Anarchist Library. First published 1903.

Torres, Bob. 2007. *Making a Killing: The Political Economy of Animal Rights.* Oakland: AK Press.

Tüfekçi, Zeynep. 2017. "Preface and Introduction." In *Twitter and Tear Gas: The Power and Fragility of Networked Protest,* edited by Zeynep Tüfekçi, ix–xxxi. New Haven: Yale University Press.

Twine, Richard. 2014. "Vegan Killjoys at the Table—Contesting Happiness and Negotiating Relationships with Food Practices." *Societies* 4: 623–39.

Twine, Richard. 2022. "Ecofeminism and Veganism: Revisiting the Question of Universalism." In *Ecofeminism: Feminist Intersections with Other Animals and the Earth,* 2nd ed., edited by Carol J. Adams and Lori Gruen, 229–46. New York: Bloomsbury Academic.

UCAR. 2022. "Shifting Ecosystems." UCAR Center for Science Education. https://scied.ucar.edu/learning-zone/climate-change-impacts/shifting-ecosystems.

von Uexküll, Jakob. 1964. "A Stroll through the Worlds of Animals and Men: A Picture Book of Invisible Worlds." In *Instinctive Behavior: The Development of a Modern Concept,* edited and translated by Claire H. Schiller, 5–80. New York: International Universities Press, Inc.

Urbanik, Julie. 2012. *Placing Animals: An Introduction to the Geography of Human–Animal Relations.* Lanham: Rowman & Littlefield.

US Congress. "H.R.418 – REAL ID Act of 2005." Congress.gov. Accessed February 4, 2019. https://www.congress.gov/bill/109th-congress/house-bill/418.

Valencia, Sayak. 2018. *Gore Capitalism.* South Pasadena: Semiotext(e).

VARK Learn Limited. 2023. "VARK Modalities: What Do Visual, Aural, Read/Write & Kinesthetic Really Mean?" VARK. https://vark-learn.com/introduction-to-vark/the-vark-modalities/.

Vergès, Françoise. 2022. *A Decolonial Feminism*. London: Pluto Press.

Véron, Ophélie, and Richard J. White. 2021. "Anarchism, Feminism, and Veganism: A Convergence of Struggles." In *Undoing Human Supremacy: Anarchist Political Ecology in the Face of Anthroparchy*, edited by Simon Springer, Jennifer Mateer, Martin Locret-Collet, and Maleea Acker, 65–88. Lanham: Rowman & Littlefield.

Volsche, Shelly. 2020. *Voluntarily Childfree: Identity and Kinship in the United States*. Lanham: Lexington Books.

Waldau, Paul. 2013. *Animal Studies: An Introduction*. New York: Oxford University Press.

Walden, Liz. 2015. "Worldwide Pet Ownership Statistics." Last modified May 13, 2015. https://www.petsecure.com.au/pet-care/a-guide-to-worldwide-pet-ownership/.

Wang, Jackie. 2018. *Carceral Capitalism*. South Pasadena: Semiotext(e).

Weil, Zoe. 2004. *The Power and Promise of Humane Education*. Gabriola Island, BC: New Society Publishers.

Weil, Zoe. 2009. *Most Good, Least Harm: A Simple Principle for a Better World and Meaningful Life*. New York: Beyond Words.

Weil, Zoe. 2016. *The World Becomes What We Teach: Educating a Generation of Solutionaries*. New York: Lantern Publishing & Media.

Welch, Craig. 2017. "Half of All Species Are on the Move—And We're Feeling It." *National Geographic*. Last modified April 27, 2017. https://www.national-geographic.com/science/article/climate-change-species-migration-disease.

Wendt, Alexander, and Raymond Duvall. 2008. "Sovereignty and the UFO." *Political Theory* 36, no. 4: 607–33.

Wergin, Jon F. 2019. *Deep Learning in a Disorienting World*. Cambridge, UK: Cambridge University Press. doi:10.1017/9781108647786.

White Jr., Lynn. 1967. "The Historical Roots of Our Ecological Crisis." *Science* 155, no. 3767: 1203–7.

White, Monica. 2018. *Freedom Farmers: Agricultural Resistance and the Black Freedom Movement*. Chapel Hill: University of North Carolina Press.

White, Richard. 2017. "Rising to the Challenge of Capitalism and the Commodification of Nonhuman Animals: Post-Capitalism, Anarchist Economies and Vegan Praxis." In *Animal Oppression and Capitalism*, edited by David Nibert, 270–94. Santa Barbara, CA: Praeger Press.

White, Richard J. 2018. "Looking Backward/Moving Forward: Articulating a 'Yes, BUT . . . !' Response to Lifestyle Veganism, and Outlining Post-Capitalist Futures in Critical Agriculture." *EuropeNow* 20.

White, Rob. 2018. "Ecocentrism and Criminal Justice." *Theoretical Criminology* 22, no. 3: 342–62.

Whitley, Cameron T., Ryan Gunderson, and Meghan Charters. 2018. "Public Receptiveness to Policies Promoting Plant-Based Diets: Framing Effects and Social Psychological and Structural Influences." *Journal of Environmental Policy and Planning* 20, no. 1: 45–63.

Williams, Krista, and Robin Downing. 2021. "Obesity in Cats." VCA Animal Hospitals. vcahospitals.com/know-your-pet/obesity-in-cats.

Winders, Delcianna J., and Elan Abrell. 2021. "Slaughterhouse Workers, Animals, and the Environment: The Need for a Rights-Centered Regulatory Framework in the United States That Recognizes Interconnected Interests." *Health and Human Rights* 23, no. 2: 21–34.

Winter, Christine J. 2022. "Introduction: What's the Value of Multispecies Justice?" *Environmental Politics* 31, no. 2: 251–57.

The Wire Staff. 2017. "Cow-Killers Will Hang, Says Chhattisgarh Chief Minister, but Admits His State Has None." *The Wire*, April 2, 2017. https://thewire.in/politics/chhattisgarh-chief-minister-will-hang-cow-killers.

Wisconsin Department of Natural Resources. 2019. "Asian Carp Control Efforts."

Wise, Steven M. 2002. *Drawing the Line: Science and the Case for Animal Rights.* Cambridge, UK: Perseus Books.

Wrenn, Corey. 2012. "Applying Social Movement Theory to Nonhuman Rights Mobilization and the Importance of Faction Hierarchies." *The Peace Studies Journal* 5, no. 3: 27–44.

Wrenn, Corey Lee. 2013. "Resonance of Moral Shocks in Abolitionist Animal Rights Advocacy: Overcoming Contextual Constraints." *Society & Animals* 21, no. 4: 379–94.

Wright, Laura. 2015. *The Vegan Studies Project: Food, Animals, and Gender in the Age of Terror.* Minneapolis: University of Minnesota Press.

Wynter, Sylvia. 2003. "Unsettling the Coloniality of Being/Power/Truth/Freedom: Towards the Human, After Man, Its Overrepresentation—An Argument." *CR: The New Centennial Review* 3, no. 4: 257–337. doi.org/10.1353/ncr.2004.0015.

Yong-Kyun, Bae, dir. 1989. *Why Has Bodhi Dharma Left for the East?* Bae Yong-kyun Productions.

Young, Ashley, Kathayoon A. Khalil, and Jim Wharton. 2018. "Empathy for Animals: A Review of the Existing Literature." *Curator: The Museum Journal* 61, no. 2: 327–43. doi:10.1111/cura.12257.

Young, V. J., and J. Vermilyea. 2020. "Imposter Syndrome: A Review." *Journal of Behavioral and Cognitive Therapy* 30, no. 1: 34–46.

Zizek, Slovak. 2008. "Nature and Its Discontents." *SubStance* 37, no. 3: 37–72.

Zuboff, Shoshana. 2020. *The Age of Surveillance Capitalism: The Fight for a Human Future at the New Frontier of Power.* New York: PublicAffairs.

About the Contributors

Kiana Avlon is a graduate of Westminster College's Master of Arts in Community Leadership program, where she studied rhetoric as it pertains to speciesism, with a focus on countering ecofascism within the animal liberation movement. She has presented research on the rhetoric surrounding houselessness in Salt Lake City and the root causes of speciesism at the Western Social Science Association conference and the Annual North American Conference for Critical Animal Studies. She grounds her research in critical animal studies, anarchism, and ecofeminism, with the goal of total liberation. Her free time is dedicated to volunteering at local animal sanctuaries.

Lucrezia Barucca is a master's student in Environmental Humanities, with a specialization in Cultural Studies, at Ca' Foscari University of Venice. She holds a BA in Languages, Literatures, Cultures, and Translation from the Sapienza University of Rome. Her bachelor's thesis critically examined the topic of the unnecessary suffering of nonhuman animals, in particular according to the spiritual understanding of famous Russian author Leo Tolstoy. Lucrezia has a wide array of academic interests, the main ones being animal liberation, veganism, the food-and-health relationship, environmental education, eco-spirituality and Buddhist studies, as well as literary studies and creative writing.

Marquis Bey is an assistant professor of African American Studies and English and core faculty in Gender & Sexuality Studies and Critical Theory at Northwestern University. Their work concerns black feminist theory, transgender and nonbinary studies, abolition, and contemporary literature. They are the author of numerous books, most recently

Black Trans Feminism and Cistem Failure: Essays on Blackness and Cisgender. Currently, Bey is at work on a three-volume collection of critical essays that assert the abolition—through the concept of "jailbreaking"—of gender, race, and class.

Darren Chang is a PhD student in the Department of Sociology and Criminology and the Sydney Environment Institute at the University of Sydney. His research interests broadly include interspecies relations under colonialism and global capitalism, practices of solidarity and mutual aid across species in challenging oppressive powers, and social movement theories.

Richard Giles recently received a doctorate in Social and Ecological Sustainability from the University of Waterloo's School of Environment, Resources, and Sustainability. Richard's dissertation focused on the theoretical and material implications of cultured meat, stemming from an ideological concern with animal life and liberation. Now working as an independent researcher, Richard is trying, probably foolishly, to find employment in the academic realm while also trying to publish work in various forms. When not focusing on these aspects of life, Richard is engaged in private animal rescue.

Paislee House is a scholar-activist who graduated from the University of Central Missouri with a degree in History, specializing in American labor rights and environmental history. Since then, Paislee has retained a strong interest in anti-capitalist critique, animal rights, and Earth liberation. Having recently left her job at a tech company in Austin, Texas, in search of something more socially positive, Paislee currently resides in Central Wisconsin, working as an equipment technician for the University of Wisconsin–Stevens Point's speech and hearing clinic.

Varun Joshi is a PhD candidate at the University of Guelph studying life-course criminology, who's currently in the proposal-writing stage. His dissertation examines the ways in which a Canadian prison slaughterhouse furthers prison as a total institution. A Punjabi Canadian,

Varun is also involved in mental health advocacy in the Punjabi community and is a part of the Men's Mental Health Forum with Soch Mental Health. Varun intends on furthering green criminology as a discipline by incorporating experiences in the Indus subcontinent to assess how hierarchies in perceiving animals are created.

Lea Lani Kinikini Kauvaka (PhD, University of Auckland; MA, University of Hawai'i; BS, University of Utah) is a researcher and educational practitioner who has worked internationally—in Aotearoa, Oceania, Hawai'i, and on Turtle Island. Her research considers how legal fictions and jurisdictions are extrapolated within Oceania. She is currently director of the Institute for Research and Engaged Scholarship at University of Hawai'i West O'ahu, working on transformative justice and community-engaged research projects.

Lynda Korimboccus is an activist-scholar who has been a committed ethical vegan and grassroots campaigner since 1999 and who is a passionate advocate of equity and justice. Her PhD research in sociology investigates the experiences of young vegan children in social institutions, such as the education system, in Scotland. Lynda has an MA in Anthrozoology, as well as undergraduate honors degrees in Philosophy, Politics, Social Psychology, and Sociology. Writing independently in the fields of vegan sociology and critical animal studies, she is also editor-in-chief of the *Student Journal of Vegan Sociology* and has taught sociology at West Lothian College, Scotland, for over fifteen years.

Sarah May Lindsay obtained a PhD in Sociology at McMaster University. Her research areas include human–nonhuman animal relations, human and nonhuman-animal shelters and housing, nonhuman companion animals, nonhuman-animal use and abuse, speciesism, abolitionism, environmentalism, social movements, disability, "disease," and deviance. She works from the intersectional perspective of critical animal studies, leveraging progressive pedagogy for social change. Lindsay's dissertation research surveys companion-animal co-sheltering policies and practices at women's emergency shelters in Ontario, Canada.

Lindsay is also co-chair of CSA's Animals in Society research cluster, council member and newsletter editor of the ASA's Animals and Society Section, assistant editor of the *Student Journal of Vegan Sociology*, organizing member of the Canadian Violence Link Coalition and Bi-Annual Conference, and member of the Animal and Interpersonal Abuse Research Group (AIPARG) and the International Association of Vegan Sociologists.

Seven Mattes received her PhD in Cultural Anthropology from Michigan State University in 2018 and currently serves as an assistant professor in the Center for Integrative Studies. Specializing in human–animal relationships in Japan, her applied research is aimed at improving disaster preparedness and resiliency for animals through policy change and direct action with nonprofit organizations. In both research and teaching, she emphasizes the significance of valuing and understanding human–animal entanglements across cultures.

Jihan Mohammed is a faculty lecturer in Vanderbilt's Department of Sociology. She holds a PhD in Sociology from Michigan State University. Originally from the Iraqi Kurdistan Region, Jihan focuses her research on ethnic and sectarian identities in the Middle East. She uses qualitative and quantitative methods to investigate how identities are constructed and deconstructed in the MENA region. Specifically, this involves looking at how ethnic and sectarian narratives impact people's attitudes and behaviors.

Joshua Russell is an associate professor in the Department of Animal Behavior, Ecology, and Conservation and the graduate program director of anthrozoology at Canisius College in Buffalo, New York. His coursework and research explore children's relationships with animals, critical pedagogies, and the applications of hermeneutic phenomenology and queer theory in human–animal studies and environmental education. He is the editor of *Queer Ecopedagogies: Explorations in Nature, Sexuality, and Education* (Springer, 2021). Joshua lives in Niagara Falls, Ontario, with his partner, Sean.

Macy Sutton is currently pursuing a Doctor of Education, with a specialization in humane education, through Antioch University. She is an occupational therapist with many years of clinical experience in different settings. In 2021, Macy shifted her career toward researching the effect of plant-based diets on human health. She is passionate about advocating for nonhuman animals and educating about interconnected oppressions. Macy lives with her loving cat, Knuckles, in Maryland.

Emily Tronetti holds a Master of Science in Anthrozoology from Canisius College and a Certificate in Applied Animal Behavior from the University of Washington. She is pursuing a Doctor of Education in Educational and Professional Practice, with a specialization in humane education, through Antioch University. Her dissertation work explores multispecies agency in the context of sanctuary education. Emily is a consultant and humane educator who teaches in various settings about topics such as animal behavior and well-being. Through her work, she aims to inspire humans to compassionately coexist with each other and the more-than-human world.

Iván Vazquez has been a member of the Utah animal rights activist community for over five years, working with the Utah Animal Rights Coalition, Anonymous for the Voiceless, and DxE as well as volunteering at local animal sanctuaries. He credits local activists, whom he eventually joined, with giving him the knowledge and support to embrace a vegan lifestyle after nine years of being a vegetarian. Iván has worked in the field of ophthalmology for the past twenty-five years. He is an openly transgender man of color who began his social and medical transition at the age of forty-one. Iván describes his experiences as "living a hundred lifetimes in only forty-three years." Some of these experiences include homelessness, domestic abuse, and racial discrimination. While he is personally connected to multiple social justice issues, his activism efforts are focused on animal liberation. In his words, "the blinders that allow us to overlook animal cruelty to the degree that we do have a huge impact on the injustices we overlook with each other, so I felt a greater sense of urgency to dedicate my effort and resources to animal rights movements."

Amanda R. Williams is a total-liberation activist who has been engaged in the animal rights movement since 2016 as well as an author and independent scholar holding degrees in English Literature and Teaching English as a Second Language. They were recognized by the Institute for Critical Animal Studies as a Critical Animal Studies Hilda Scholar of the Year in 2022. Amanda enjoys researching and writing on the interplay of animal liberation and other social justice struggles. As their day job, Amanda manages a database for Austin Pets Alive!, one of the largest no-kill companion-animal rescues in the country. A Midwesterner through and through, they can be found birding in Central Wisconsin when not spending time with their partner Paislee, their dog Reese, and their two cats, Tycho and Zinn.

About the Editors

Erin Jones holds a BSc in Anthropology and Psychology from Trent University, an MSc in Anthrozoology from Canisius College, and a PhD in Human–Animal Studies from the University of Canterbury's New Zealand Centre for Human–Animal Studies. Erin's primary research interests are the dog–human relationship, the power dynamics of petkeeping based on the paradigm of human exceptionalism, and concepts around canine consent. Erin is a certified dog behavior consultant and accredited dog trainer with the International Association of Animal Behavior Consultants, a certified professional dog trainer with the Certification Council for Professional Dog Trainers, and an accredited animal behavior consultant with Companion Animals New Zealand. She is the owner of Merit Dog Project, an educational platform for assisting dog caregivers and those involved in dog education, and an instructor at the IAABC Foundation.

Nathan Poirier is a tutor and adjunct instructor at Lansing Community College, with graduate specializations in (critical) animal studies and women's and gender studies, as well as advanced degrees in anthrozoology, mathematics, and sociology. Nathan co-edited the book *Emerging New Voices in Critical Animal Studies: Vegan Studies for Total Liberation* (Peter Lang, 2022) and has several interdisciplinary and transdisciplinary publications in diverse animal studies and environmental journals and books.

 **Mark Suchyta** is a teacher, activist, researcher, and artist whose work broadly focuses on how humans can better coexist with other animals and the rest of nature. His scholarship has appeared in scientific journals such as *Social Forces*, *Human Ecology Review*, and *Agriculture and Human Values*. He also works on a semi-annual zine series with his partner, Ren Suchyta-Korany, called *A More-than-Human Society*. Mark is currently a lecturer at Butler University in Indianapolis, where he teaches courses on environmentalism and human–animal relationships, as well as introductory sociology courses. When he is not busy working, Mark enjoys spending his time with his partner and his four rescued parakeets, Opa, Whimsey, Aspen, and Rainford.

 **Sarah Tomasello** is an independent scholar who received bachelor's degrees in Anthropology and Religious Studies and a Master of Science in Anthrozoology from Canisius College. Throughout her studies and publications, Sarah's work has focused on the intersections between decolonization, animal rights, and wildlife conservation. She is especially interested in improving conservation initiatives so that they are respectful and inclusive of Indigenous communities, as well as more compassionate toward the nonhuman individuals they impact. Sarah has several publications in (critical) animal studies journals and books.

About the Publisher

Lantern Publishing & Media was founded in 2020 to follow and expand on the legacy of Lantern Books—a publishing company started in 1999 on the principles of living with a greater depth and commitment to the preservation of the natural world. Like its predecessor, Lantern Publishing & Media produces books on animal advocacy, veganism, religion, social justice, humane education, psychology, family therapy, and recovery. Lantern is dedicated to printing in the United States on recycled paper and saving resources in our day-to-day operations. Our titles are also available as ebooks and audiobooks.

To catch up on Lantern's publishing program, visit us at www.lanternpm.org.

facebook.com/lanternpm
instagram.com/lanternpm
tiktok.com/@lanternpmofficial